OUTSIDE THE

Also by Martin Westlake and published by Agenda

Slipping Loose: The UK's Long Drift Away From the European Union

OUTSIDE THE EU

OPTIONS FOR BRITAIN

Edited by
Martin Westlake

agenda
publishing

First published in 2020 by Agenda Publishing

Agenda Publishing Limited
The Core
Bath Lane
Newcastle Helix
Newcastle upon Tyne
NE4 5TF
www.agendapub.com

ISBN 978-1-78821-312-7 (hardcover)
ISBN 978-1-78821-313-4 (paperback)

British Library Cataloguing-in-Publication Data
A catalogue record for this book is available from the British Library

Typeset by JS Typesetting Ltd, Porthcawl, Mid Glamorgan
Printed and bound in the UK by TJ Books Limited

CONTENTS

ACKNOWLEDGEMENTS

I owe a huge debt of gratitude to all of the contributors to this book: in the first place, for agreeing at rather short notice to pen chapters; in the second place, for having drafted such authoritative and clear analyses; in the third place, for having agreed to, and respected, a very tight submission schedule.

Editing this book has been a joy and I have learned so much. I fervently hope that the book will enjoy a wide readership, particularly among UK and EU policy-makers. The learned analyses it contains can surely help all sides in understanding why and how countries take the paths they do and what sort of pathways the UK–EU tandem might like to consider as the future relationship develops, as it must.

I would like to thank the publishers, Agenda, and my commissioning editor, Alison Howson, for having taken on this title and turned it around so rapidly and handsomely. I would like to thank Thorfinnur Omarsson for digging out the original text of the European Free Trade Agreement.

I would like to thank those who have been sharing the lockdown with me: Godelieve, Claire and Oliver. It's nice to have company, especially when the company is so nice. And I would like also to thank those who were close in spirit, Emily and Tristan, and accompanied me – at an appropriate distance – on my daily laps of the *Parc Josaphat* as the book progressed.

Last but not least, I would like to thank Godelieve for her patience and support as yet another manuscript neared completion.

Martin Westlake
Brussels

ABBREVIATIONS

AAT	Agreement on Air Transport
AFMP	Agreement on the Free Movement of Persons
ASEAN	Association of Southeast Asian Nations
CETA	Comprehensive and Economic Trade Agreement (EU–Canada)
CFTA	Comprehensive Free Trade Agreement
CTA	Common Travel Area
DCFTA	Deep and Comprehensive Free Trade Area
DSM	Dispute Settlement Mechanism
DUP	Democratic Unionist Party
EC	European Community
ECHR	European Court of Human Rights
ECJ	European Court of Justice
ECSC	European Coal and Steel Community
EEA	European Economic Area
EEC	European Economic Community
EESC	European Economic and Social Committee
EFTA	European Free Trade Association
EPA	Economic Partnership Agreement
FCO	Foreign and Commonwealth Office
FTA	Free Trade Agreement
GATS	General Agreement on Trade in Services
GATT	General Agreement on Tariffs and Trade
GDP	gross domestic product
GNI	gross national income
IFA	Institutional Framework Agreement
IMF	International Monetary Fund
ISDS	Investor State Dispute Settlement
JCD	Joint Committee Decision
MFN	most favoured nation
MRA	Mutual Recognition Agreement
NAFTA	North American Free Trade Agreement
NATO	North Atlantic Treaty Organization
NGO	non-governmental organization

OCT — Overseas Countries and Territories
OECD — Organisation for Economic Co-operation Development
OEEC — Organisation for European Economic Cooperation
OT — Overseas Territory
PCA — Partnership and Cooperation Agreement
PESCO — Permanent Structured Cooperation
PRS — Public Regulated Service
PTA — Preferential Trade Agreement
SIS — Schengen Information System
SPS — sanitary and phytosanitary
STRI — Services Trade Restrictiveness Index
TBT — Technical Barriers to Trade
TEU — Treaty on European Union
TFEU — Treaty on the Functioning of the European Union
TPP — Trans-Pacific Partnership
TRIPS — Trade-Related Aspects of Intellectual Property
TRQ — tariff rate quota
TTIP — Transatlantic Trade and Investment Partnership
UKTF — Task Force for Relations with the United Kingdom
UKTPO — UK Trade Policy Observatory
UNCTAD — United Nations Conference on Trade and Development
WA — Withdrawal Agreement
WCO — World Customs Organization
WTO — World Trade Organization

CONTRIBUTORS

GEORGES BAUR is a Senior Research Fellow with the Liechtenstein-Institute, Bendern (Liechtenstein). He has held the posts of Assistant Secretary-General of EFTA and Deputy Head of Mission of the Principality of Liechtenstein to the EU in Brussels. He is a member of the Swiss Bar Association.

NAZAR BOBITSKI (Bobytskyi) is a former Ukrainian diplomat. He held various positions in the central office of the Ministry of Foreign Affairs of Ukraine, the Embassy of Ukraine in Belgium and the Netherlands, as well as the Mission of Ukraine to the EU. He is currently setting up and managing a permanent Brussels office of the Ukrainian Business and Trade Association, a non-profit Ukrainian association representing the voice of Ukrainian business to the EU institutions in Brussels.

ALAN BOLLARD is a Professor of Practice at the School of Government, Victoria University of Wellington, New Zealand. Between 2012 and 2018 he was Executive Director of the APEC Secretariat based in Singapore. He was Governor of the Reserve Bank of New Zealand, 2002–12, and from 1998 to 2002 he was Secretary to the New Zealand Treasury. He has served as New Zealand's Alternate Governor to the International Monetary Fund, the Asian Development Bank and the World Bank.

MARTYN BOND is Senior Distinguished Fellow at Regent's University London. Both as the BBC's Berlin correspondent and as London Press Correspondent for the Council of Europe he has long experience of commenting on European affairs. Between 1989 and 1999 he was Head of the Office of the European Parliament in the UK. He has been a Senior Fellow of the Salzburg Global Seminar since 1985 and a Visiting Professor of European Politics and Policy at Royal Holloway, University of London, 2003–13.

VASCO CAL was an economic adviser (2009–16) to the President of the European Commission, José Manual Barroso, in the Bureau of European Policy Advisers. He was a Member of the Private Office of the Commissioner for Budget and

Financial Programming, Dalia Grybauskaité (2004–09), and a Member of the Private Office of the Commissioner for Justice and Home Affairs, António Vitorino. He has also served as a Member of the European Economic and Social Committee (1986–2000) and as a Member of the EFTA Consultative Committee (1974–2002).

GIJS DE VRIES is a Visiting Senior Fellow at the European Institute of the London School of Economics (LSE). He previously served as the Deputy Minister of the Interior of the Netherlands and as the representative of the Dutch government in the European Convention, which drew up the European Union's draft constitutional treaty. Between 2004 and 2007 he was the European Union's Counter-Terrorism Coordinator. He is a founding member of the European Council on Foreign Relations and a former lecturer in international relations at the University of Leiden.

ALEXANDER DOWNER is Executive Chair of the International School for Government at King's College London. From 2014 to 2018 he was Australian High Commissioner to the UK. Prior to that, he was Australia's longest-serving Minister for Foreign Affairs, a role he held from 1996 to 2007. In addition to a range of other political and diplomatic roles, he was the UN Secretary General's Special Adviser on Cyprus, working on peace talks between Turkish and Greek Cypriots. He is currently Chairman of the UK think tank Policy Exchange.

KURT HÜBNER is Jean Monnet Chair for European Integration and Global Political Economy at the University of British Columbia. He is actively involved in a number of national and international research networks and, in recent years, has held visiting positions at Hebrew University in Jerusalem, University of Birmingham, National University of Singapore, LUISS University in Rome, Sciences Po in Grenoble, Waseda University in Tokyo and Ben Gurion University of the Negev in Israel.

SELIM KUNERALP is a retired Turkish diplomat who was Deputy Secretary General of the International Energy Charter, Head of the Permanent Delegation of Turkey to the World Trade Organisation and Head of the Permanent Delegation of Turkey to the European Union. He has served variously as Turkish Ambassador to South Korea and Sweden, the Deputy Undersecretary for Economic Affairs, Director General for Policy Planning and Director General for the European Union.

SIR MICHAEL LEIGH is Senior Adjunct Professor of European and Eurasian Studies, at the Johns Hopkins University School of Advanced International

Studies, Bologna, Senior Fellow, Bruegel, Brussels, and Senior Adviser on public policy and government affairs at Covington, Brussels. He served as Director-General for Enlargement of the European Commission (2006–11); Deputy Director-General for External Relations (2003–6); and cabinet member and official at the European Commission (1977–2003).

CHRISTOPHER LORD is Professor at ARENA, the Centre for European Studies at the University of Oslo. He writes mainly on democracy and legitimacy and the European Union, but has a longstanding interest in the history of the United Kingdom and European integration.

DAVID PHINNEMORE is Professor of European Politics and Dean of Education at Queen's University Belfast, Northern Ireland. He is also a Visiting Professor at the EU International Relations and Diplomacy Studies Department at the College of Europe, Bruges.

SEBASTIAN REMØY is Executive Vice President and Global Head of Public Affairs at KREAB (a global strategic communications agency), where he also leads the trade and competition practice. As a Norwegian national, he worked in the EEA Coordination Division of the EFTA Secretariat in Brussels. He also worked in the International Trade Administration – US Department of Commerce, and the US Congress – Office of Technology Assessment, Washington, DC.

ALASTAIR SUTTON is a former European Commission official who has prac-tised EU and international law in Brussels for 30 years. Among his clients were the governments of Jersey, Guernsey, Alderney, the Isle of Man, Bermuda and Gibraltar. He is an English barrister, practising in Brick Court Chambers in London and Brussels and is an *avocat* at the *Barreau francophone de Bruxelles*.

MARTIN WESTLAKE is a Visiting Professor in Practice at the LSE's European Institute and a Visiting Professor at the College of Europe, Bruges. During a 30-year European career, he worked in the Parliamentary Assembly of the Council of Europe, the EU's Council of Ministers and the European Commission, with the European Parliament and in the European Economic and Social Committee, where he served as Secretary-General (2008–13).

L. ALAN WINTERS is Professor of Economics and Director of the UK Trade Policy Observatory at the University of Sussex. From 2008 to 2011 he was Chief Economist at the British government's Department for International Development, and from 2004 to 2007 Director of the Development Research Group of the World Bank. He has advised, *inter alia*, various UK government departments, the OECD, the Commonwealth Secretariat, the European Commission, the European Parliament, UNCTAD, the WTO, and the Inter-American Development Bank.

STEPHEN WOOLCOCK is Associate Professor of International Relations at the LSE. Before joining the LSE he worked on trade and EU policy at Chatham House and for the private sector. In 1999 he established the International Trade Policy Unit at the LSE to bridge the gap between academic and policy work. He has served as a consultant to the European Parliament, European Commission, OECD, Commonwealth Secretariat, the UK and other governments.

FOREWORD

For me, as a convinced European, Europe has always been about far more than a market. Europe is mostly about preserving and promoting a way of life: our values, the things that we care about, our civilization, the things which go to make up our European identity. The United Kingdom is incontestably an important part of European civilization and therefore it must remain a part of the European dream. From that broader point of view, Brexit is deeply regrettable and will have profound consequences, but it is not the end of the story. A new relationship between the EU and the UK must be found and, as this book will show, all sorts of models have evolved that may illuminate and perhaps even inspire the negotiators' work. We know the equation they have to solve and that has not changed for a long time: how can the UK remain as distant as possible from European political integration while benefiting as much as possible from European economic unification? Different solutions have been found in the past, and will need to be found in the future.

It would be a mistake, in that context, to confuse the current negotiating stances of the two sides with what that relationship will turn out to be in the longer run. From a swift glance at the "to-do" list – the telephone directory of issues that will need to be settled and negotiated – it is clear that it is simply impossible for everything to be done within one year, nor even within two or three, were an extension to the transitional period to be requested and agreed. That was true before the Covid-19 crisis erupted and is even more true now. What is possible, and hopefully probable, is some sort of an interim agreement that settles most of the issues that need to be settled in the short term and establishes some general principles according to which all the other issues will be negotiated in due course. And then there will be, as in any agreement, implementation schedules or sequences or transitions. At least from the trade agreement point of view, such a staggered process would appear to be a "no-brainer".

It would be a mistake, also, to confuse political rhetoric with underlying relationships. Governments and ministers and European Commissions and European commissioners come and go, but the United Kingdom will always remain a great trading nation and the European Union will surely remain its major trading partner. It is in their mutual interest that this should remain the case. People on both sides of the Channel will not forgive their leaders if the many commercial linkages that have grown up since 1973, and indeed since 1945, were to be summarily severed or allowed to erode away. Having championed the internal market because of its benefits, the UK must be well aware of the costs of leaving it. Clearly, the best relationship will be one that is mutually beneficial and where trade is hampered as little as possible.

At the same time, the scale and unique nature of the challenge that both sides face should not be underestimated. No member state has ever exited the European Union before. The United Kingdom has not been alone in managing its own trade relations since 1973. The EU has a long-established trade policy. In voting to leave the EU in 2016, the UK decided what it did not want, but it has yet to decide exactly what it does want – and, I suspect, it does not yet know exactly. To say that to negotiate under these circumstances is challenging is an understatement. That is not to underestimate the goodwill of the negotiators, merely to point to the scale of the challenge they face.

As Sir Michael Leigh suggests in his Afterword, the Covid-19 crisis and its massive consequences should concentrate minds and encourage the negotiators and their leaders to avoid additional major shocks to the system. Professor Winters cogently demonstrates in his chapter how a relationship based on "WTO rules" alone would be extremely costly, but it would not be a total apocalypse, not least because the EU trade regime within the WTO is an open one. Such an outcome should, I stress, be avoided if at all possible. But, in any case, whatever might happen in the short term, "WTO rules" alone cannot and will not be the end state for the EU–UK relationship which should, it seems clear to me, be some sort of Free Trade Agreement "plus". That, inevitably, will require a viable dispute resolution mechanism. Here, negotiators should not get hung up on the principle. The WTO has its Dispute Settlement System. The EU has its Court. A pragmatic solution can surely be found. The same goes for regulatory proximity, about which the WTO rulebook does not say much, and which is nowadays, much more than in the past, the real playing field to be levelled.

And then there is the rest: all those areas, from culture, education and sport through to technology, transport, security and defence, to give just a few examples, where the absence of the UK would simply be unimaginable. As Gijs de Vries reminds us, it is impossible to imagine a European security and defence policy without some sort of involvement of the UK, a founding member of NATO, a fellow European nuclear power (together with France) and a fellow permanent member of the UN Security Council (again, together with France). And, as Martyn Bond's chapter points out, the UK remains an active member of the Council of Europe, an organization that it did so much to create. The United Kingdom, with its strong attachment to the rule of law and human rights, will surely remain an important player in that broader concert of Europe.

That is why, as a passionate European and a great admirer of the United Kingdom, I remain convinced not only that the UK will remain a part of the European dream but that it must.

PASCAL LAMY
Director, World Trade Organisation, 2005–13
European Commissioner for Trade, 1999–2004
Honorary President, *Notre Europe*

Europe endless – Kraftwerk

INTRODUCTION

Martin Westlake

On 23 June 2016, the people of the United Kingdom voted to leave the European Union. On 31 January 2019, the UK formally left. The question as to whether the UK would "really" leave was thus definitively answered. Although, under the terms of the Withdrawal Agreement, a transitional period running until 31 December 2020 is currently under way (and may be extended, once only, for one or two years), the UK is now, in EU terms, a third country. Although it was never imagined that it would be used by the UK, Treaty on European Union (TEU) Article 50 has served its purpose and is no longer relevant. The only way back into the EU would be through the provisions of TEU Article 49, which would see the UK applying again for membership as a third country. All of the UK's hard-won accumulated exceptionalism has gone for all time: no more rebate, no opt-out of the single currency and the Schengen agreement on the dismantlement of frontiers, no opt-in to justice and home affairs provisions, no February 2016 New Settlement. All gone.

Thus, one question has been definitively answered, but another remains open. Just what sort of future relationship will the UK enjoy with the EU? This is a question of obvious significance for both sides and yet, strangely if understandably, it was hardly debated, let alone answered, in the run-up to the 23 June 2016 Brexit referendum. Moreover, it is a question that, ultimately, can only be answered by both sides together. Equally understandably, once the referendum result *was* known, debates began, both in the UK and in the EU, about what the answer to the question might be, bookended by debates about what it *could* be and what it *should* be. Almost immediately, alternative models were suggested, and these tended to be associated with particular countries; for example, "Norway", "Canada +", "Switzerland", "Singapore on the Thames", "Ukraine" and so on. But what exactly do such models entail, and how have they evolved? What are their perceived advantages and disadvantages, especially for the countries concerned?

EXPERT ANALYSES

A first idea behind this study, therefore, is to contribute to the ongoing debate by bringing together a team of acknowledged experts in their fields to examine these existing models – to the extent that they *are* models – and how they evolved, and to consider how relevant, or not, they might be to the case of the future UK–EU relationship.

In Chapter 2, Vasco Cal reviews the history of Portugal's relationship with the EU and shows how Portugal, as a small, postcolonial trading nation that has tried other forms of government and sought other possible multilateral arrangements, has come to the pragmatic conclusion that only full EU membership is a viable option for the country, constraining though it may be in several regards. Portugal therefore accepts all of the regulatory centralization that is involved in assuring the internal market, but it does not necessarily accept the logic for federalization going beyond that. Cal shows also how Portugal brought its own experience to bear in ensuring that the European Economic Area was more beneficial to its non-EU member states than might otherwise have been the case.

In Chapter 3, Sebastian Remøy considers the case of Norway and its membership of the European Economic Area (EEA). Like Portugal, Norway is a European country that enjoyed a close trading relationship with the UK and cleaved close to it through both the European Free Trade Association (EFTA) experiment and the first applications for European Economic Community (EEC) membership in the 1960s. Unlike Portugal, it has opted to remain outside the EU, although nevertheless staying very close to it. Remøy charts the origins and development of the EEA. He considers its complicated architecture and mechanics and its asymmetric power balances, in both the EFTA and the EU pillars. Economically and politically advantageous, but democratically disadvantageous, the EEA arrangement works for Norway but, Remøy concludes, would not for the UK. On the other hand, he argues, it will be difficult for the UK to avoid the gravitational pull of the EU's Single Market.

In Chapter 4, Georges Baur considers the case of Switzerland, another smaller European country that has had difficulty in finding an appropriate and comfortable relationship with the burgeoning EU. Baur recounts how a popular referendum diverted Switzerland from its intended membership of the EEA and turned potential full EU membership into a distant prospect. The alternative relationship, a complicated series of bilateral agreements and "softer" forms of cooperation, is intensely disliked by the EU, which has been holding out for the establishment of some sort of overarching institutional framework, although that would not resolve some of the outstanding awkward issues that have arisen. Given its particular constitutional arrangements, Switzerland sees little alternative to current practice, but from the EU point of view there is no such thing as the "Swiss model".

In Chapter 5, Selim Kuneralp recounts how Turkey's tactical request for early membership of the EU was diverted into a conditional first stage of a customs union (a unique requirement for a candidate country), which was only finally completed, in formal terms, in 1995. He recounts how Turkish industry, particularly the car industry, has since thrived. But there are nevertheless downsides to the arrangement. In particular, Turkey must align with the EU's trade policy without any say in its elaboration and has to accept restraints on its ability to conduct an autonomous trade policy with neighbouring countries. As the EU's Single Market was consolidated, so the customs union became increasingly incomplete. At the same time, as the renewed Turkish accession talks have slowed to an effective halt, so attention has turned back to completion of the union, but its asymmetric demands make it a far from optimal arrangement, even for a country in a theoretical accession perspective, let alone the contrary.

In Chapter 6, Nazar Bobitski considers the EU–Ukraine Association Agreement, described as the most advanced framework of relations ever concluded between the EU and a third country. The elaboration of the agreement took place against the backdrop of a complicated and conflict-ridden geopolitical landscape and was a first concrete realization, within the context of the new, post-Lisbon Treaty European Neighbourhood Policy, of a new type of integration without the ultimate perspective of EU membership. Impressively comprehensive in its scope, the agreement's potential is only slowly being realized. Its basic logic is to encourage convergence and a close relationship, and it is therefore of less relevance to a country set on the right to diverge. Moreover, its comprehensive scope might be considered of less relevance to a country currently determined to avoid such an approach, although the mechanics of its implementation could be of interest.

In Chapter 7, Kurt Hübner considers the EU–Canada Comprehensive and Economic Trade Agreement (CETA), which was mentioned frequently as a potential model for the UK in the hours and days after formal Brexit occurred at the end of January 2020. He documents the asymmetrical nature of what is effectively a preferential trade agreement, with an imposing regulatory and economic giant on one side. He considers the complicated implementation mechanisms (various joint committees) and the inherent logic of economic and regulatory closeness through partial alignment. Something like CETA could yet become an option for negotiators, were a "hard Brexit" to be avoided, but would take time to negotiate.

In Chapter 8, L. Alan Winters sets out the stark reality of a "World Trade Organization (WTO) rules"/"no deal" situation for the United Kingdom, detailing the massive shock to UK trade and the major cost to UK consumers that it would represent. And these shocks would come at a time when the WTO's potential to resolve disputes and function fully has been badly undermined by the actions and inaction of the Trump administration.

In Chapter 9, Alan Bollard recounts the history and development of Singapore before examining its political, social and economic model and its trade strategy. Singapore is not what British and EU politicians seem to think it is, being neither low tax, nor low regulation, nor open trade. "Singapore on the Thames" is political shorthand, therefore, for a model that does not exist.

In Chapter 10, Stephen Woolcock examines how UK membership of the Comprehensive and Progressive Trans-Pacific Partnership (CPTPP) might sit with UK's "Global Britain" option. He argues that seeking membership of the CPTPP would satisfy the political aim of projecting the concept of "Global Britain" and, if achieved, would also provide the UK with a seat at a table at which trade rules are shaped in a significant region. But UK accession to CPTPP would offer no shortcut to better access to potential growth markets in the Asia-Pacific region, nor would it be likely to have any noticeable benefits for UK economic growth and employment. Trade benefits would depend on the terms negotiated with each existing CPTPP member and these would be unlikely to exceed those that UK businesses enjoy already through the existing EU bilateral agreements. There would also be important democratic ramifications.

DIFFERENT PERSPECTIVES

A second idea behind this study is to look at Brexit from various different perspectives. Thus, in Chapter 1 Christopher Lord looks at the other end of the UK's relationship with the European integration process: the beginning. In 1954, having decided against participating in the talks launched after the 1950 Schuman Declaration, the UK signed an Association Agreement with the newly established European Coal and Steel Community. The agreement was the first of its kind. What did it deliver? Might it have delivered more? Could it have been put to better use? Were opportunities missed? And what insights might that experience give into the sort of arrangement that the UK and the EU might now negotiate?

In Chapter 11, Alexander Downer considers how, in 1973, Australia's and New Zealand's economies coped with a sudden loss of preferential market access, following the UK's accession to the EEC, obliging both economies to find other markets and models. Are there lessons in that experience from which the UK could learn? Downer believes there might be, but they would inevitably come with initial painful adjustments and subsequent reforms, always assuming that alternative markets could be found.

Lastly, in his Afterword, Sir Michael Leigh looks at the other side of the coin. The UK may have definitively left the EU but what is the EU itself likely to become in the years ahead, especially given the geopolitical context of shifting balances between the EU, Eurasia and the USA in world affairs? He considers several different scenarios. Each of them would have consequences for the UK–EU relationship, possibly creating other options which, combined with changing political circumstances in the UK, particularly in a Covid-19 world, might result in an as yet unenvisaged future relationship.

ASSOCIATED ISSUES

A third idea behind this study is to look at different issues related to the Brexit process that will have to be managed or resolved in one way or another. Thus, in Chapter 12, Alastair Sutton looks at the cases of the UK Crown Dependencies, overseas territories and Gibraltar. How far will their status be changed by Brexit? How far will the UK seek to look after their interests, and how far, given the economic consequences of the Covid-19 crisis, will it be able to do so?

In Chapter 13, David Phinnemore looks at the thorny conundrum that is the island of Ireland and, in particular, at the implementation of the Protocol to the Withdrawal Agreement on Ireland and Northern Ireland. The latter will, clearly, enjoy some differentiated treatment relative to the rest of the UK, but how will this be squared with the North's very special political circumstances?

In Chapter 14, Gijs de Vries examines the possible nature of the UK's future relationship with the EU in the context of internal and external security and defence policy. Paradoxically, the UK has played a leading role in developing the Union's internal security and yet has consistently blocked the development of the EU's external defence capacity. In any case, some arrangement will surely have to be found, but that, as de Vries documents, may take some time.

Last but not least, in Chapter 15 Martyn Bond considers the doubts about the UK's continued membership of the Council of Europe, an organization it helped to create in 1948–9 but which also requires its member states to pool their sovereignty, although to a much lesser degree.

LESSONS FOR OTHERS?

As Pascal Lamy points out in the Foreword, Brexit is unique; *du jamais vu*. Leaving aside the special cases of Algeria in 1962 and Greenland in 1985, it is the first example of a country deliberately withdrawing from the EU and consequently hindering and almost certainly changing, if not diminishing, its existing trading patterns. However, there are other countries dotted around the European continent, not currently member states, who have not yet settled on their future relationships with the EU as it, and they, evolve. A fourth idea behind this study is, therefore, that the analyses collected together here might also be of use to those countries as they ponder their futures. In, or out? Near, or far? What sort of near? What sort of far? At what price? Economic, democratic?

As several contributions to this volume attest, there are demonstrable economic advantages to full membership of the EU. Many current member states would also argue that membership brings clear political advantages. But these advantages are, potentially, offset by perceived disadvantages in terms of democracy, autonomy and national identity. In turn, those perceived disadvantages can be offset by opting for something less than full membership. However, anything less than full membership also comes with economic and political disadvantages. Meanwhile, European countries have come to understand that the EU is a trade and regulatory giant, exercising the "Brussels effect", whether they are in it or outside it.

As the studies in this book demonstrate, each country makes its own calculation about what relationship is most appropriate. That calculation will, in one way or another, take into account a country's history, its traditions, its size and its sense of itself and of its future. That calculation will also consider perceived advantages and disadvantages, economic and other (political, democratic, constitutional). The UK is no different in that regard. And nor are the 27 European countries currently subsumed within the EU although, as with Portugal, their membership obfuscates very different routes to what seems for the time being to be the same destination. Who now remembers, for example, that Austria, Finland, Ireland, Malta and Sweden were previously neutral countries, let alone that Malta was until very recently "non-aligned"? Yet these were once, not so long ago, important signifiers for these countries' identities and futures.

In any case, it could be argued that Brexit is not quite the aberration that it is currently considered to be, nor European integration the beneficent one-way perpetual motion process that it is frequently portrayed as being: Algeria (1962) was the first territory to leave the EEC, followed later by Greenland (1985) and now by the UK (2020); Europe has said definitively "no" to Morocco (1987) and "no, but" variously to Greece and Turkey (1959), Spain (1962), the UK, Norway, Ireland and Denmark (1963, 1967), and Andorra, Monaco and San Marino (2012); and, the other way around, the people of Norway (1972, 1994) and Switzerland (1992) preferred not to join, while Iceland (2013) decided to suspend accession negotiations; the people of Denmark (2000) and Sweden (2003), meanwhile, voted not to join the euro, and the people of Denmark (2015) voted not to opt in to various justice and home affairs provisions. A complete list would also include the many referendum setbacks for the Maastricht

Treaty (Denmark), Nice Treaty (Ireland), Constitutional Treaty (France, the Netherlands) and the Lisbon Treaty (Ireland) and all the many exceptional-isms granted to various member states through rebates, opt-ins, opt-outs, treaty annexes, declarations and other fixes that have cumulatively and collectively enabled the EU "show" to remain "on the road".

And nor should organized, integrated "Europe" be understood as only being about the EU. As Martyn Bond reminds us in Chapter 15, the 47-member Council of Europe is also working, in less obvious, more time-consuming but effective ways, at organizing and integrating this broader Europe, and nor should the Organization for Security and Co-operation in Europe, with 50 European countries among its membership of 57, be forgotten in this context, nor should various regional organizations be overlooked (the Nordic Council, for example).

In closing, I should perhaps point out that I have adopted a light editorial hand throughout this book, letting the experts speak for themselves. The point, for me as editor, is to illuminate the ongoing debate, not to take sides in it. In his Afterword, Michael Leigh points to the changing geopolitical nature of the world, particularly in Covid-19 times. Who knows how the world might change? But, for as long as they both still exist, the UK and the EU will continue to coexist and interrelate. That much is certain and, ultimately, a way will be found.

1

LESSONS FROM THE PAST? THE 1954 ASSOCIATION AGREEMENT BETWEEN THE UK AND THE EUROPEAN COAL AND STEEL COMMUNITY

Christopher Lord

INTRODUCTION

It was one of the strangest cabinet meetings in British political history.[1] Yet it was also one of the most important. The three leading members of the government – the prime minister (Clement Attlee), the foreign secretary (Ernest Bevin) and the chancellor of the exchequer (Stafford Cripps) – were absent, either on holiday or in hospital. It was thus a depleted cabinet that decided on 2 June 1950 to decline the invitation to participate in the talks which led to the formation of the European Coal and Steel Community (ECSC).

The meeting was chaired by the Deputy Leader of the Labour Party, Herbert Morrison, who would later say that the "Durham miners would not wear" participation in a ECSC.[2] Still, a full cabinet would probably not have decided differently. Although the UK was not being asked at that stage to accept a coal and steel community under an independent supranational authority, it was being asked to confine any talks to that option. Given that Bevin had earlier described the Council of Europe in a magnificently mixed metaphor as a "Pandora's Box full of Trojan Horses"[3] he was unsurprisingly also opposed to any "ultimatum on pooling the coal and steel industries of Great Britain with those of other countries".[4]

A common interpretation[5] is that the UK stumbled into a fateful self-exclusion from what would become the European Communities through a mixture of accident, conceit, incompetent preoccupation with the internal politics of the Labour Party ("the Durham miners will not have it") and suspicion of forms of European integration with supranational institutions and federal ambitions ("a Pandora's box full of Trojan Horses"). That suspicion may also have been self-defeating. Had the UK accepted the invitation to the talks it might have bent them to its own preferences for a more intergovernmental form of cooperation. As Edmund Dell put it, the UK might have "sucked the federalism" out of the ECSC had it remained in the talks[6] (after all, even without the UK the ECSC emerged with a Council of Ministers that had not been a part of Jean Monnet's original design of the Schuman Plan).

Instead, the UK ended up with a modest Association Agreement with the ECSC, agreed in December 1954. The association, as we will see, was useful. Yet it is little remembered. Nor is it much discussed in the literature on the UK and European integration.[7] Both the UK and the Six soon turned their attention to other initiatives. By 1955 the Six were already discussing plans to supplement the sectoral ECSC with a more general-purpose European Economic Community (EEC), which would be agreed in the Treaty of Rome (1957), and a European Atomic Energy Community (which, together with the ECSC, were known as the European Communities). In 1958 the UK responded with a plan for a wider European Free Trade Area of 15 members of the Organisation for European Economic Co-operation. When that initiative failed, the British government concluded in 1961 that it had little alternative but to apply for full membership of the European Communities.[8]

However, for fear that any negotiation with the UK might unravel the Communities, and aware of how difficult it had been even to negotiate those Communities between themselves, the Six famously insisted that the UK should accept all existing institutions, policies and commitments (the *acquis communautaire*) unchanged. "Swallow the lot and swallow it now" was how the official in charge of the 1970–1 negotiations, Con O'Neill, described what was expected of the UK.[9] That meant the UK joined in 1973 on largely disadvantageous terms that only made sense on the assumption that the costs of continued self-exclusion would be even higher than the costs of inclusion. Policies it could have shaped by joining in the 1950s – rather than settling for a modest association agreement – became burdens of late entry in the 1970s. Thus began a sour relationship.[10]

Now the UK is once again a non-member, it is worth revisiting the Association Agreement of 1954. Looking forwards, does it have any lessons for any future association between the UK and EU after Brexit? Looking back, might it have been a mistake not to stick with association, rather than seek full membership after 1961? Those questions might seem a hopeless mixture of the speculative and the anachronistic. The UK and the European Union of the 2020s are both hugely different from their equivalents of the 1950s. Yet, there are constants: first, in the reasons why the UK then, as now, found itself a non-member; and second, in what it means to be a non-member and in options available to democracies that are closely affected neighbours of a European Community or Union without being a member of it.

In what follows, then, I trace the winding path between the decision in June 1950 not to participate in the Schuman talks, and the Association Agreement of December 1954. I distinguish respectively the constitutional, foreign policy and political economy dimensions of the UK's search for an association with the ECSC, before concluding with some tentative questions and observations for speculative debates about association after Brexit and the counterfactual debate on whether the UK might have done better to seek further associations rather than full membership after 1961.

ASSOCIATION AS A CONSTITUTIONAL SOLUTION

With all the normal caveats about nothing being historically inevitable, there is something of a continuous storyline from the cabinet meeting on 2 June 1950 to the vote to leave the European Union on 23 June 2016. Many members of the British governments – both Labour (1945–51) and Conservative (1951–64) – which rejected fuller participation in the ECSC would have recognized the central argument of the Leave campaign in 2016 that the UK should not participate in any form of European Community in which it did not have full control of its own laws.

Attlee claimed in the House of Commons debate on the Schuman Plan that his government was "enthusiastic about European Unity ... but it was no good being enthusiastic for the wrong method"; and the High Authority proposed in the Schuman Plan was, in Attlee's view, decidedly the wrong method. As he put it, the Authority was "utterly undemocratic and responsible to no one".[11] Sir Anthony Eden made a similar argument on taking up responsibility for questions of European integration on his return to the Foreign Office in the new Conservative government (1951–64): "Much of the criticism of our policy stems from a failure to distinguish between cooperation in Europe and the federation of Europe ... It is only when plans for uniting Europe take a federal form that we cannot take part, because we cannot subordinate ourselves or the control of British policy to federal authorities."[12]

What, though, made institutional and constitutional questions fundamental was that they shaped the relationship the UK *did* form with the ECSC as well as reasons for not participating as a founding member. During 1950–1 the British government defined, but did not publish, the intergovernmental form of coal and steel community in which it might have been prepared to participate.[13] In the meantime it expected "to find means of associating with whatever organizations may emerge from successful schemes of integration".

So, all eventualities seemed to be covered: if the ECSC negotiations failed, the UK would be ready with an intergovernmental proposal of its own; if the negotiations succeeded, the UK would seek to associate with any ECSC. Association would just be a standard international agreement. It would be limited to cooperation to mutual advantage. The UK would not be bound by the decisions of supranational institutions or committed to a process of further integration. The Schuman declaration had been clear; the ECSC was supposed to be the first step in a continuing process of federation. Hence, Foreign Office officials warned, the UK should only join if it was prepared "to be hustled along the road to full federation through the creation of supranational institutions controlling a widening range of functions".[14] Otherwise it should just associate.

Once, however, the ECSC negotiations succeeded, tensions emerged on just what the UK government meant by association.[15] A joint declaration in September 1951 of the foreign ministers of France, the UK and the USA claimed that "the UK desires the closest possible association with the European continental community at all stages of its development".[16] Yet a cabinet meeting two months earlier had not only rejected the option of partial membership that the Six had intriguingly and unexpectedly included in the draft treaty. The cabinet also rejected any formal instrument of association in favour of just appointing a permanent delegation to the High Authority. As a note to the foreign secretary put it, a formal association would be "difficult to negotiate and would not be essential for the close and friendly relationship we have in mind. It would be better to allow consultation to develop on a case-by-case basis."[17]

The same question of whether the UK wanted an ambitious or modest association emerged as soon as the new Conservative government took office on 26 October 1951. Within weeks, Churchill circulated a memo to the cabinet arguing we "are with but not of Europe. Our attitude is that we help, we dedicate, we participate, but we do not merge and we do not forfeit our insular or Commonwealth character."[18] Yet Churchill was determined that dedication or participation should mean something more than what he considered "socialist" hostility to the ECSC. The Eden Plan of 1952, accordingly, attempted to take the initiative by proposing that any member of the Council of Europe should be able to associate with the ECSC or the then proposal for a European Defence Community. The Eden Plan addressed the wider question of the division of Western Europe into "ins" and "outs" from any supranational communities in a way that went beyond the UK's own needs for any association.

However, to make the plan work, Eden proposed that the ECSC and European Defence Community would use the institutions of the Council of Europe. As François Duchêne put it, the Eden Plan thus came across as a "bizarre attempt to subordinate the federal Community to the intergovernmental Council of Europe".[19] Monnet even told the British government that if any attempt was made to impose the Eden Plan he would simply ask the ECSC Court to "declare it unconstitutional",[20] an interesting early indicator that any European Community might understand itself as an autonomous legal order.

With little support among the Six, the Eden Plan was dead well before the European Defence Community was voted down by the French Assembly in 1954. The Association of December 1954 was, therefore, a bilateral agreement between the UK and the ECSC. That, however, had curious constitutional implications. The UK shielded itself from constitutional implications by merely associating with the ECSC. But its association was a step in the constitutional development of the European Communities: a "non-state" associated with a "real state, and a large one"[21] without that agreement being mediated by the ECSC's member states.

What should we make of the Association Agreement of 1954? A core difficulty was that avoiding supranational commitments was only a part of what British governments wanted from any relationship with an ECSC. While in hindsight the cabinet meeting of 2 June 1950 was a parting of the ways, that was not how things appeared at the time. The interdepartmental committee of officials that advised the cabinet on the Schuman Plan felt that it was "unlikely by refusing to join in now on the French terms we shall be prevented from participating in European discussions in some manner later on".[22] Attlee assured the French ambassador, René Massigli, of his hope that "at a later stage we might be able to come in more fully".[23]

Abstention was not the core of British policy.[24] Rather, British governments sought influence without membership. Here there were various conceptions of "influence". One was that the UK would be able to negotiate as an equal, even if the Six formed themselves into a block actor through the ECSC. Bevin told Massigli that, once the Six had decided between themselves what they wanted, the UK "as a country with a great steel and coal industry would meet the new European organization, whether that took the form of a supranational or governmental authority". A solution would then allow the "two systems" to "operate".[25]

Another view implied that the UK would be a de facto veto holder over any European Communities. Reflecting on the Coal and Steel and Defence Communities, the permanent under-secretary's committee of top Foreign Office officials argued that the Six would not be able "to put their federal ideas into practice without at least the blessing and probably the active participation of the UK".[26] A final idea was that the UK would be able to lead any process of European integration from the outside, not least as "a bridge between West Europe and North America".[27] In Peter Hennessy's beautiful analogy, it was "as if Britain could be the manager of the football team without joining the other six on the playing field".[28]

FOREIGN POLICY AND ASSOCIATION

It was their foreign policy doctrine that made it thinkable to British governments that they could influence any European Community from the outside and unthinkable that they should not seek to do so. The governments of the 1950s subscribed to what Hennessy has called the "geometric conceit" that only the UK was at the intersection of the three circles of the free world; the Commonwealth, North America and Western Europe.[29] Here, constitutional and foreign policy arguments for staying out of any supranational European Communities overlapped. The UK could not be a trusted intermediary between all three circles if it were committed to integration with just one of them.

Yet the three circles doctrine also implied limits to how far the UK could stay out of any European Community. Eden warned against the "naive view that the Anglo-American relationship or the Commonwealth provided alternative routes for Britain which would enable it to dispense with a close European association".[30] The three circles doctrine was the product of insecurity as much as conceit. If the UK's relationships with each of the circles were interdependent, they could unravel together as much as reinforce one another.

However, the difficulties of influencing any European Community from the outside became obvious from the very process of attempting to associate with the ECSC. It was not always easy to define a third way between full membership and no relationship at all; or to identify a form of association that did not just reproduce objections to participating as a full member; or to achieve what the UK might want from an association in ways that were acceptable to a group of countries trying to establish themselves as a newly formed club with some meaningful differences between rights and obligations available to members and non-members.

In June 1951, the new chancellor of the exchequer, Hugh Gaitskell, cautioned against "a purely informal and *ad hoc* relationship". As he put it, the "industrial giant that looks like being created across the Channel could do us considerable harm". It would be dangerous "to drift into a condition of hostility" with it.[31] A Treasury memo added: "In the narrow sense of making bargains on coal and steel, we could probably get on well enough outside. But if we wish the Community to develop along the right lines, we need to develop as close relationships as possible."[32] Yet, for Morrison, now foreign secretary, whether the Six would be prepared to "limit their plans" so that the UK "might eventually be associated with them"[33] was now a question to be asked, rather than something to be assumed. Others in the Foreign Office worried that cherry-picking or cakeism *avant la lettre* in seeking "the obligations and rights that benefit us" while "rejecting those that do not" would only "invite a rebuff" at some cost to the credibility of British policy.[34]

Suspicion of the UK's motives also limited its influence. While the Eden Plan fanned suspicion that the UK wanted to supervise the ECSC, the UK was, for the most part, debilitated from proposing much at all for fear of the "utmost political odium"[35] that might follow from being perceived as wanting to sabotage any European integration. Here the UK most feared the "odium" of the United States, which helped broker the agreement between the Six. The UK had been right that the ECSC would not be agreed without external help, but wrong to assume that it had any monopoly on external leadership.

Already by the end of 1950, the Foreign Office was beginning to doubt its ability to take positions on a process of which it was as not a part: "we are in the awkward position of having to consider a text without having taken part in any of the discussion and bargaining that led up to it".[36] By 1951 the Cabinet Office worried that the UK position was at risk of becoming absurd. Schuman himself wanted UK comments on anything in the draft ECSC Treaty that might later smooth the way to an association agreement. Yet, still uncertain what to propose, government policy was now to avoid comment until all the Six ratified the treaty.

Still, the idea of association remained coherent. The UK and the ECSC could cooperate to their mutual advantage without anyone having to accept unwanted constitutional arrangements: without the supranational six being subordinated to a wider intergovernmental agreement or without the UK being bound by supranational decisions. Peaceful co-existence was possible (to use another 1950s term from the Cold War). But that was, arguably, because the Association Agreement of 1954 focused on interdependencies and questions of political economy, rather than foreign policy ambitions or retaining UK influence over further European integration, as the following section explains.

THE POLITICAL ECONOMY OF ASSOCIATION

From the point of view of Franco-German reconciliation, coal and steel could hardly have been better choices to initiate a process of sectoral cooperation in Western Europe. From a point of view of persuading a Labour government to participate in a European Community that conferred powers on an independent authority those industries could hardly have been worse chosen. Coal had only just been nationalized and steel was still in the process of being nationalized. Coal and steel were considered the "commanding heights" of the mid-twentieth century. The power to influence investment in coal and steel following their nationalization was expected to be the main means by which Labour governments would introduce an element of economic planning and ensure full employment.

Many in the labour movement had struggled for a generation to bring coal and steel into public ownership. They were not now about to share control of those industries with six other countries whose politics and governments they suspected of being at best unstable and at worst exposed to the influence of monopoly capitalism. As Kenneth Morgan has put it, "the Labour Party was from top to bottom hostile".[37] Reduced to a majority of six in the February 1950 election and expecting to have to fight another election soon, the Labour government was in no position to risk a rebellion in its own party by seeking anything more than an association with the ECSC.

The Conservative government of 1951–64 was not constrained in the same way. It would base demand management on cuts in income tax rather than varying investment in coal and steel. It was also freer to focus on one form of interdependence that could require cooperation between the coal and steel industries of the UK and those of the Six. Given the enormous scale and indivisibilities of capital formation in coal and steel, it would be easy for producers in any one country to miscalculate output and investment with adverse effects on the overall stability of economic cycles across the UK and Western Europe. The government's economic adviser advised the 1950–1 Attlee government that there would be great advantage "in the co-ordination of investment, regulation or production in a slump".[38] A working party of officials on the ECSC Treaty advised the 1951–5 Churchill government: "it would be in our interests to see a satisfactory balance of demand and supply … Instability brings dangers of violent price wars".[39] Hence, when, in 1952, the UK established a permanent delegation to the ECSC, conversations turned to ways in which cooperation could avoid either overproduction or shortages in coal and steel. That was also important to the 1954 Association Agreement.[40]

CONCLUDING LESSONS: BACK TO THE FUTURE?

The 1950s were a different world. Yet there may be lessons for any attempt to design an association between the UK and EU after Brexit. The EU can only negotiate an association as a bloc actor. That logical and legal necessity confers strategic advantages on members who may, in any case, need to prioritize relationships with one another, given they are constrained to cohabit the policies and institutions of the Union. Without full information about the preferences of members and without being a part of their preference formation a non-member may then suffer problems of bounded rationality in making its bargaining moves.

Perhaps an even deeper difficulty is that the Union operates as a club good. There are other explanations and justifications for the Union's political, legal and normative order. But one of them is that the Union is a structure of rights and obligations for the provision of key collective goods that its members cannot provide separately. But that presupposes an ability to exclude free riders. The Union cannot be the Union without tediously and inflexibly insisting that rights and benefits really cannot be had without obligations and costs. Yet a non-member may, in turn, be unable to take on some of those obligations without contradicting some of the reasons for not wanting to be a member in the first place. Membership and non-membership are closely related. The relationships members can offer non-members are constrained by the obligations of membership; and reasons for not being a member limit the relationships a country can have with the Union as a non-member. All these difficulties will constrain any association after Brexit. All constrained the search for association between 1950 and 1954 and explain why the eventual association was one of mutual advantage rather than mutual obligation. It identified where the UK and the ECSC would need to discuss and coordinate, but did not commit to much more than that.

So, should the UK have stuck to associating for reasons of mutual advantage rather than seeking to take on the obligations of membership after 1961? That suggestion would turn much historical interpretation on its head. It would mean the great mistake of the UK's relationship with the European Union was not the cabinet meeting of 1950 that turned down the invitation to the Schuman talks but that of 1961 that decided to apply for membership of the European Communities. Political economy tells us there should have been significant "gains from trade" to be had from concentrating just on mutually advantageous associations. In contrast, the bid for full membership perpetuated foreign policy delusions and constitutional phobias.

For decades, British Eurosceptics would argue that a fraud had been perpetuated on the British people by joining without explaining the constitutional significance of membership. Yet, in part, that was because British governments did not seek to explain membership as much as change its nature. Alan Milward noted how Con O'Neill "put on paper a truth that could scarcely be uttered": namely, that a "large if unavowable part of our objective in negotiating membership from 1961–3 was precisely that of changing the character of the Community".[41]

A focus on further associations rather than membership might have been more honest both with British Eurosceptic opinion and the European Communities. It might have allowed the UK and the Communities to manage aspects of their interdependence while acknowledging institutional differences.[42] But, for associations to do that, they need to be based on an understanding of the large differences between membership and non-membership. They cannot be attempts to perpetuate membership by other means.

Notes for Chapter 1

1. Most of the documents used in this chapter are available in R. Bullen and M. Pelly (eds), Documents on British Policy Overseas 1950–1952, Series II, Vol. 1, *The Schuman Plan, the Council of Europe and Western European Integration* (London: HMSO, 1986). However, I also list the full references below to give the reader an idea of the importance of the sources.

2. K. Morgan, *Labour in Power 1945–1951* (Oxford: Oxford University Press, 1985), 420.

3. A. Bullock, *Ernest Bevin: Foreign Secretary 1945–1951* (London: Heinemann, 1983), 659.

4. Record of a conversation with Mr Bevin at the London Clinic, 2 June 1950, PRO [CE 2677/2141/181]. Bullen & Pelly, 135.

5. E. Dell, *The Schuman Plan and the Abdication of British Leadership in Europe* (Oxford: Oxford University Press, 1995).

6. *Ibid.*, 289–90.

7. Although, for exceptions, see W. Diebold *The Schuman Plan: A Study in Economic Co-operation 1950-1959* (New York: Praeger, 1959); R. Ranieri, "Inside or outside the magic circle? The Italian and British steel industries face to face with the Schuman Plan and European Coal Iron and Steel Community" in A. Milward *et al.* (eds) *The Frontier of National Sovereignty: History and Theory 1945-1992* (London: Routledge, 1993); D. Spierenberg & R. Poidevin, *The History of the High Authority of the European Coal and Steel Community: Supranationality in Operation*, (London: Weidenfeld & Nicolson, 1994); J. Young, "The Schuman Plan and British Association" in J. Young (ed.) *The Foreign Policy of Churchill's Peacetime Administration 1951-1955* (Leicester: Leicester University Press, 1988).

8. R. Griffiths, "A slow one hundred and eighty degrees turn: British policy towards the Common Market 1955–1960" in G. Wilkes (ed.) *Britain's Failure to Enter the European Community 1961-63* (London: Frank Cass, 1997), 35–50.

9. Quoted in P. Ludlow, "'Swallow the lot and swallow it now': Britain is, and was, deluded about its negotiating power with the EU", LSE Blog, 22 November 2017, https://blogs.lse.ac.uk/brexit/2017/11/09/swallow-the-lot-and-swallow-it-now-britain-is-and-was-deluded-about-its-negotiating-power-with-the-eu. Retrieved 7 February 2020.

10. S. George, *An Awkward Partner: Britain in the European Community* (Oxford: Oxford University Press, 1998).

11. House of Commons Debates, 27 June 1950, columns 2169–71.

12. Mr Eden to HM Representatives Overseas, "United Kingdom attitude to European Integration", 15 December 1951, PRO [F.O.953/1207]. Bullen & Pelly, 790–1.

13. Conclusions of a Meeting of the Cabinet, 4 July 1950 PRO [CAB 128/18]. See also Report by a Committee of Ministers, 1 July 1950, PRO [CAB 129/40]. Bullen & Pelly, 234–9, 247–50.

14. "Background to the problem of European integration", Memorandum of the Permanent Under Secretary's Committee of the Foreign Office, 9 June 1951, PRO [ZP 18/20]. Bullen & Pelly, 587–94.

15. Minutes of a Meeting of the Economic Policy Committee held at No. 10 Downing Street, 24 July 1951, PRO [CAB 134/228]. Bullen & Pelly, 674–6.

16. Declaration of the Foreign Ministers of France, the United Kingdom and the United States. F.R.U.S. 1951, Vol. 3, 1306–8.

17. Brief by Sir R. Makins for the Secretary of State, 23 July 1951, PRO [CE(W) 1543/390]. Bullen & Pelly, 673.

18. Memorandum by the Prime Minister, 29 November 1951, PRO [C (51) 32].

19. F. Duchêne, *Jean Monnet: The First Statesman of Interdependence* (New York: Norton, 1994), 237.

20. *Ibid.*, 238.

21. *Ibid.*, 261.

22. "Integration of French and German Coal and Steel Industries". A Report by a Committee of Officials, 2 June 1950, PRO [CAB 129/40]. Bullen & Pelly, 137–8.

23. Record of Mr Attlee's Conversation at lunch with the French Ambassador, 7 June 1950, PRO [PREM 8/1428]. Bullen & Pelly, 165–6.

24. C. Lord, *Absent at the Creation: Britain and the Schuman Plan 1950–2* (Aldershot: Dartmouth, 1996) and C. Lord, "'With but not of', Britain and the Schuman Plan: a reinterpretation", *Journal of European Integration History* 4:2 (1998), 23–46.

25. Bevin to Hayter, 31 August 1950, PRO [WF 1051/13]. Bullen & Pelly, 299–300.

26. Minutes of a Meeting of the Permanent Under-Secretary's Committee, 29 March 1951, PRO [ZP 18/1]. Bullen & Pelly, 457–62.

27. Memorandum for the Permanent Under-Secretary's Committee, 13 February 1951, PRO [ZP 18/19]. Bullen & Pelly, 393–400.

28. P. Hennessy, *Having It So Good: Britain in the Fifties* (London: Penguin, 2006), 288.

29. *Ibid.*

30. E. Shuckburgh, *Descent to Suez: Diaries 1951–6* (New York: Norton, 1986), 17–18.

31. Memorandum by Mr Gaitskell, 17 July 1951, PRO [CAB 134/230]. Bullen & Pelly, 646–50.

32. The Schuman Plan. Brief by Mr Pitblado, 20 July 1951, PRO [T 229/753]. Bullen & Pelly, 655–6.

33. Mr Morrison to HM Representatives in Western Europe, 16 April 1951, PRO [ZP18/1]. Bullen & Pelly, 488–90.

34. See Roger Makins' views recorded in the Minutes of the Economic Steering Committee, 9 July 1951, PRO [CAB 134/264]. Bullen & Pelly, 633.

35. Makins to Strang, 28 June 1950, PRO [CE3353/2141/181]. Bullen & Pelly, 225.

36. Mr Wilson to Viscount Hood (Paris), 25 November 1950, PRO [CE 5735/2141/181]. Bullen & Pelly, 349–51.

37. Morgan, *Labour in Power*, 419.

38. Hall to Attlee, 21 June 1950, PRO [PREM 8/1428].

39. Report of the Working Party of Officials on the Treaty Constituting the European Coal and Steel Community, 31 December 1951, PRO [FG (WP) (51) (43)].

40. W. Feld, "The Association Agreements of the European Communities: A comparative analysis", *International Organization* 19:2 (1965), 229.

41. A. Milward, "Childe Harold's pilgrimage" in J. Noakes, P. Wende & J. Wright (eds) *Britain and Germany in Europe 1949–1990* (Oxford: Oxford University Press, 2002), 62.

42. C. Wurm, "Britain and West European integration 1948–9 to 1955: politics and economics" in Noakes, Wende & Wright (eds) *Britain and Germany in Europe 1949–1990*, 27–48.

2

FROM THE EUROPEAN FREE TRADE ASSOCIATION TO THE EUROPEAN ECONOMIC COMMUNITY AND THE EUROPEAN ECONOMIC AREA: PORTUGAL'S POST-SECOND WORLD WAR PATH

Vasco Cal

PORTUGAL AND THE SECOND WORLD WAR

The long authoritarian rule of António de Oliveira Salazar (1932–68) and the democratic transition following the 1974 Carnation Revolution were the main factors determining Portugal's post-Second World War position regarding European organizations. Following a 28 May 1926 military coup d'état against the democratic regime, Salazar was appointed finance minister and granted extraordinary powers to enable the country to avoid imminent financial collapse. On 5 July 1932 he was appointed as Portugal's one hundredth prime minister. A new constitution was drafted, with Salazar as its guiding spirit. Taking a leaf out of the book of other authoritarian and fascist regimes at that time, he organized a popular referendum on 19 March 1933 to approve his Constitution but also to consolidate his powers and vision.

The resulting *Estado Novo* (New State) effectively established an anti-parliamentarian, corporatist and authoritarian form of governance that would last until 1974. Salazar rapidly outlawed political parties, imprisoned opposition leaders, instituted censorship of the press and reorganized the state, imitating many of the features of the regime of his contemporary in Italy, Benito Mussolini, including the creation of a secret police service, the "State Defence and Surveillance Police" (*Polícia Internacional e de Defesa do Estado*) which, profiting from technical assistance from Nazi Germany's Gestapo, established concentration camps and tortured prisoners.

Salazar consolidated his hold on power during the 1930s, surviving abortive uprisings and a 1937 assassination attempt. During the 1939–45 war, the Portuguese government adopted a "neutral" position, aiming to preserve its profitable economic trade with Germany but also wishing not to jeopardize its centuries-old alliance with the United Kingdom (the Anglo-Portuguese Alliance, ratified by the Treaty of Windsor in 1386, remains to this day the oldest extant alliance in the world). Portugal's neutrality also meant that its overseas territories were less at risk of invasion and occupation. However, following the December 1941 entry of the United States into the war and the strategic importance for the Allied forces of the Azores, the Portuguese government was forced to align itself more closely with the Allies, while remaining theoretically neutral.

This alignment, and Portugal's tacit complicity with the British and Americans in particular, effectively created the conditions that enabled the country to participate in some of the key postwar conferences about the reorganization of European, and the creation of transatlantic, structures. Thus, Portugal was among the founder nations that signed the 4 April 1949 North Atlantic Treaty, and therefore became a founder member of the North Atlantic Treaty Organization (NATO), and it was among the founder nations that established the Organisation for European Economic Cooperation (OEEC) in 1948 and hence of the Organisation for Economic Co-operation and Development (OECD) that superseded it in September 1961.

PORTUGAL JOINS THE EUROPEAN FREE TRADE ASSOCIATION

Portugal did not, however, participate in the 1948 conference in The Hague that led to the 5 May 1949 signing of the Treaty of London and the subsequent creation of the Council of Europe, with its emphasis on human rights and the rule of law (Portugal would not join the organization until 22 September 1976), and nor did it respond to Robert Schuman's 9 May 1950 declaration, with its explicitly stated goal of the federation of Europe. Portugal was subsequently not among the participating countries in the 1955 Messina Conference and the 1955–6 Spaak Committee, nor among the signatories of the 25 March 1957 Treaty of Rome, which had agreed to the creation of a European Economic Community (EEC) with a customs union and common policies, including agriculture. But Portugal *did* join the rival 1956–8 conferences promoted by the United Kingdom, within the framework of the OEEC, with a view to creating a broader free trade area between the six EEC founder member states and the remaining 11 OEEC member European countries.

However, Portugal's primary strategic concern at that time – to save its colonies – made it difficult for the country to adopt a definitive position. Despite international pressure, Salazar had rebuffed a 1950 request from India's prime minister, Jawarharlal Nehru, to hand over Portugal's enclaves in India and had amended the constitution so that its colonies became overseas "provinces" and hence an integral part of its territory, enabling him to affirm Portugal's status as a pluricontinental nation (a concept borrowed from the fourteenth century) and not as a colonial empire. In addition, a distinction had rapidly developed between the most developed countries (the United Kingdom, Norway, Sweden, Switzerland, Austria, Denmark) and the less developed (Greece, Turkey, Ireland, Portugal, Iceland). Portugal could not risk being outside of the different arrangements being discussed. At the same time, Portugal noted well the strong opposition from the most developed countries to the demands from some of the less developed countries for financial support and for a thirty-year transition period.

Given all of this, the Portuguese government decided, with tactical shrewdness, not to ask for any financial support and instead to concentrate on demands related to tariff reductions, and the creation of a "special case" status for itself. This nuanced tactical approach was welcomed by some of the more developed countries, particularly Norway and Switzerland,[1] and Portugal's specific situation was explicitly recognized in the reports for the creation of the proposed broader European Free Trade Area (EFTA). Following repeated clashes between the British and the (rightly) suspicious French delegations during the negotiations, the French counter-proposed a multilateral association agreement (the European Economic Association) but negotiations thereafter became bogged down until on 15 November 1958 an impatient and irritated French president, General Charles de Gaulle, unilaterally rejected the British free trade agreement (FTA) proposal. The negotiations were at an end.

At first the collapse of the negotiations seemed to have doomed Portugal's tactical approach. But in the spring of 1959 the six most developed countries invited Portugal to join them in negotiating a smaller free trade area that would give them collectively some of the benefits of eliminating customs barriers. Negotiations began in Switzerland.[2] On 20 November 1959 the resulting European Free Trade Association Treaty was initialled in Stockholm. Portugal had been a full party to the negotiations throughout. The Portuguese negotiators, well aware that their country was the only one[3] of the less developed European countries invited to take part in the negotiations, had maintained their previous tactics of not asking for any financial support but, instead, of requesting special case status and hoping to benefit from tariff dismantlement concessions in the new free trade area. Ultimately, those concessions would become Annex G of the 1959 EFTA Stockholm Convention.[4]

On 12 January 1960, the European Free Trade Association Treaty was signed in the Golden Hall of the Prince's Palace in Stockholm. Portugal joined Austria,

Denmark, Norway, Sweden, Switzerland and the United Kingdom as one of EFTA's seven founder members. In the same year Portugal joined the General Agreement on Tariffs and Trade, the International Monetary Fund and the World Bank. Given Portugal's political system and status as a still authoritarian, still colonial and non-democratic state, this was something of a coup, especially when compared and contrasted with similarly authoritarian Spain, which became a NATO member in 1992 (as seen above, Portugal was there from the beginning, in 1949) and a member of the OECD in 1961 (again, Portugal was a founder member in 1948) and would never become an EFTA member.

Although overshadowed by the progress being made by the "inner six" in the steadily evolving EEC, the EFTA also enjoyed quiet success. Finland became an associate member in 1961 and by 1966 most tariffs within EFTA had been abolished and it had become a free trade area for industrial products. Portugal's participation in EFTA and the more open economic area it created had a profound impact on the growth, development and modernization of the country's economy, with increases in foreign direct investment, participation in the international division of labour, and exports, and all this against the backdrop of very high economic growth rates throughout the 1960s.

That this positive impact was not even greater was due to Portugal's increasingly fragile situation. This included a still authoritarian regime; sapping colonial wars that ended up consuming 35 per cent of the country's budget; strong migratory flows to other European countries; high energy dependence; a very weak education system; and low infrastructure investment. Moreover, under the country's industrial policy, the so-called "Industrial Conditioning Law", all significant investment needed approval from the government and protection for domestic producers, no matter how inefficient, was guaranteed.

In 1968 Salazar suffered a debilitating brain haemorrhage (he died in 1970) and was replaced by Marcelo Caetano, but the authoritarian model of governance continued. Changes in the world economic situation at the beginning of the 1970s, with Richard Nixon's 15 August 1971 abandonment of the gold standard and the increase in oil prices that followed, created new challenges for the Portuguese economy. The United Kingdom, together with Denmark, left EFTA in 1972 and joined the EEC on 1 January 1973. In 1972 Portugal, like the other remaining EFTA countries, negotiated a preferential trade agreement with the EEC; in Portugal's case primarily to maintain its access to the UK market. But the burden of the country's colonial wars, with an army of 350,000 in three different African theatres of operation (Angola, Mozambique and Guinea-Bissau), was becoming increasingly difficult to manage. In effect, it was an impossible situation that the Caetano regime was unable to solve.

THE DEMOCRATIC TRANSITION AND EU MEMBERSHIP

In the end, a peaceful 25 April 1974 military coup (the "Carnation Revolution"), coupled with a civil resistance campaign, overthrew the government and triggered a confused and turbulent two-year revolutionary process, with a coup and counter-coup ultimately leading to the postwar country's first free elections on 25 April 1975. The resulting constituent assembly began work on drafting a new constitution. As they watched these, at first uncertain, developments, governments and political parties in Europe and the US took varying positions about the Portuguese democratic process. Notably, Henry Kissinger, then US secretary of state, considered Portugal to be a lost case that should be isolated so as not to create contagion in similar cases, particularly Greece and Spain, which were also in the process of overturning their authoritarian regimes. The EEC as a whole took a more nuanced wait-and-see position while also reinforcing support to like-minded Portuguese political parties.

An immediate effect of the 1974 coup was a rapid and complete process of decolonization, leading to profound shocks to the Portuguese economy. In November 1975, EFTA – of which Portugal remained a member state – decided to establish a fund to support the development and restructuring of Portuguese industry. The fund was set up in 1976 and started operating on 1 February 1977. The establishment of the fund was a result of discussions at the EFTA Consultative Committee during 1975, at which representatives of the Portuguese social partners with the support of Swedish representatives of industry argued for the need to show concrete solidarity with a fellow member state and to help reinforce its modernization and economic development. Thanks to flexible and close relations between EFTA's Consultative Committee and the member states' ministers the proposal was rapidly adopted by the EFTA Council.[5]

The new Portuguese Republic's first general election, held on 25 April 1975, resulted in a plurality of votes for the Socialist Party, and its leader, Mário Soares, subsequently became prime minister. Determined to return Portugal's economy to the European-encouraged growth rates of the 1960s, on 28 March 1977 Soares applied for membership of the EEC. The new democratic government in Spain followed soon after (28 June 1977). Greece had applied on 12 June 1975.

The negotiations with Portugal and Spain took almost nine years. Although it had made much economic progress during the 1960s, Portugal was still a relatively less developed country. Decolonization and the revolutionary period had additionally taken their toll. In 1975 Portugal's per capita gross domestic product (GDP) had reached 52.3 per cent of the EC-12 average. As when the country joined EFTA, Portuguese negotiators were therefore faced with the task of protecting industry and agriculture, trying to negotiate derogations, exemptions and transition periods, this time with the additional task of protecting the changes resulting from the nationalization processes of the 1974–5 period. The European Commission taskforce nevertheless drove a hard bargain, its attitude being that, "we did not ask you to become a member state, you yourself asked for accession, you must accept the *acquis communautaire*".

The attitude taken by the new conservative Greek government, returned in November 1977, was very different. The pro-European prime minister, Constantine Karamanlis, reportedly organized a day-long meeting with all of Greece's chief negotiators to take stock of the situation. They presented the long list of demands under negotiation and the difficulties presented by the EEC side. At the end of the day, so eyewitnesses reported, he concluded sharply, "you do not understand how the EEC works, first you enter and then you negotiate. Let's put all of these demands to one side and get in." As a result of these pragmatic tactics and the support of influential member states – France in particular – Greece became a member state on 1 January 1981, five years before Portugal and Spain.

But, in reality, it was not the complexity of the negotiations with Portugal and Spain that contributed to such a long delay. The real reason was the protectionist attitude of some member states, above all France, mainly concerned about competition with Spanish agriculture. Jacques Chirac, French agriculture minister at the time, was strongly opposed to the accession of the Iberian countries from the beginning, and it was only with the election of François Mitterrand as French president on 10 May 1981, and the support of the new Socialist government, that negotiations progressed; and, even then, not very quickly.

In 1978 the European Economic and Social Committee (EESC), an EU advisory body, organized what was to become a surreal event. Representatives of the social partners of the three candidate countries were invited to attend the EESC's plenary session where an opinion on the accession of the three Mediterranean countries would be discussed and adopted. The rapporteur was a French representative from the agriculture sector and the draft opinion was *against* the accession of the three countries![6]

To accelerate the last phase of the accession negotiations, Portuguese negotiators pragmatically decided that, since many of the regulations and directives concerning the internal market were adopted by unanimity, it should simply agree and close as many files as possible. Then, in 1985, after the end of the negotiation phase and when ratification procedures had already been launched, the Portuguese and Spanish prime ministers were invited to attend the European Council meeting in Milan which adopted a new strategy to create the Single Market. This decision was the basis for the Single European Act signed in February 1986, which set the European Community the objective of establishing a Single Market by 1992 and, to that end, changed the voting procedures in most areas of the internal market from unanimity to qualified majority.

The unbalanced situation created among the member states, whereby some of them were not fully prepared or willing to open their national markets, gave birth in February 1987 to the so-called Delors I Package of budgetary reforms, setting out proposals which would provide the Community with the resources necessary to attain the objectives of the Single Act, proposing a multiannual financial framework for the European budget and the doubling of the regional development funds so as to address the structural challenges of the less developed regions.

The proposals met with strong resistance from some member states, the UK among them, and the proposals were not adopted by the European Council in Copenhagen in December 1987. It was only in February 1988 that it became possible to reach an agreement and the European Community's (EC) financial framework until 1992 was adopted. The creation of a new resource function of gross national income to reflect the relative prosperity of contributing member states was one of the most important decisions taken and its impact on the efficacy of the budget lasts until today.

But the proposal on resources was not the only difficulty encountered. European Commission President Jacques Delors had to intervene strongly at the Commission meeting that adopted the draft regulations concerning the priorities of the Structural Funds, supporting the positions of the Greek and Portuguese commissioners in giving priority to the indicator of GDP per capita in purchasing power standard terms. Others, including the Spanish and Italian commissioners, wanted to define less developed regions by using an indicator mixing GDP per capita with unemployment rates. Delors pointed out that unemployment rates were already dealt with in the second objective, "regions in industrial decline", hence addressing, among others, many regions of the UK. He refused to put the subject to a vote.[7]

THE EUROPEAN ECONOMIC AREA

The Single Market also created new challenges for the EFTA countries. The 1972–3 trade agreements between individual EFTA member states and the EEC had essentially been concerned with the elimination of customs duties on industrial products. Although the 1957 Treaty of Rome had laid down the free movement of goods, persons, services and capital as objectives for the EEC, member state reluctance, combined with de facto unanimity for decision-making, meant that these objectives remained largely unachieved. However, the introduction of qualified majority voting by the Single European Act and the associated "1992" project of more than 300 legislative proposals to be adopted, creating a Single Market and applying the four freedoms, would necessarily threaten EFTA countries' continued access to the EEC market.

This prospect encouraged several EFTA states, led by Sweden, to ponder applying for accession to the EC itself. In 1989, Delors, who feared that further enlargement would impede the ability of the Community to complete internal market reform and establish monetary union, proposed as an alternative the creation of a European Economic Space, later renamed the European Economic Area (EEA), and the negotiations to enlarge the new Single Market to all the EFTA countries began. As a former EFTA country, Portugal was particularly involved in the conception of the EEA and in the negotiations themselves, doing its best to make them a success and thus to preserve the special relationship between the European Union and its member states and the EFTA countries, reflecting their proximity and the importance of their economic ties.

The resulting agreement was signed in Porto on 2 May 1992 and entered into force on 1 January 1994.[8] But history, as the EU was learning, particularly after the 9 November 1989 fall of the Berlin Wall, refused to stand still. Austria applied for full membership of the EC in 1989, followed, between 1991 and 1992, by Finland, Norway, Sweden and Switzerland. Norway's accession to the EC was subsequently rejected in a referendum. On 6 December 1992, the Swiss people rejected the EEA agreement in a referendum. (Switzerland subsequently froze its EU application.) Thus, from the outset, EEA membership did not extend to all EFTA member states.

Since Chapter 3 will deal in detail with the EEA, this chapter will limit itself to a few general observations. As a contemporary press release described it:

> The Agreement lays the foundations for an efficient, unified market modelled on the EC's Single Market, with common rules and conditions of competition, backed up by the necessary machinery and arbitration arrangements, and based on equality, reciprocity and an overall balance of advantage, rights and obligations for the Contracting Parties.

In addition to implementing the four freedoms, the EEA Agreement aimed to strengthen and expand the EU's relations with the participating EFTA countries by a process of extensive and balanced cooperation: in fields relating to economic activity which directly affect the four freedoms, so-called "horizontal" policies, including social policy, consumer protection, the environment, statistics and company law; and in areas subject to Community flanking policies outside the four freedoms, in the form of EFTA participation in Community programmes, projects and actions concerning research and development, the environment, social policy, information services, education, training and youth, small and medium-sized enterprises, tourism, the audio-visual sector and civil protection. In the interests of narrowing the social and economic disparities within the EEA, the participating countries agreed to establish a financial mechanism to provide assistance in the form of interest rate subsidies and grants to regions corresponding to the EU Structural Fund Objective No 1 (that is, regions in Portugal, Ireland, Greece and Spain).[9]

PRAGMATISM OR IDEALISM?

The Maastricht Treaty, signed in 1992, transformed the EC into the European Union and established, among other things: a citizenship common to nationals of all member states; an economic and monetary union, paving the way to the creation of the euro; and a common foreign and security policy. The Treaty deeply changed the nature of the European project although this was not fully understood until later developments. Since then, if not before, two different narratives have developed in parallel at EU level.

One narrative sees the sovereignty of the member states and the role of the European Council (bringing together the heads of state or government) and the Council of the European Union (bringing together sectoral ministers) as the most important features of the EU's original and *sui generis* model, and hence an arrangement not easy to qualify in comparison with other models. The other narrative argues that constant progress towards a more federal model is the only way and that the "bicycle will fall over if it stops moving". To the latter narrative was added the ambiguity of the role of the European Parliament, with its powers reinforced by each Treaty change to respond to German concerns about the EU's democratic deficit but which was itself suffering from a deficit of credibility and decreasing participation rates in European elections (with the exception of the last elections in May 2019, which saw an increase in turnout from 42.61 to 50.62 per cent).

Nor were these two narratives being played out on the same field. The first was based in real power and the real politics of the member states, with the latter intervening when needed to avoid future problems, as member states did at the 2007 Intergovernmental Conference that approved the final draft of the Lisbon Treaty, signed at the end of the Portuguese presidency, with its clear message to the other institutions that the EU should concentrate only on what was already decided, and could not keep adding new themes to "show off" or continue to attempt to satisfy the disparate initiatives of the European Parliament. The second narrative, present in so many articles in the press and conference polemics, was barely visible on the negotiating table of the member states.[10]

These two narratives did not develop only at the European level, but also impacted on internal politics in many member states, with various political parties and leaders adopting public positions about their preferences for the future of the European Union. But those positions were rarely followed by concrete action at European level, where real politics continued to impose themselves and member states' representatives adopt positions according to their own national interests or what they seem to believe those interests might be. In any case, in reality, at elite level, only the first of those two narratives ever applied to Portugal in its relations with the EU. Immediately after accession, the country's main challenge was to win a specific programme that would support and finance the modernization of Portuguese industry. Subsequently, the *Programa Específico de Desenvolvimento da Indústria Portuguesa* (the specific programme for the development of Portuguese industry)[11] was approved and financing guaranteed, but Portuguese negotiators had thus seen from the outset that the best strategy would always be to be in from the outset and to fight, from within, for options in Community policies that would best suit the interests of the country.

However, for such a strategy to be successful the country would need to build alliances with other member states with similar interests, as was indeed the case when it suggested the creation of the group of "friends of cohesion (policy)", a group that until now has been able to counterweigh the much more powerful "net contributors" group in the Multi-Annual Financial Framework negotiations every seven years; or the more informal group of ministers of agriculture that is mainly interested in ensuring a higher budget for that particular policy area; or the group of member states that were at the origin of the Schengen Agreement, an area where, in pre- (and hopefully post-) Covid-19 times, internal border checks have largely been abolished; or the support for stronger ties between the European Union and South America and/or with African countries, continents where Portugal still had/has links and influence.

It has been a long time since discussions first took place after the Second World War about the creation of a free trade area in Europe. Present world affairs and the current challenges facing the European Union raise doubts about the future of the European project itself. But not for the Portuguese establishment. After the end of empire and the illusions of a "pluricontinental" Atlantic community involving South America, the Portuguese are necessarily engaged in the European construction process but, at the same time, are very far from supporting any kind of federalist approach. Indeed, Portugal's pro-European Union consensus was severely tested during the period of financial assistance following the post-2008 world financial crisis.[12]

What can the post-Brexit United Kingdom glean from Portugal's postwar experience? It is, perhaps, that the position of all European countries, whether inside or outside the European Union, is necessarily a function of their history, on the one hand, but also of hard-headed calculation about where their best economic interest lies. For a small, postcolonial, Atlantic-oriented, trading economy like Portugal, there was never an optimal alternative to full membership of the "club", whether the club in question was EFTA or, later, the EU. It remains to be seen whether for a much larger, postcolonial, Atlantic-oriented, trading economy like the United Kingdom, such an optimal alternative exists.

Notes for Chapter 2

1. The report recognizing the specificity of the Portuguese case was drafted by Johan Merlander, a Norwegian representative, and supported by Gerard Bauer, a Swiss representative. The UK and Sweden were most opposed to Portuguese participation, arguing that a free trade agreement was only for developed countries.

2. The first informal meeting was held in Switzerland and, thanks no doubt to the good and supportive relationship between the Portuguese and the Swiss, Portugal received a surprise invitation to attend. Other interested countries were informed only afterwards and, since Portugal was present from the outset, its subsequent participation in the first formal negotiation meeting came as no surprise. See, for example, N. Andresen Leitao, "O convidado inesperado: Portugal e a fundação da EFTA, 1956–1960", *Analise Social* 171 (2004), http://www.scielo.mec.pt/pdf/aso/n171/n171a02.pdf; E. Santos Alipio, "O processo negocial da adesão de Portugal à EFTA 1956–1960", http://www.fmsoares. pt/aeb/biblioteca/indices_resumos/resumos/015978.htm.

3. Iceland, also part of the group of the less developed European countries during the 1956–58 negotiations, only finally became a member of EFTA in 1970.

4. See https://lovdata.no/dokument/TRAKTATEN/traktat/1960-01-04-1/KAPITTEL_ 8#KAPITTEL_8.

5. Although Portugal left EFTA in 1985 and joined the EEC, the remaining EFTA members decided to continue the Portugal Fund, which originally took the form of a low-interest loan from the EFTA member countries to the value of US$100 million. Repayment, initially scheduled to start in 1988, was postponed until 1998. The Portugal Fund has now been dissolved.

6. The memories of this surreal meeting came to my mind years later when, in 2002, as an official of the European Commission in charge of the Economic and Social Cohesion report, I was drafting the guidelines for the regional policy of the ten candidate countries that would become member states in 2004. The approach of European negotiators then was completely different, pushing for rapid accession even before all conditions had been met.

7. As a member of the European Economic and Social Committee (EESC), I participated in the working group to prepare the opinion on these Regulations, and another surreal situation arose when the representative of the Commission, from DG REGIO, came to our first meeting and attacked and criticized the position adopted by the college of commissioners and supported the position that had been defeated in the college! A quick call to the private office of the (Greek) commissioner in charge of the file solved the problem. The head of his private office attended the meeting and afterwards kept following the process throughout. Even then, only with an amendment presented in the plenary session to the draft opinion prepared by the working group was it possible to include the clear sentence that the EESC "agrees and supports the proposal of the Commission" (on the indicator of GDP per capita to define the less developed regions).

8. See https://www.efta.int/eea/eea-agreement.

9. European Commission Background briefing MEMO 93/55: https://ec.europa.eu/commission/presscorner/detail/en/MEMO_93_55. This financial mechanism was first proposed in the opinion that I drafted in the Economic and Social Committee about the EEA and it was not part of the original negotiation guidelines drafted by the European Commission. When I first presented the proposal, the European Commission negotiator did not want to take it into consideration because it "was not included in the negotiation guidelines and will make negotiations more difficult". In fact, it did not. The proposal was easily accepted by the EU member states' negotiators and the EFTA countries also considered the proposal to be fair and agreed to include it in the Agreement, signed in Porto during the Portuguese Presidency in 1992.

10. I remember an insider saying in the 1990s that only two EU member states were less reticent towards the concept of a federal Europe, Italy and Belgium. Nowadays, not even those two countries are sympathetic to such a federalist vision. Only the UK, and then apparently mainly for domestic political reasons, seems to believe that the "bicycle" is still running and that the march towards a federal Europe still proceeds apace.

11. A programme to support Portuguese agriculture was included in the results of the accession negotiations, but not for industry. Only after membership was it possible to obtain such support.

12. In effect, Portugal was suffering the consequences of its now traditional strategy of being in at the beginning. Like several other member states' economies, it was simply not ready for the burdens of full membership of the euro from the outset. Yet the imposition of strict rules of budget discipline, the role of the European Central Bank and the European Commission (at the time with José Manuel Barroso, former prime minister of Portugal, as its president) during the Troika's interventions to overcome the crisis were never understood in Portugal as being the consequences of the economic policy that had to be followed after the creation of the euro and Portugal's immediate participation in it.

3

NORWAY AND THE EUROPEAN ECONOMIC AREA: WHY THE MOST COMPREHENSIVE TRADE AGREEMENT EVER NEGOTIATED IS NOT GOOD ENOUGH FOR THE UK

Sebastian Remøy

The "Norway Option" was a term that cropped up repeatedly in the UK's Brexit debates. Possibly this caused some confusion to a good number of Britons, but for many the term became a shortcut for the idea of the United Kingdom remaining in the Single Market without being a member of the EU. That is the deal that Norway and Iceland (since 1994) and Liechtenstein (since 1995) have with the EU, via their participation in the 1994 European Economic Area (EEA) Agreement. These three states are in the European Free Trade Association (EFTA), and are known as the EEA EFTA states. Switzerland is also in EFTA, but it is not in the EEA, having opted not to join after a referendum in 1992. Switzerland has its own very different arrangement with the EU, managed through numerous bilateral agreements, as Georges Baur describes in Chapter 4.

The EEA agreement is complex and unique. There is no other trade agreement between trading partners anywhere in the world that comes close to resembling it. Perhaps the most remarkable aspect of the agreement is that its negotiation is perpetual. It is never completely or finally negotiated. This is because every time the EU legislates to update and improve the Single Market, the EU and the EFTA states talk with each other to see whether and how that legislation should be incorporated into the EEA Agreement. Together, each year, the EU and the EEA EFTA states make several hundred Joint Committee Decisions (JCDs), with or without technical adaptations, to incorporate EU legal acts into the EEA Agreement. It is the only example of a *dynamic* trade agreement that ensures *homogeneity* of market conditions between the parties to the agreement. "Dynamic" and "homogenous" are central terms in EEA parlance, because they uphold the principle of a level playing field that is an essential requirement for full participation in and integration into the Single Market.

WHY A EUROPEAN ECONOMIC AREA?

A question that has not been asked enough by participants in the Brexit debate is why the EEA Agreement came into being in the first place. Understanding the answer to this would have helped people to realize the trade-offs that were being made when favouring one model over another; for example, a simple trade agreement that is essentially limited to removing tariffs over an agreement that fully integrates a country into the Single Market.

Already in the 1984 Luxembourg Declaration, the EFTA countries had agreed with the EU that they wanted to deepen their cooperation with the European Community (EC) and create a "European Economic Space".[1] As Vasco Cal describes in Chapter 2, they already benefitted from tariff-free trade on primarily industrial products with the EC via a number of trade agreements that were put in place in the 1970s. However, with the establishment of the Single Market project in the mid-1980s which, among other things, sought to enable free movement of services, capital, persons and goods, removing non-tariff and technical barriers to trade, it became quickly apparent that those trade agreements would no longer be fit for purpose; at least not if economic operators and individuals from the EFTA countries were to have an equal level of access to the Single Market as those from the EU.

The conceptualization of the EEA Agreement and the construction of the framework for the internal market happened, not-coincidentally, during Jacques Delors' presidency of the European Commission. He asked the question, "How far are the EFTA States willing to go in their cooperation with the Community?" concerning the construction of a European Economic Space. If the EFTA states did not want to get left behind concerning the construction of and participation in the Single Market, then they would have to beef up the institutional structure of EFTA, and establish a pillar with parallel structures to the EU.[2] Such a pillar would reflect and match some of the decision-making powers of the Council, the treaty surveillance capabilities of the Commission and the judicial powers of the European Court of Justice (ECJ). There would also be an appropriate interlocutor in the EFTA pillar for the European Parliament, and the same for the (advisory) European Economic and Social Committee (EESC).

TWO PILLARS

Before trying to understand why the UK has now rejected the "Norway Option", I would like to take a closer look at how the EEA Agreement works. There is an institutional structure to the EEA Agreement that supports its functioning. This is known as the two-pillar structure (Figure 3.1). There is an EFTA pillar and an EU pillar.

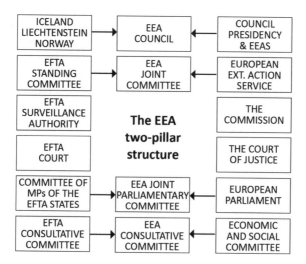

Figure 3.1. The institutional structure of the EEA Agreement

Source: EFTA Secretariat.

A new legal order was established, EEA law, that was parallel to EU law, so that the same result should be delivered whether a practice or an event took place in an EFTA state or an EU state.

Practically all EU legislation that is relevant to and necessary for the functioning of the internal market is taken into the EEA Agreement to ensure homogeneity across the EEA. Ambassadors from Iceland, Liechtenstein and Norway in EFTA's Standing Committee meet numerous times annually with EU representatives from the European External Action Service to make the several hundred JCDs each year that incorporate newly adopted EU legislation into the EEA Agreement. This is all overseen at the political level in the EEA Council in meetings between ministers from the EEA/EFTA states and representatives from the Council Presidency and the European External Action Service.

Before JCDs are made there are a lot of information exchanges and discussions between Commission officials and representatives from the EFTA states who participate in the Standing Committee's subcommittees and working groups. This preparatory work is essential so that EU legal acts can be smoothly incorporated into the national law of the EEA EFTA states, and preferably at the same time as the laws come into effect on the EU side.

The EU Commission and the EU Court of Justice in the EU pillar and the EFTA Surveillance Authority and the EFTA Court in the EFTA pillar have the competences to monitor, discipline and adjudge the correct implementation and interpretation of the provisions of EEA law. Individuals and economic operators have access to both EU and EFTA authorities to claim their rights under the agreement as well as before national courts.[3]

Despite the diagram in Figure 3.1, the pillars are clearly not of equal girth and stature. The EU side represents just short of half a billion citizens in 27 member states. The EFTA pillar stands for three countries with less than 6 million people. The three EFTA countries have only a little more than 1 per cent of the total population of the EEA. Of that 1 per cent over 90 per cent is accounted for by a single country: Norway. There is a very unequal balance of power between the pillars in the EEA Agreement, and among the EEA EFTA states within the EFTA pillar there is another unequal balance of power. What enables this political machinery to continue to exist and to function is a very solidly engineered and designed binding international association agreement.

These imbalances were not always so pronounced, though. In 1992, when the EEA Agreement was signed, there were seven EFTA and 12 EU signatories. This association between the EU and EFTA was never going to be a "marriage of equals", but neither did anyone envisage that it would end up being as lop-sided as it is today. Switzerland in a referendum voted not to join in December 1992 so the Agreement entered into force on 1 January 1994 without the Swiss. Then, Austria, Finland and Sweden acceded to the European Communities on 1 January 1995,[4] hopping from the smaller EFTA pillar to the already much larger EU one. The asymmetry between the two pillars became even more evident. Then, in 2004, ten new mainly central European countries joined the EU, followed a few years later by Bulgaria and Romania (2007) and, more recently, Croatia (2013), further expanding the EU pillar.

There are people in the EFTA states who support the UK joining, or more correctly rejoining, EFTA, and then also rejoining the EEA.[5] They would welcome a beefing up of the EFTA pillar and a dilution of Norway's dominance of it. What better way to do this than by getting a wealthy G7 economy with nearly 70 million inhabitants to hop across to the other side? There are others, however, who feel that the UK could destroy the EEA. Especially from Norway, although they are not alone, the opinion is voiced that the UK is too big for the EFTA pillar in the EEA, and that because the good functioning of the Agreement depends so much on consensus decision-making, these same voices feel it is not well suited to a country that is prone to an "exceptionalist" way of thinking.

The EEA Agreement was not envisaged by all involved in its construction as a permanent fixture in the European economic and political landscape. Some viewed it as a temporary waiting and preparatory space for countries entering into the EU. The fact that it has survived for so long is, again, a testament to the ingenuity of its construction and adaptability.

THE FOUR FREEDOMS

A central objective of the EEA Agreement is to extend the internal market to the EEA EFTA states. Free movement of goods, services, persons and capital is extended to Iceland, Liechtenstein and Norway. In order to enable this to happen, and for there to be a level playing field between the EFTA countries and the EU member states, the three EFTA countries consent to incorporate EU internal market legislation into national law. They agree to do this unanimously, via JCDs between the EEA EFTA states and the EU, within the two-pillar structure mentioned above. In 2019, for example, the EEA Joint Committee met eight times and adopted 319 decisions incorporating 708 legal acts. Since it came into force in 1994, more than 11,000 legal acts have been incorporated into the EEA Agreement and implemented into Norwegian law. About half of these remain in force today.

It is important to note that, should one of the EFTA countries not agree to the adoption of a JCD, the decision is also blocked for the other EFTA countries. Put another way, each pillar speaks with one voice. This is known as the unanimity principle in the EEA Agreement, and is one reason why some in the EFTA pillar, and most notably in Norway, were concerned that if the UK joined the EFTA pillar in the EEA many decisions could be blocked that the other 30 EEA states would want to adopt.

The cost to an EFTA state of being able to fully participate in the internal market, without being a member state of the EU, is both political and financial. Looking at the political, Norway has no commissioner, practically no permanently employed civil servants in the European Commission and the other EU institutions, no members of the European Parliament and no seat at the European Council and the Council of Ministers. In short, it does not participate in decision-making. This does not mean that it does not have an ability to influence decisions, but it has no vote. Norway also makes substantial financial contributions to numerous projects in EU member states, and to funding programmes of the EU such as Horizon Europe. The idea is that, if it wants to participate in the Single Market, Norway should contribute to the evening out of economic and social disparities within it. Third, Norway and the other two EEA EFTA states have to follow ECJ jurisprudence, even if it is the EFTA Court that delivers judgements on the EFTA side.

WHAT'S IN IT FOR NORWAY?

One might ask why Norway accepts this deal. Why should it agree to be in an important international project to construct an internal market in Europe, without participating in the decision-making structures that manage that project? Norway accepts the rules and pays its dues but self-excludes itself from the democratic rule making of the whole endeavour. It is perhaps a bit like being a resident/owner in an apartment block, paying the condominium fees, accepting the rules and charges agreed by the block, but giving up one's vote and all rights to participate in decisions taken by the managing residents' association.

Norway, however, has not had the greatest of experiences with participation in unions, stretching far back into the previous millennium. Having entered into the Union of Kalmar with Denmark and Sweden in 1397, Norway found itself over subsequent centuries to be the lesser party in various constellations with the one and the other, until finally it wrested itself free from its 90-year-old union with Sweden in 1905, gaining independence and full control over its foreign and commercial policies.

With their country being far away from Brussels, somewhat on the periphery of the continent and with a relatively small population, quite a few Norwegians questioned whether Norway would ever exert enough influence in Brussels for its interests to be taken sufficiently into account and safeguarded. Furthermore, Norway had valuable resources – hydrocarbons and fish – that it wanted to control, as well as a heavily subsidized agricultural sector that it wished to preserve. EC membership raised the spectre within the population that it could lose all this: its independence and sovereignty, the ability to administer its own natural resources without interference from European bureaucrats and politicians, and the possibility to sustain agricultural and economic activity in rural and coastal communities.

The results of two referenda held on membership in 1972 and 1994 were close, but in the end with small majorities (53.5 and 52.2 per cent respectively) the "no" campaigns won, using among others the arguments set out above. Debates on EC/EU membership were fierce and awoke passions on both sides. No government since 1994 has dared put the question to Norwegians for a third time. The EEA is a political compromise for Norwegians. It enables the country to enjoy many of the economic benefits of membership, yet still preserve aspects of its sovereignty that it did not wish to subjugate to, cede to, pool or share with (pick your term) a supranational Union.

The EEA Agreement excludes full free trade in agriculture and fisheries and allows Norway to stay out of the Common Agricultural Policy and Common Fisheries Policies. It also contains what some refer to as a right of reservation, Article 102, which they say means that EFTA states can reject EU legislation that otherwise would be deemed to be EEA relevant. Others, however, say that Article 102 is no such thing, as it urges the parties to the Agreement to find a solution, and if one cannot be found after six months, then the relevant part of the treaty can be suspended.[6] This can have serious consequences for economic operators and individuals relying on that particular aspect of the accord. Those in Norway who are against EU membership, but who support EEA participation, claim that Norway has preserved its sovereignty because of this right of reservation, and the EEA's status under the auspices of an international treaty rather than as part of a supranational institution.

Article 102 is not a joker card that allows the EEA EFTA states free rein to cherry pick. The fact that an intention to invoke the right of reservation has only been communicated once to the EU, and that this was never put into effect, is an indication that doing so could cause harm and serious disruption to the economic interests to one, several or all parties to the agreement.[7]

THE UK IN EFTA AND THE EEA

The "Norway Option" before and after the referendum was heavily referenced in the UK Brexit debate as one of several potential models for the country's future relationship with the EU. It came to represent the closest level of integration into the Single Market without actually being a member of the Union.

Gradually, however, the option's popularity began to wane among both dovish Remainers and dovish Leavers who had initially viewed it as a middle way between membership and "hard Brexit" or even a no deal scenario where the UK would trade under World Trade Organization terms. After some time, they understood that the compromises the UK would have to make were not politically acceptable, except perhaps for a limited transitional period. These would have included:

- acceptance of practically all Single Market rules, with no participation in decision-making;
- substantial financial contributions;
- free movement of persons, as inseparable from the other three freedoms, of goods, capital and services; and
- ECJ jurisdiction.

All of the above was pretty much ruled out already in January 2017, when Theresa May, shortly after becoming UK prime minister, announced in her Lancaster House speech that there would be participation neither in the Single Market nor in the Customs Union.[8]

It is important to point out that participation in the Single Market is not the same as *access* to that market. Even countries with no comprehensive free trade agreements with the EU (for example, the USA and India) have access to the Single Market, after dealing with the impediments of tariff and non-tariff barriers. Neither is participation in the Single Market the same as tariff-free access via comprehensive free trade agreements such as those that South Korea, Japan, Vietnam and Canada enjoy.[9] Participation, in the way that the EEA EFTA states enjoy it, involves full immersion in the four freedoms of goods, services, capital and persons and also involvement in horizontal and flanking policies and programmes. This is only possible through a dynamic and, to the greatest extent possible, simultaneous process of rule assimilation that enables the preservation of homogenous market conditions.

After Theresa May's various statements at Lancaster House, Mansion House, in the House of Commons, and before, during and after various EU Summits and negotiations, it became clear that EEA membership or anything similar to it was a no-go for her, and for the party and the government that she led. The closest she ever got to a plan for closer integration with the Single Market was the Chequers plan, where there was consideration of a common rulebook for trade in some goods. But that pick-and-mix approach to Single Market involvement was never going to be acceptable to the EU. Also, the idea that the UK would go from being one of 28 countries that collectively determined the rules of the Single Market, to having equal weight on its side, with the entire EU and its remaining 27 member states on the other side, was never going to fly, even if it only applied to some products. Anyway, it was ultimately rejected in the UK Parliament, including by quite a large number of MPs from her own party.

From the EU perspective, what frustrated the EU negotiators to a considerable extent was the mixed political messaging coming from the May government. Having rejected participation in the Single Market and the Customs Union relatively early on, it made no sense to promise UK businesses frictionless trade with the EU. Not even Norway (in the Single Market of the EEA) nor Turkey (in a customs union agreement with the EU) enjoy entirely frictionless trade. As the EU's chief Brexit negotiator, Michel Barnier, made clear on several occasions, the only way to achieve frictionless trade was to be in both the Single Market and the Customs Union.

TAKING BACK CONTROL

Perhaps the most obvious reason why the Norway option would not work as a long-term form of association for the UK with the EU is that it would go directly against the idea that the UK should fully take back control of its law making. The EEA EFTA states are essentially rule-takers, even taking into consideration the "right of reservation" in Article 102 of the EEA Agreement. It would make no political sense for the UK to go from a situation where it had representation and a vote in the decision-making bodies of the EU to one where it had virtually none. The fact that Norwegian experts and representatives enjoy non-voting participation in some several hundred expert, programme and comitology committees, as well as in many of the EU's regulatory agencies, should not be confused with participating in the ultimate decision-making processes of the EU. Norway can make all the noise it wants to if it does not like or wants to amend a new or revised rule of the Single Market, but as already stated, it has no seat at the Council or in the Parliament when votes are counted, and there is no Norwegian sitting in the College of the European Commission.

EEA membership would only have made sense for the UK if, for a longer temporary period, it had wished to stay in the Single Market after having left. It could perhaps have bought itself five or six years to negotiate a special agreement with the EU. The transitional period that is part of the Withdrawal Agreement is not equivalent to the EEA Agreement. There is no two-pillar structure, no similar information-sharing and decision-making apparatus, no surveillance authority or EFTA court to enable and ensure the dynamic and reliable continuation of homogeneity in the Single Market. The transitional arrangement in the Withdrawal Agreement merely freezes the status quo between the UK and the EU for a very limited period of time, in between the day that the UK left on 31 January 2020 and the establishment and entry into force of a new relationship, or a situation where there is no deal at all. This would either be at the end of 2020, or the end of 2021 or 2022, to be decided by July 2020. At time of writing, UK legislation determines that it would be at the end of 2020.

Were the UK government to have decided that it would have liked that breathing space that EEA membership could have provided, it would have had to convince all four EFTA states to accept it back into the organization, and then the three EEA EFTA states and all 27 EU EEA states would have had to agree to the UK re-entering the EEA as an EFTA state. Changing the structure of EFTA and then the EFTA pillar within the EEA would have been a substantial task, and only worth doing for a longer period of time if it were to be done at all. And, as mentioned previously, bringing the much larger UK into the EFTA family, with its tendency to object to, or ask for all sorts of opt-outs from, European policies, was not an idea that was greeted with relish in the EFTA pillar of the EEA. The prospect was certainly not welcomed by Norway, whose government was quite vocal in discouraging the UK from pursuing the notion.

They needn't have worried. There was no political appetite for this in the Conservative Party, except for a few isolated proponents.

The Labour Party's idea of participation in the Single Market and the Customs Union would have got closer to achieving the frictionless trade that Theresa May's government had initially promised but, as many pointed out, what would be the point of leaving on the one hand, retaining most of the privileges and obligations of EU membership, but losing all influence in decision taking on the other? Moreover, this would have been practically difficult to achieve as neither EFTA nor the EEA are customs unions. EFTA has trade agreements with 44 countries, so fitting the UK into the EFTA pillar of the EEA while it was in a customs union with the EU would have required quite some re-engineering.

A LOST OPPORTUNITY?

The UK joined something in 1973 that was often referred to as the Common Market. Some people say that UK politicians had ample opportunity to understand that the EU was destined to go further than that. The words "ever closer union" were already contained in the preamble of the 1957 Treaty of Rome. The UK went in with eyes wide open, they say.

However, for countries mainly interested in the commercial aspects of the European project there is a tough dilemma (touched on by Vasco Cal in Chapter 2): it can participate as a member of the EU, with the risk of being drawn more deeply than it desires into the political aspects of the project; or it can be in the Single Market via the EEA, without properly taking part in the rule making of that market. Norway has chosen the latter. The UK *had* chosen the former but, fearing that it was on a train that was speeding way beyond the destination of its preference, it decided to jump off.

A question for the architects of European integration is whether there could not be a more equitable way to organize a multi-speed Europe, so that those countries that just wished to participate in the Single Market would not have to be excluded from its decision-making bodies. If Norway, and eventually the UK, wished only to participate in the Single Market, would it have been possible to have members of the European Parliament who only participated in votes and committee meetings concerning Single Market laws? Could Norway have sent ministers to Council meetings only to take part in discussions and decisions relevant to reform of the Single Market, and likewise, could it have had a commissioner who would only be involved in College meetings of relevance to its own limited participation?

We already see via enhanced cooperation and in the management of the eurozone that there are ways for countries to exclude themselves from certain projects, without having to be outside of the European institutions as a whole. However, to view the development of an internal market as a purely commercial or economic endeavour might be to underestimate its political essence. Free movement of persons is a deeply political facet of the Single Market, and without it there is no real free movement of goods, services or capital. The passporting of financial services is also the result of a profoundly political decision to harmonize rules across the entire internal market, in part so that laborious and continual mutual recognition processes and equivalence determinations are not necessary, but more importantly because it strengthens the trust and confidence of economic operators in ways that are essential in order for a Single Market to function. Harmonization of technical standards, mutual recognition of qualifications, the transfer of social benefits, cross-border healthcare provision, merger clearance and anti-trust enforcement, the negotiation of trade accords on behalf of all member states: these and so many other things underpin the functioning of the internal market, and they are political commitments. So one might say there is no Single Market without a certain level of political integration.

Even if Britain and Norway were able to be in the European Union for only the commercial aspects of European integration, there would also be the issue of its structure and governance. So, it was not only a question of *what* the EU does, or will want to do in the future, but *how* it does it which also became a central issue of the Brexit debate. The EU is a supranational organization. This limits the legal capacity of decision makers in member states to take some decisions without external constraints. It does involve therefore some loss of national sovereignty.[10] The "take back control" mantra of the pro-Brexit side pushed some sensitive buttons in the UK, asserting that the country had lost the ability to manage its own affairs in accordance with its national interest. Immigration was a primary example of this.[11] Fisheries was another. We will see how much more control of these and other issues the UK achieves after the transition period ends. Realpolitik is to a much greater extent the name of the game outside of supranational structures, so it will be interesting to see how the UK manages its relationship with the EU when the balance of power is so unequal and not in its favour.

Norway, via the EEA, docks onto this political project without participating in the processes that drive it. It has been able to swallow the democratic consequences of this for just over 25 years, by claiming that it has not ceded sovereignty to a supranational organization. The extent to which Norway has preserved its sovereignty within its current form of association to the EU is a subject of hot political and academic debate in Norway.

Any country for whom the EU is an important trading partner will feel the power of the "Brussels effect".[12] The EU, as a relatively wealthy market of nearly half a billion consumers, has such a strong gravitational force that its standards and regulations for the production and trading of goods and services are quite frequently also adopted globally. The UK, as one of the big four powers of the EU, was an important influencer in shaping those EU and then global standards, not least in financial regulation.

On the outside now, the UK will have to rely much more on its expertise and creativity in certain sectors to influence European and global standards, if it wants to. Norway does so, for example, in the development of standards for the offshore oil and gas industry and in aquaculture, where its expertise is much valued. But remember it also benefits from non-voting participation in EU agencies, and expert, comitology and programme committees. That, to a large extent, is enabled through the EEA Agreement, and while it cannot be compared to actual participation in the EU's decision-making processes, it does give Norway a fighting chance to shape some important decisions in the areas that matter most to the country. The UK will have to decide what level of independence it wants from EU institutional and regulatory bodies. The further the separation and the more divergence it seeks to achieve, the less influence it will have on European and often global standards. Ultimately, in many sectors it may anyway have to adopt EU standards, because that is where 46 per cent of UK exports currently go, and because the "Brussels effect" means that these standards eventually become global industry norms.

CONCLUSION

The EEA is the best trade agreement in the world, if one measures it in terms of establishing homogenous market conditions between the parties, and thereby liberalizing and facilitating trade to the greatest extent possible. The trade policy wonk in me wishes that this were the option the UK had gone for once 51.89 per cent of the British people decided that the UK should leave the EU. A Norway-style solution, with some additional engineering to enable the UK to stay within the Customs Union, would to a very great extent have diminished the economic and social disruption caused by the UK leaving the EU.

However, the democrat in me tells me that this is all wrong. A country should not accept more than 700 legal acts in a year into its national legislation without having had a say and vote throughout the formative process of each act. People talk about a democratic deficit in the EU, and in the EEA they speak about a double democratic deficit. My opinion is that there is plenty of democracy in EU law making. The 705 elected representatives of the European Parliament make sure of that, and so do ministers, prime ministers and presidents from elected governments when they meet in the Council and the European Council to take decisions.

But, unless it were for a limited period of time, as a transition to something else, the EEA Agreement would have exacerbated the frustrations of both sides in the UK's Brexit debate. The Leavers would have said we have not taken back, and in fact we have lost more, control; and they would have been correct. And the Remainers would have said the deal we have today is not as good as the deal we had before; and they would also have been correct.

As a Norwegian, I accept the compromise my country has made in the form of EEA membership. However, I do not agree that as a small country on the periphery of the continent Norway's voice would be lost if it were to join the EU. In recent years Irishmen and women have held the positions of president of the European Parliament, EU commissioners for trade, for agriculture and for the internal market, secretary-general of the Commission, director general for trade, and president of the Council of the European Union. For a country with a population of 5 million on the edge of the continent, Ireland exerts a lot of influence on EU policy-making. Norway could too, but it would have to be absolutely certain that it kept sufficient control of its marine and natural resources and that it was allowed to continue to organize its society and its international engagement in a way that corresponded with widely held national values and objectives, and without unmanageable external interference. That confidence is not yet in place: while about 61 per cent of the population support continued membership of the EEA, only 28 per cent would vote to join the EU.[13]

Norway and the UK are on different trajectories now. Both are outside, but one will stay close to the EU, and the other seems to have set a course for a more distant orbit. One thing is certain, however: taking into account both countries' geographical location and historical trading relations, there is very little chance of (or sense in) trying to escape from the gravitational pull of the Single Market, and consequently there is no getting away from the laws that make it function.

Notes for Chapter 3

1. Luxembourg: ministerial meeting between EFTA countries and the EC and its Member States Joint Declaration, 9 April 1984.

2. S. Norberg, "From Luxembourg to Oporto: how the Creation of the Single Market brought about a dynamic and homogenous European Economic Area", *EFTA Bulletin: The European Economic Area and the Internal Market – Towards 10 Years* (1993), 8–11.

3. For an account of the construction of the two pillars, and the role of EFTA's supervisory and judicial functions; see S. Norberg, "Joint dispute settlement and interpretation: a precondition for participation in the EU internal market?" in *The Art of Judicial Reasoning: Festschrift in Honour of Carl Baudenbacher* (Cham, CH: Springer, 2019).

4. M. Westlake, *Slipping Loose: The UK's Long Drift Away from the European Union* (Newcastle upon Tyne: Agenda Publishing, 2019), 73.

5. The UK was a founding member of EFTA from 1960 until it joined the EC in 1973. It was also a member of the EEA, via its membership of the EU, until it left.

6. For this reason, jurists say there is no "right of reservation" in the EEA Agreement, as there are sanctions for failing to agree to incorporate internal market *acquis* into the agreement. The term is however used frequently in political circles. "Right of veto" is also sometimes used to describe Article 102, to the abhorrence of legal experts who claim that this is entirely incorrect.

7. In 2011 the Norwegian (Labour-led) government warned the EU of its intention to invoke the right of reservation with respect to the Third Postal Services Directive,

but the decision was postponed, and the directive was eventually adopted by a new coalition government in 2014.

8. Lancaster House Speech, 17 January 2020.

9. These agreements contain much more than just tariff elimination, most often including chapters on procurement, trade in services and cooperation on competition enforcement, as well as regulatory dialogue in key sectors, among other things. But they are not dynamic, and they do not involve the establishment and maintenance of regulatory homogeneity.

10. N. Nugent, *The Government and Politics of the European Union* (Basingstoke: Palgrave Macmillan, 2003), 475.

11. There is an argument that the EU permitted the UK more control over policies than the UK public was led to believe. There are countries inside the EU/EEA that require immigrants from other EU countries to register with the authorities within three months of arrival if they intend to stay longer, and then, before six months elapse, they must prove that they have employment or sufficient funds to sustain themselves and to cover the costs of health insurance. Norway does this. If the UK had done this, would its population have felt that its government had so little control over immigration from the EU?

12. As discussed by Anu Bradford in *The Brussels Effect: How the European Union Rules the World* (Oxford: Oxford University Press, 2020).

13. Opinion poll by Sentio, 1,000 people asked between 12–18 November 2019: https://norwaytoday.info/news/more-norwegians-favour-the-eu-and-the-eea/.

4

SWITZERLAND: STRIKING HARD BARGAINS WITH SOFT EDGES

Georges Baur

Switzerland, not unlike the United Kingdom, always had a somewhat awkward, if not difficult, relationship with Europe, especially with the European Union. On the one hand, Switzerland is geographically situated at the centre of the continent and therefore highly dependent on being on good terms with its surrounding neighbours, all of them being EU member states, with the exception of Liechtenstein. On the other hand, Switzerland always saw itself as being special: neutrality, (semi-)direct democracy and strong federalism are seen as being in the DNA of the country and, thus, largely incompatible with EU membership.[1]

In this chapter I will first describe how the current situation with the so-called "Bilateral Agreements" came about and what exactly they are. I will then look at how the Bilateral Agreements work and at their advantages and disadvantages. I will then consider how such an approach would work with the UK and what kind of precedent might be set by it.

HOW THEY CAME ABOUT

After the Second World War, Switzerland, like other European countries, went on its quest for an ideal form of cooperation. The above political sensitivities were seen as obstacles to joining any international organization which was seen as being "political". Thus, it took three referenda for Switzerland to join the United Nations, and accession to the EU was always seen as being very difficult and, indeed, has stood no chance of being accepted in a referendum to this very day. For Switzerland, therefore, foreign policy was always foreign *trade* policy. When some Western European states in 1960 joined around the UK to set up the European Free Trade Association (EFTA) as an alternative to the European Economic Community (EEC), Switzerland was among them.[2]

Since then, Switzerland has cautiously tried to deepen its relations with the (now) EU. Next to concluding the odd agreement to facilitate trade in special fields, such as watches or insurance, in the early 1990s it embarked, together with the other EFTA states at that time, on a venture which would link these states to the EU's internal market. In 1992 the European Economic Area (EEA) Agreement was signed and should have entered into force on 1 January 1993. This was, however, not to be: on 12 December 1992, Swiss voters rejected participation in the EEA project. Consequently, the EEA entered into force a year later than planned, and without the Swiss.

There was no simple "plan B". Switzerland tried to convince the EU to at least conclude certain sectoral ("bilateral") agreements that would facilitate relations between them. After five years of negotiations, in 1999 Switzerland and the EU signed a first set of seven sectoral agreements. In 2004 a second set followed. The system of Switzerland–EU bilateral agreements currently comprises about 20 main agreements and 100 other bilateral agreements.[3]

These sectoral agreements, seen as a tool to gain access to the EU's internal market, differ in many ways from the EEA Agreement. Compared with the latter, two main differences should be highlighted: first, the absence of a comprehensive approach; second, there is no overarching institutional framework that would allow for the dynamic development and coherent interpretation of legislation. Hence, the aim of guaranteeing homogeneity among the two parties cannot be achieved.

The EU always saw these sectoral agreements as provisional, until Switzerland either joined the EEA in a second attempt or, perhaps, even joined the EU. However, in 2006 the Swiss Federal Council (government) declared that either outcome was only a remote option, whereas bilateralism was seen as being the best way to proceed in relations with the EU. The EU's reaction to this was to argue that, if this set of very different sectoral agreements was to be the basis for mutual cooperation, it needed to be supplemented by an institutional framework. Between May 2014 and December 2018, the EU and Switzerland therefore conducted negotiations on an Institutional Framework Agreement (IFA). A draft was published, but not signed by the Swiss government. There has since been no further movement, and the issue remains pending.

Meanwhile, the EU has demonstrated, through certain actions, what it means to be a (real) third country: the European Commission's equivalence decision with regard to the Swiss stock exchange was de facto withdrawn and the Commission threatened not to update the Mutual Recognition Agreement (MRA, see below) anymore, thus rendering Swiss industrial exports more cumbersome and costly. The signal is clear: in the absence of an IFA, the Bilateral Agreements as they stand will erode.

WHAT IS THE "SWISS MODEL"? 1. THE HARD
BARGAINS: (SPECIFIC) SECTORAL AGREEMENTS

In the Beginning: A Few Agreements with Narrow Scope

In the ten years after the foundation of EFTA, and despite it being one of the organization's aims, bringing about a free trade area between the two groups of Western European countries (the "inner six" and the "outer seven") proved difficult to achieve. There were, however, minor agreements that were concluded bilaterally between the (then) EEC and Switzerland. These were typically narrow in scope, such as the 1967 Watch Agreement[4] or the 1967 Tariff Agreement on cheese.[5]

The European Free Trade Zone

A breakthrough to a fundamentally new development occurred in 1969 after the EEC summit in The Hague. In that meeting, the EEC in principle agreed to enlarge the Communities through the accession of new members as well as to conclude free trade agreements with those EFTA countries which were not likely to ask for membership. Meanwhile, more bilateral agreements were to follow, such as the 1989 Insurance Agreement.[6] However, by far the most important element in this network of agreements was the 1972 Free Trade Agreement between the EEC and Switzerland, which regulates, in particular, the reduction or elimination of customs duties in bilateral trade in industrial products and processed agricultural products. This agreement still is the basis for trade in goods between Switzerland and the EU.

First Set of Sectoral Agreements (Bilateral Agreements I)

Following the 6 December 1992 rejection of Switzerland's participation in the EEA by its people and the cantons, Switzerland embarked, as early as 1994, in bilateral negotiations with the EU, which resulted in seven agreements (Bilateral Agreements I) on:

- free movement of persons (Agreement on the Free Movement of Persons, AFMP);
- technical barriers to trade (MRA);
- public procurement (Procurement Agreement);
- agriculture (Agricultural Agreement);
- land transport (Land Transport Agreement);
- air transport (Agreement on Air Transport, AAT); and
- research (Research Agreement).[7]

These agreements were signed in 1999 and entered into force in 2002 after their approval in another referendum.[8] At the time, the conclusion of these Bilateral Agreements I was an important element of the reform efforts of the 1990s, which went hand in hand with a relatively high unemployment rate (by Swiss standards). Many Swiss companies were suffering from their unfavourable position regarding market access compared to their competitors based in the EU. Thus, the issue of securing market access by removing regulatory differences and trade barriers was of great importance.[9]

Second Set of Sectoral Agreements (Bilateral Agreements II)

A second set of agreements concluded subsequently, the Bilateral Agreements II, took into account other economic interests, and expanded cooperation between Switzerland and the EU to new areas beyond the existing framework. The agreements of the second package[10] are:

- the Schengen and Dublin Association Agreements;
- the Savings Taxation Agreement;
- the Anti-Fraud Agreement;
- the Agreement on processed agricultural products[11] revising Protocol No. 2 of the 1972 EU–Switzerland free trade agreement (FTA);
- the Environment Agreement;
- the Agreement on Statistical Cooperation;
- the MEDIA (programme) Agreement;
- the education programmes; and
- the Pensions Agreement.[12]

Further Agreements

In addition, other agreements have been concluded between Switzerland and the EU:

- the Agreement between Switzerland and Europol;
- the Agreement between Switzerland and Eurojust;
- the Agreement on Customs Facilitation and Security;
- the Competition Cooperation Agreement;
- the Satellite Navigation Agreement;
- the Participation Agreement to the European Asylum Support Office; and
- the Arrangement for Armed Collaboration with the European Defence Agency.[13]

Finally, it should not be forgotten that Switzerland pays a contribution to the "reduction of economic and social inequalities in the enlarged EU" of currently

CHF 1 billion (2004 accession countries), CHF 257 million (Bulgaria and Romania) and CHF 45 million (Croatia). A further CHF 1.302 billion have been earmarked for a second contribution.[14]

WHAT IS THE "SWISS MODEL"? 2. THE SOFT EDGES: "AUTONOMOUS ADAPTATION", MUTUAL RECOGNITION, EQUIVALENCE AND UNILATERAL "CASSIS DE DIJON"

"Autonomous Adaptation"

Given the sectoral-only compatibility of Swiss law with that of the internal market, there are areas which are not subject to any formal obligation of adaptation to EU law. It is, however, in the economic interest of Switzerland to legislate as closely as possible to EU law in order to create as few difficulties as possible for Swiss exports. Out of that need was born the Swiss concept of autonomous adaptation ("*autonomer Nachvollzug*", "*reprise autonome*").[15] When European law is adopted without the existence of a legal obligation in this regard, there is, of course, a wide variety of ways to do this. The term "autonomous adaptation" is used when the European model is adopted in Swiss law more or less unchanged. The European influence can, however, also be exhausted in a more general inspiration that does not differ fundamentally from the influence of other preparatory work, for example on a legislative bill. Of course, if the adjustment is based not on economic incentives but on pressure or conditions, there can no longer be any talk of an "autonomous" process. This is, for example, the case where compatibility with European law is a prerequisite for access to the EU's internal market.[16]

Mutual Recognition, Equivalence and Unilateral "Cassis de Dijon"

The most recent example for such an autonomous adaptation is the unilateral introduction of the *Cassis de Dijon* principle,[17] according to which Switzerland unilaterally allows products corresponding to EU standards to access its market.[18] Because Switzerland did not join the EEA, the FTA with the EU of 1972 remained the basis for bilateral trade in industrial products. Under that agreement, however, the Swiss Federal Court had refused to adopt the case law of the European Court of Justice on the free movement of goods. This was notably the case[19] with regard to the *Dassonville*,[20] *Cassis de Dijon*[21] and *Keck* rulings.[22]

Hence Switzerland did not benefit from the *Cassis de Dijon* principle, as is the case in the EEA. Rather, there are still numerous technical barriers to trade that, among other effects, contribute to excessive prices in Switzerland. Considering the domestic political difficulties that inevitably accompany Switzerland–EU relations, and given the lack of enthusiasm on the EU's part to enter into further sectoral agreements, especially those that would only benefit Switzerland (such as on financial services, for example), any negotiation on a bilateral agreement introducing the *Cassis de Dijon* principle was out of the question. Therefore, the Swiss legislator decided to introduce the *Cassis de Dijon* principle autonomously and apply it unilaterally to products from the EEA.[23] This was done by amending the Federal Technical Barriers to Trade (TBT) Act.[24] These amendments entered into force on 1 July 2010. The introduction of the *Cassis de Dijon* principle was expected to lead to lower prices for consumers, facilitating trade with the EEA states and thus saving well over CHF 2 billion annually.[25]

HOW DOES IT WORK?

The Problem of No Institutional Framework

The absence of an overarching institutional framework is seen as a "key feature" of the "Swiss model".[26] Since 2006, when it became clear that Switzerland would neither join the EU in the near future, nor attempt a second referendum on the EEA,[27] the EU has increasingly expressed its dissatisfaction with the Bilateral Agreements it once entered into with Switzerland. It bears repeating that the EU only accepted this piecemeal approach at the time on the assumption that Switzerland might either try again to join the EEA or then join the EU altogether. None of this happened. At the EU's insistence, therefore, Switzerland agreed to negotiate with the EU an IFA in order to bring the relationship between the EU and Switzerland closer to the standards mentioned above.

Incoherent Institutional Functionality

Only the Schengen and Dublin Association Agreements, together with the Agreement on Customs Facilitation and Security, contain provisions on their own adaptation.[28] These adaptations are discussed in the respective Joint Committees created by the Agreements. All changes to the other bilateral agreements can only be done by way of the formal revision procedure: that is, negotiation, treaty revision and ratification. From the Swiss point of view, this has the advantage that changes cannot be imposed by the EU. Furthermore, Switzerland is – for now – in a position where it can delay, and de facto block, unwanted amendments. A prominent example is the so-called Union Citizenship Directive[29] that Switzerland – despite the EU's insistence – has until now refused to incorporate into the AFMP. This leads to disruption with regard to the pre-supposed "equivalence of legislation".[30]

Contrary to the EEA Agreement, in the case of Switzerland there are no common authorities to supervise the correct implementation and application of the agreements. The only exception is the AAT, where the European Commission is given some supervisory powers with regard to Switzerland as well.[31] Switzerland's reluctance to grant supervisory powers to non-Swiss authorities is rooted in the aforementioned strong view on sovereignty. The exception of the AAT seemed, however, justified given that air transport is ultimately a global issue and mostly technical.

Judicial enforcement is not expressly covered in any of Switzerland's current agreements with the EU and therefore lies with the European Court of Justice (ECJ) for EU member states and the Swiss Federal Court for Swiss parties. In some exceptional cases, judicial competence may either partly lie with the courts of the EU, as in the AAT, or with an arbitration panel.[32]

Dispute settlement between the EU and Switzerland normally lies with the respective sectoral Joint Committee. And if such a political process does not settle the dispute, there is, quite simply, no further remedy. Either party can simply "camp" on its position. An example of this is Switzerland's unilateral introduction of so-called "flanking measures against social dumping", which are seen by the EU as protectionist barriers to competition.[33] Discussions in the Joint Committee on the AFMP[34] have led nowhere. Again, "equivalence of legislation" is at stake.

In the case of Switzerland, legislative homogeneity has, until now, been difficult to achieve. Only two agreements contain explicit rules about parallel or homogeneous interpretation: the AFMP and the AAT. However, as long as there is no duty to adapt the bilateral agreements in a dynamic manner, any commitment of the homogeneous development of the *acquis* is merely political and down to the goodwill of the parties, and all the more so if it cannot be enforced by dispute settlement. An example is, again, the Swiss refusal to amend the AFMP by introducing the Union Citizenship Directive.

Finally, there is the problem of potentially diverging jurisprudence with regard to identical or similar wording. This dates back to the interpretation of the EU–Switzerland FTA. In 1979, the Swiss Federal Tribunal held, with regard to its Articles 13 and 22 vs Articles 30 and 36 EEC Treaty, that different aims may lead to different interpretations.[35] The ECJ replied in kind in the Polydor case.[36] Hence, the so-called "Polydor principle".[37] This is now standard, as the ECJ has consistently argued: Switzerland did not subscribe to the project of an economically integrated entity with a Single Market, therefore it did not join the EU's internal market, and therefore does not enjoy the same rights.[38]

ADVANTAGES, DISADVANTAGES AND AN UNFINISHED REMEDY

The Swiss View: Fit for Purpose

According to the majority view in Switzerland, there is no suitable alternative to the bilateral "model": "negotiating a deeper free trade agreement would be too time-consuming and not necessarily guarantee adequate access to the internal market. Similarly, the advantages of joining the European Economic Area (EEA) would not justify the inevitable loss of sovereignty."[39] The possibility of EU membership is officially not even considered anymore.

The EU's View: A Cumbersome, Provisional, Piecemeal Approach Not to be Repeated

Taken altogether, the Bilateral Agreements between the EU and Switzerland are a very fractured set of agreements that do not follow any common rules. As seen above, only two Agreements are "dynamic". Some are updated through the formal revision procedure, while others are updated by the decisions of their respective Joint Committees. In the case of the AFMP, even that competence varies, depending on the annexes. And, while most of the Bilateral Agreements may be Association Agreements according to Article 217 Treaty on the Functioning of the European Union, some are mixed agreements, while others are not. All of this leads to extremely difficult and potentially incoherent management of the agreements.

In particular, the EU sees a danger with regard to the "equivalence of legislation". This and the lack of a comprehensive institutional framework leads to an overall different treatment by the EU compared with Switzerland's fellow EFTA members: Iceland, Liechtenstein and Norway. For example, the latter were, because of their membership in the EEA Agreement, exempt from EU safeguard measures regarding steel products, whereas Switzerland was not.[40] Switzerland is in the process of rearranging its relationship with the EU. In late 2018 the EU and Switzerland concluded negotiations on a draft IFA covering existing and future bilateral market access agreements.

Remedy: An IFA

Since 2006, when it became clear that Switzerland would neither join the EU in the near future, nor attempt a second referendum on the EEA, the EU has increasingly expressed its dissatisfaction with the Bilateral Agreements it once entered into with Switzerland. It again bears repeating that the EU only accepted the piecemeal approach at the time on the assumption that Switzerland might either try again to join the EEA or then join the EU altogether. None of this happened. Upon the EU's insistence, Switzerland had agreed to negotiate an IFA with the EU in order to bring the relationship between the EU and Switzerland closer to the standards mentioned above.

Such an agreement would establish a common framework for five of the several Bilateral Agreements, namely those on the free movement of persons, including the right of establishment and the posting of workers, land transport, civil aviation, TBT/MRA and agriculture. Several other agreements, most notably the EU–Switzerland FTA, are not included. There would be a dispute settlement mechanism whereby the parties, if they failed to arrive at a consensus in the Joint Committee, could choose to bring the dispute before an arbitration panel. This panel is bound to refer questions of interpretation of EU law to the ECJ. The decisions of the ECJ are binding upon the arbitration panel and, hence, the parties.

Once it had finalized the IFA negotiations in November 2018,[41] the Swiss government did not sign the agreement but, rather, launched a consultation exercise with all Switzerland's major parties and stakeholders. In the feedback the government received, the three most contested elements in the IFA were:

- including the Swiss so-called "flanking measures", adding national measures to the rules on posting of workers as per the AFMP, as Swiss trade unions fear this would facilitate more "social dumping";
- incorporating rules on state aid, as cantons fear their cantonal banks would lose their privilege to extend state guarantees for savings; and
- eventually incorporating the Union Citizenship Directive,[42] as this is seen by some to further open up Switzerland to foreign immigration.

The Swiss government requested "clarifications" on these points. The EU refused to reopen or renegotiate the agreement but, rather, urged the Swiss to move.[43] For the time being, it seems therefore that the IFA is deadlocked.

The Threat of Eroding Bilateral Agreements

Given the delay in finalizing the IFA, the EU grew increasingly irritated and declared that in the absence of such an overarching agreement, not only would no new agreements[44] be concluded, but the Bilateral Agreements would be allowed to "erode".[45] That would mean that, for example, the MRA would not be updated anymore, which might lead to ever-receding access for the Swiss industry to the internal market, or only at much higher costs than today. A current example is the problem with regard to the next update concerning medical devices. While part of the new EU-Regulation 2017/745[46] has already been incorporated into the MRA, a large part is still missing. In the EU, this part was planned to apply as of 26 May 2020.[47] The EU has stated that it is not willing to agree to an updating decision in the Joint Committee. At the same time, it argues that, in the absence of this update, the entire chapter on the mutual recognition of conformity assessments can no longer be applied. Already before this, the EU had started to downgrade the relationship: although in terms of subject matter not linked in any way to the IFA, in 2017 the European Commission began to make a political link, announcing that it would renew its equivalence decision regarding the Swiss stock exchange regulations only if Switzerland would take positive steps towards the IFA. Having decided in favour of equivalence on a temporary basis on two occasions, in summer 2019 the European Commission did not renew its decision.

COULD THE SWISS MODEL WORK FOR THE UK?

Aims of the Parties

Given its economic size and importance in security terms, there is good reason to expect that the EU would wish for the UK to be in a very close relationship with it.[48] The EU is therefore offering a Comprehensive Free Trade Agreement (CFTA) ("New Partnership Agreement").[49]

The UK government started from a position that intended to secure a relationship that is "broader in scope than any other that exists between the EU and a third country".[50] The UK clearly expected "to be treated as a privileged partner of the EU, and arguably in a manner that confers on it unique privileges unavailable to other European states". Hence, "neither a 'Norway model' nor a 'Switzerland model'" were considered.[51]

Before commencing negotiations with the EU, the UK government in its approach to negotiations with the EU changed its ambitions: a CFTA should be at the core of the new relationship. Essentially, it should be a broad range FTA "on the lines of the FTAs already agreed by the EU in recent years with Canada and with other friendly countries". That "CFTA should be supplemented by a range of other international agreements covering, principally, fisheries, law enforcement and judicial cooperation in criminal matters, transport, and energy". On institutional matters the UK government states that "all these agreements should have their own appropriate and precedented governance arrangements, with no role for the Court of Justice".[52]

It Works as a Model for the Bilateral UK–Switzerland Trade Agreement

Meanwhile, the UK has been pursuing its "Global Britain" free trade agenda, although not with as much success as it had hoped. However, the UK has been able to conclude a trade agreement with a relatively important trading partner, namely Switzerland. It will seamlessly enter into force at the end of the transitional period.

The overall "deal" between Switzerland and the UK actually consists of a package of several agreements. First, there are several standalone agreements, essentially copies of certain bilateral agreements, such as the Agreements on Air and Land Transport or Social Security in place between Switzerland and the EU, and so were already in force between the two countries when the UK was an EU member state. Then there is the UK–Switzerland Trade Agreement, an agreement which itself is a framework agreement referring to several other agreements that are to be applied *mutatis mutandis*.

This is supplemented by an additional Memorandum of Understanding by which the parties confirm to revise, if necessary, the annexes to the incorporated agreements, to replacing or modernizing the UK–Switzerland Trade Agreement and consider to extend their henceforth bilateral relationship by incorporating provisions on additional areas, such as trade facilitation, trade in services, protection of intellectual property rights, labour, environment, trade remedies and dispute settlement.[53]

Hence, the UK bilaterally has already transposed the structure it wishes to have with the EU.

CONCLUSION

When approaching new negotiations, the EU normally thinks in terms of established models.[54] This path-dependent behaviour seems not to be caused in order to proceed in line with established principles, but also because on the part of the EU there is "a wariness of precedent setting".[55] "Concerns exist that a departure from existing models would impact on existing relations with third countries, particularly with regard to the more extensive consultation arrangements envisaged by the UK."[56]

It is quite clear that when negotiating more formalized relationships with third countries the EU will do anything to prevent them from "cherry-picking". There must be a balance of rights and obligations measured against the EU's interests. The EU will therefore not allow countries "to separate out the four freedoms of its internal market and insists on a role in decision-making being the preserve of member states". For all these reasons, "it prefers to work with and is therefore arguably constrained by existing arrangements".[57]

However, we know as well that the EU clearly does not want to repeat the "Swiss model".[58] This is due in part to the fact that the EU regards the current structure with Switzerland as provisional and rather cumbersome. On the latter point the experience is, especially regarding the "equivalence of legislation", not satisfactory. Therefore, the EU will do the utmost to prevent the "Swiss model" from being repeated. On the former point, the EU therefore denies that there is a "Swiss model", exactly because it fears such a precedent being held up against it as a model by the UK.

The end of that story is still open.

Notes for Chapter 4

1. C. Kaddous, "Switzerland and the EU: current issues and new challenges under the draft Institutional Framework Agreement" in S. Gstöhl & D. Phinnemore (eds), *The Proliferation of Privileged Partnerships between the European Union and its Neighbours* (Abingdon: Routledge, 2020), 68.

2. Kaddous, "Switzerland and the EU", 69.

3. A list can be found at https://www.eda.admin.ch/dam/dea/fr/documents/publikationen_dea/accords-liste_fr.pdf (French) or https://www.eda.admin.ch/dam/dea/de/documents/publikationen_dea/accords-liste_de.pdf (German) (accessed 30 April 2020).

4. Agreement of 30 June 1967 concerning products of the clock and watch industry between the European Economic Community and its member states and the Swiss Confederation, additional agreement OJ L 118, 30.4.1974, p. 12.

5. Tariff agreement with Switzerland negotiated under Article XXVIII of GATT on certain cheeses of the exposition 04,04 of the Common Customs Tariff, signed in Geneva on 29 June 1967; OJ L 257, 13.10.1969, p. 5.

6. Agreement of 10 October 1989 between the Swiss Confederation and the European Economic Community concerning direct insurance other than life assurance, OJ L 205, 27.7.1991, pp. 3–44.

7. Agreement of 21 June 1999 between the Swiss Confederation on the one hand, and the European Community and its member states on the other, on the free movement of persons, OJ L 114, 30.4.2002, pp. 6–22. Agreement of 21 June 1999 between the Swiss Confederation and the European Community on mutual recognition in conformity assessment, OJ L 114, 30.4.2002, pp. 369–429. Agreement of 21 June 1999 between the Swiss Confederation and the European Community on certain aspects of public procurement, OJ L 114, 30.4.2002, pp. 430–67. Agreement of 21 June 1999 between the Swiss Confederation and the European Community concerning trade in agricultural products, OJ L 114, 30.4.2002, pp. 132–368. Agreement of 21 June 1999 between the Swiss Confederation and the European Community on the carriage of goods and passengers by rail and by road, OJ L 114, 30.4.2002, pp. 91–131. Agreement of 21 June 1999 between the Swiss Confederation and the European Community on Air Transport, OJ L 114, 30.4.2002, pp. 73–90. Agreement on Scientific and Technological Cooperation between the European Union and the European Atomic Energy Community and the Swiss Confederation associating the Swiss Confederation with the Horizon 2020 framework program for research and innovation and the research and training program of the European Atomic Energy Community complementing the Horizon 2020 framework program and regulating the participation of the Swiss Confederation ITER (an international nuclear fusion research and engineering project) activities carried out by Fusion for Energy, OJ L 370, 30.12.2014, p. 3.

8. Message concerning the approval of sectoral agreements between Switzerland and the European Community of 23 June 1999, FF (Swiss Federal Journal, French) 1999, p. 5440.

9. For further details see M. Oesch, *Switzerland and the European Union* (Zurich: Dike, 2018), 21–2.

10. For further information see Oesch, *Switzerland and the European Union*, 22.

11. Agreement of 26 October 2004 between the Swiss Confederation and the European Community amending the Agreement between the Swiss Confederation and the European Economic Community of 22 July 1972 as regards the provisions applicable to processed agricultural products, OJ L 23, 26.1.2005, pp. 19–48.

12. Agreement of 26 October 2004 between the Swiss Confederation, the European Union and the European Community on the Association of the Swiss Confederation in the Implementation, Application and Development of the Schengen *acquis*, OJ L 53, 27.2.2008, pp. 52–79. Agreement of 26 October 2004 between the Swiss Confederation and the European Community on the criteria and mechanisms for determining the state responsible for examining an asylum application lodged in a member state or in Switzerland, OJ L 53, 27.2.2008, pp. 5–17. Agreement of 26 October 2004 between the Swiss Confederation and the European Community providing for measures equivalent to those provided for in Council Directive 2003/48/EC on the taxation of savings income in the form of interest payments, OJ L 385, 29.12.2004, pp. 30–49. Cooperation Agreement of 26 October 2004 between the Swiss Confederation, of the one part, and the European Community and its member states, of the other part, to combat fraud and any other illegal activity affecting their financial interests, OJ L 46, 17.2.2009, pp. 8–35. This agreement has not yet entered into force. However, Switzerland has been applying the agreement early since 2009 to EU member states that have also ratified the agreement and made a declaration on its early implementation. Thus, the agreement is already applied by Switzerland, the EU and several member states. Agreement of 26 October 2004 between the Swiss Confederation and the European Community amending the Agreement between the Swiss Confederation and the European Economic Community of 22 July 1972 as regards the provisions applicable to processed agricultural products, OJ L 23, 26.1.2005, pp. 19–48. Protocol No. 2 of 22 July 1972 concerning certain processed agricultural products, OJ L 300, 31.12.1972, pp. 191–282. Agreement of 26 October 2004 between the Swiss Confederation and the European Community concerning the participation of Switzerland in the European Environment Agency and in the European Environment Information and Observation Network, OJ L 90, 28.3.2006, pp. 37–47. Agreement of 26 October 2004 between the Swiss Confederation and the European Community on statistical cooperation, OJ L 90, 28.3.2006, pp. 2–20. Agreement of 11 October 2007 between the Swiss Confederation and the European Community in the audiovisual field, establishing the terms and conditions for the participation of the Swiss Confederation in the Community program MEDIA 2007, OJ L 303, 21.11.2007, pp. 11–23. Agreement between the European Union and the Swiss Confederation establishing the terms and conditions for the participation of the Swiss Confederation in the "Youth in Action" programme and in the action programme in the field of lifelong learning (2007–13), OJ L 87, 7.4.2010, pp. 9–18 (not in force any longer). Agreement of 26 October 2004 between the Swiss Federal Council and the Commission of the European Communities to avoid the double taxation of retired officials of the institutions and agencies of the European

Communities residing in Switzerland, SR/RS [German/French] 0.672.926.81, not published in the OJ.

13. Agreement of 24 September 2004 between the Swiss Confederation and the European Police Office, SR/RS 0.362.2. Agreement between Switzerland and Eurojust of 27 November 2008, SR/RS 0351.6. Agreement of 25 June 2009 between the Swiss Confederation and the European Community on the facilitation of checks and formalities in the transport of goods and on customs security measures, OJ L 199, 31.7.2009, pp. 24–42. Agreement of 17 May 2013 between the Swiss Confederation and the European Union concerning cooperation on the application of their competition laws, OJ L 347, 3.12.2014, pp. 3–9. Cooperation agreement of 18 December 2013 between the Swiss Confederation, on the one hand, and the European Union and its member states, on the other, on European satellite navigation programs, OJ L 15, 20.1.2014, pp. 3–17. Arrangement of 10 June 2014 between the Swiss Confederation and the European Union on the modalities of its participation in the European Asylum Support Office, OJ L 65, 11.3.2016, pp. 22–37. Framework for cooperation between the European Defence Agency and the Federal Department of Defence, Civil Protection and Sports of the Swiss Confederation, see https://register.consilium.europa.eu/doc/srv??=ENXF=ST%2017172%20211%20INIT.

14. Kaddous, "Switzerland and the EU", 70–1.

15. See more extensively, for example, F. Maiani, "Legal Europeanization as legal transformation: some insights from Swiss 'Outer Europe'" in F. Maiani, R. Petrov & E. Mouliarova (eds), *European Integration Without EU Membership: Models, Experiences, Perspectives*, EUI MWP, 2009/10, 4–9; Oesch, *Switzerland and the European Union*, 139–53.

16. A. Heinemann, "Rechtliche Transplantate zwischen Europäischer Union und der Schweiz" in L. Fahrländer *et al.*, *Europäisierung der schweizerischen Rechtsordnung* (Zürich: Dike, 2013), 20.

17. For more details, see G. Baur, "Mutual recognition and EFTA" in A. Albors-Llorens, C. Barnard & B. Leucht (eds), *Cassis de Dijon: Forty Years On* (forthcoming).

18. An introduction can be found in Oesch, *Switzerland and the European Union*, 149–51.

19. Most recently, Swiss Federal Court in *Physiogel*, Judgment of the Swiss Federal Court of 6 September 2006, 2A.593/2005, consideration 6.

20. Judgment of 11 July 1974, *Procureur du Roi v Benoît and Gustave Dassonville*, C-8/74, ECLI:EU:C:1974:82.

21. Judgment of 20 February 1979, *Rewe-Zentral AG v Bundesmonopolverwaltung für Branntwein*, C-120/78, ECLI:EU:C:1979:42.

22. Judgment of 24 November 1993, *Keck and Mithouard*, C-267/91 and C-268/91, ECLI:EU:C:1993:905.

23. A general introduction can be found in Oesch, *Switzerland and the European Union*, 149–51.

24. Bundesgesetz über die technischen Handelshemmnisse (THG)/Loi fédérale sur les entraves techniques au commerce (LETC), 6 October 1995, SR/RS 946.51.

25. C. Perritaz & N. Wallart, "Les conséquences économiques de la révision de la loi sur les entraves techniques au commerce", *Die Volkswirtschaft/La Vie économique* 10–2008, 23.

26. M. Vahl & N. Grolimund, *Integration without Membership* (Zurich: Europa Institut & Brussels: CEPS, 2006), 111.

27. With the ratification of the second round of bilateral treaties, the Swiss Federal Council downgraded its characterization of full EU membership of Switzerland from a "strategic goal" to an "option" in 2006, Swiss Federal Council, "Rapport Europe 2006", 06.064, 28.06.2006, FF 2006 6461, p. 6620 [French].

28. Oesch, *Switzerland and the European Union*, 42–3.

29. Directive 2004/38/EC of the European Parliament and of the Council of 29 April 2004 on the right of citizens of the Union and their family members to move and reside freely within the territory of the member states amending Regulation (EEC) No. 1612/68 and repealing Directives 64/221/EEC, 68/360/EEC, 72/194/EEC, 73/148/ EEC, 75/34/EEC, 75/35/EEC, 90/364/EEC, 90/365/EEC and 93/96/EEC; OJ L 158 of 30.4.2004, pp. 77–123.

30. Kaddous, "Switzerland and the EU", 73.

31. For example, Article 18 (2) AAT.

32. C. Tobler & J. Beglinger, *Grundzüge des bilateralen (Wirtschafts-)Rechts Schweiz-EU*, Vol. 1 (Zurich: Dike, 2013), 32.

33. Council of the EU, "Council conclusions on EU relations with EFTA countries", Brussels, 20.12.2012, para. 32.

34. Swiss Federal Council, "Botschaft zur Genehmigung der sektoriellen Abkommen zwischen der Schweiz und der EG" (explanatory message on the sectorial agreements between Switzerland and the EU), Bundesblatt, 1999 pp. 6128–449, p. 6316 [German].

35. Judgment of the Swiss Federal Court of 25 January 1979, *Bosshard Partners Intertrading AG v Sunlight AG*, BGE/ATF 105 II 49, a.k.a. ("OMO").

36. Judgment of 9 February 1982, *Polydor Limited and RSO Records Inc. v Harlequin Records Shops Limited and Simons Records Limited*, C-270/80, ECLI:EU:C:1982:43.

37. For more details see G. Baur, *The European Free Trade Association* (Cambridge: Intersentia, 2020), 121–2.

38. Judgment of 7 March 2013, *Switzerland v Commission*, C-547/10, ECLI:EU:C:2013:139, paras 78 and 79.

39. For more details see: https://www.avenir-suisse.ch/en/publication/bilateral-treaties-what-else/ (accessed 30 April 2020).

40. European Commission, "Trade: Commission imposes provisional safeguard measures concerning imports of a number of steel products", press release IP/18/4563, 18 July 2018.

41. (Swiss) Federal Department of Foreign Affairs, "Accord facilitant les relations bilatérales entre l'Union européenne et la Confédération suisse dans les parties du marché intérieur auxquelles la Suisse participe", 23 November 2018, https://www.eda. admin.ch/dam/dea/fr/documents/abkommen/Acccord-inst-Projet-de-texte_fr.pdf [French].

42. See note 29.

43. Council of the EU, "Council conclusions on EU relations with the Swiss Confederation", press release 116/19, 19.2.2019.

44. Such as the proposed Energy Agreement.

45. (Swiss) Federal Department of Foreign Affairs FDFA, "Institutional agreement between Switzerland and the EU: key points in brief", 7.12.2018, https://www.eda.admin.ch/dam/dea/en/documents/abkommen/InstA-Wichtigste-in-Kuerze_en.pdf (30.4.2020); joint declaration by Andreas Schwab, chair of the European Parliament Delegation for Northern Cooperation and for relations with Switzerland and Norway and to the EU-Iceland Joint Parliamentary Committee and the European Economic Area (EEA) Joint Parliamentary Committee (DEEA Delegation) and Hans-Peter Portmann, Chair of the Swiss Federal Assembly Delegation to the EFTA Parliamentary Committee and for Relations with the European Parliament (EFTA/EU Delegation) and the undersigned Members of the European Parliament and the Swiss Federal Assembly on the Draft Institutional Framework Agreement (IFA) between Switzerland and the EU on the occasion of the 38th interparliamentary meeting between Switzerland and the EU on 27 and 28 November 2019 in Strasbourg, https://www.europarl.europa.eu/cmsdata/189505/Final%20draft%20joint%20declaration%20with%20signatures_27.11.19-original.pdf (accessed 30 April 2020).

46. Regulation (EU) 2017/745 of the European Parliament and of the Council of 5 April 2017 on medical devices, amending Directive 2001/83/EC, Regulation (EC) No 178/2002 and Regulation (EC) No 1223/2009 and repealing Council Directives 90/385/EEC and 93/42/EEC, OJ L 117, 5.5.2017, p. 1.

47. Now delayed as the underlying Council decision will, due to Covid-19, only be taken in the autumn.

48. D. Phinnemore, "UK withdrawal from EU membership – the quest for cake" in Gstöhl & Phinnemore, *The Proliferation of Privileged Partnerships*, 158.

49. UK Task Force, "Draft text of the Agreement on the New Partnership with the United Kingdom", 18.3.2020, https://ec.europa.eu/info/sites/info/files/200318-draft-agreement-gen.pdf (accessed 30 April 2020).

50. UK Government, "The future relationship between the United Kingdom and the European Union", 12.7.2018, p. 7, http://www.gov.uk/government/publications/the-future-relationship-between-the-united-kingdom-and-the-european-union (accessed 30 April 2020).

51. Phinnemore, "UK withdrawal from EU membership", 158.

52. UK Government, "The future relationship with the EU – the UK's approach to negotiations", February 2020, 3.

53. For further details see G. Baur, "Post-2020 UK–Switzerland Trade Agreement also for the EU?" Blog (2020), Efta-Studies.org.

54. Phinnemore, *The Proliferation of Privileged Partnerships*, 168.

55. *Ibid.*, 169.

56. European Commission, Foreign, Security and Defence Policy (Slides), TF50 (2018) 50 – Commission to EU27, 15.6.2018, https://ec.europa.eu/commission/sites/beta-political/files/slides_on_foreign_security_defence_policy.pdf (accessed 30 April 2020).

57. Phinnemore, *The Proliferation of Privileged Partnerships*, 170.

58. "The Brexit effect: Brussels tries to blunt the Swiss model", *Financial Times*, 2 October 2018.

5

THE CUSTOMS UNION BETWEEN TURKEY AND THE EUROPEAN UNION

Selim Kuneralp

Selim Kuneralp

INTRODUCTION: EARLY APPLICATION FOR MEMBERSHIP, TO ASSOCIATION, TO CUSTOMS UNION

Turkey applied to join the European Economic Community (EEC) on 31 July 1959, barely a year after the Treaty of Rome creating the Community had entered into force. The decision to apply was taken exclusively for political reasons. Relations between Turkey and Greece had deteriorated sharply after the first of many crises erupted over the Crown Colony of Cyprus, the UK government having made it clear that it was going to vacate the island as part of the gradual demise of the British Empire. Greece had applied to join the Community in June 1959. It was therefore important for the then leaders of the Turkish Republic to do the same, so as not to be left behind.

The response of the EEC to both countries was that they were not ready for membership, because their economies were at a much lower level of development than that of the six original members of the Community. Instead, the two applicant countries each signed an Association Agreement with the EEC, Greece in June 1961 in Athens, Turkey on 12 September 1963 in Ankara. The agreements were similar in their structure. Each country was offered a process of gradual economic integration that would prepare it for a customs union, to be completed at an (originally unspecified) date and that would, in turn, serve as a stepping stone to full membership of the Community.

It cannot be sufficiently stressed that economic integration and the establishment of a customs union were not perceived as being ends in themselves but, rather, as instruments to prepare the two countries for full membership of the Community. In the case of Turkey, this objective was explicitly recognized in the Preamble to the Association Agreement, which stated, "Recognizing that the support given by the European Economic Community ... will *facilitate the accession of Turkey to the Community at a later date.*" Article 28 of the same agreement further stated that, "As soon as the operation of this Agreement has advanced far enough to justify envisaging full acceptance by Turkey of the obligations arising out of the Treaty establishing the Community, *the Contracting Parties shall examine the possibility of the accession of Turkey to the Community*"[1] (emphasis added).

Thus, the Association Agreement was essentially a non-binding declaration of intent which called on the parties to undertake some unspecified groundwork to prepare Turkey for the establishment of a customs union. The agreement was accompanied by financial assistance protocols under which grant aid was allocated to Turkey to help raise its level of development. This preparatory stage was expected to be followed at the end of a five-year period by the next phase, called the transitional stage, during which Turkey and the Community were to establish a customs union.

It is important to note that as a non-member state, Turkey was not expected to join *the* Customs Union that the member states of the EEC were gradually establishing among themselves at the same time but, instead, to create with the Community a separate union whose basic principles, such as a common external tariff and the elimination of tariffs and non-tariff measures, were identical in theory but somewhat different in practice.

Soon after the end of the preparatory phase, an Additional Protocol to the Association Agreement was concluded on 23 November 1970. The Additional Protocol set out a detailed programme of work that was to be followed throughout the transitional period and that would follow the preparatory phase and culminate in the foreseen final phase of the Association, namely, the completion of the Customs Union between Turkey and the European Communities.[2] It contained detailed provisions for the gradual elimination of tariffs between the two parties and the adoption by Turkey of the EC's Common Customs Tariff. Because of the continued disparity in the levels of development between the two sides, it was foreseen that the transitional period would last 22 years from the date of the entry into force of the Protocol; that is, after it had been ratified by both parties. Ratification duly occurred on 1 January 1973, which meant that the two sides had until 1 January 1995 to complete the Customs Union. Because of the asymmetric nature of the Association, the Communities undertook to fulfil their side of the deal almost immediately, on 1 January 1971, and eliminated import tariffs on products covered by the Protocol; namely, industrial products.

Since the Customs Union was not an end in itself but, rather, a means of preparing Turkey for full membership of the Communities, the Protocol also contained provisions dealing with agriculture, movement of persons and services, right of establishment, alignment of economic policies (particularly competition), taxation and commercial policy. Generally speaking, these provisions envisaged a standstill in policies, which meant that neither side would, in its relations with the other, raise obstacles that had not existed at the time of the entry into force of the Protocol. There were also provisions for the coordination of efforts so as to align Turkish legislation and practice in the areas covered with those of the Communities. The main idea was that, for the Customs Union to function properly, it would have to be accompanied by measures that would ensure a level playing field between the two sides.

The Protocol was accompanied by commitments to continue regular material assistance that would be provided in the form of financial protocols, of which there were four in the end.

The standstill commitment on movement of persons and the right of establishment were particularly valuable for Turkey which, at that time, was supplying large numbers of workers to European Community (EC) member states, chiefly Germany, but also France, Belgium and the Netherlands. This particular provision has proved to be a serious bone of contention between Turkey and its Community partners because, soon after the entry into force of the Protocol, Germany, followed by other member states, started rapidly to introduce restrictions on movements of labour, as a result of the economic recession that followed the 1973 oil shock.

From the very beginning, the Additional Protocol, with its concrete schedule aimed at gradually laying the ground for the establishment of a customs union between the two parties, was a highly contentious issue in Turkey. The conventional wisdom at the time was that Turkey's industrialization could only take place behind very high protective barriers and that Turkish industry should aim at meeting the needs of the domestic market without being too concerned about exports. In other words, the country's economic development strategy was based on import substitution.

Consequently, on the eve of the signature of the Protocol, the government substantially raised the level of the Turkish tariff which meant that the threshold from which the gradual reductions would take place would be much higher than had been envisaged when the Protocol was being negotiated. Only a few months after the signature of the Protocol and even before it had been ratified, the government (which had replaced the one that had signed the Protocol) sent its foreign minister to the Community capitals to ask for a revision of the Protocol.

Despite the profound unpopularity of the Protocol and the EC–Turkey Customs Union that was its ultimate objective, the first few tariff reductions were implemented. However, they were soon frozen, allegedly as a result of the oil crisis of 1973, which badly affected Turkey, a country that relied (as it still relies) almost entirely on imports for its consumption of oil. Soon afterwards, the reductions were reversed so that, by 1975, the Turkish tariff was back at the level at which it had been at the time of the signature of the Protocol. Meanwhile, no serious effort was made to align Turkish legislation in any of the areas covered by the Protocol.

THE CUSTOMS UNION: ADVANTAGES AND DISADVANTAGES

There followed in Turkey a long period of political and economic instability which precluded the country from taking any steps to liberalize its economy, let alone prepare itself for a customs union that might ultimately pave the way for its accession to the Communities. Following a September 1980 military coup, political relations with the Communities were frozen. The accession of Greece to the EC in January 1981 complicated matters further, as for many years the country followed a policy of blocking any kind of dialogue with Turkey.

Meanwhile, the EC continued to implement its zero-tariff policy on imports of industrial products from Turkey. As one of the world's major cotton producers, Turkey's textile industry was naturally very competitive, and it met a large part of the Communities' need for cotton yarn at a cheap price. The 1973 accession of the UK to the Communities changed this situation. The UK's cotton yarn industry, which had spearheaded industrialization in the nineteenth century, was by then long since outdated and uncompetitive. However, British governments were not yet ready to allow the cotton yarn industry to go under. At the same time, the Additional Protocol's standstill clause prevented the introduction of new non-tariff barriers to imports of industrial products from Turkey.

At first, anti-dumping duties were imposed but, soon enough, a somewhat ingenious solution was found; namely, the negotiation of industry-to-industry quota agreements. These agreements, whose scope expanded over the next 20 years, had the advantage for Turkish exporters of raising the price they obtained for their exports and guaranteeing them a permanent share in the EC market. Successive Turkish governments, conscious of their failure to abide by the obligations contained in the Protocol, did not object to this situation.

The quantitative restrictions on Turkish exports of cotton yarn also had an unexpected effect. They forced Turkish industrialists to use surplus cotton yarn locally, which meant moving to higher value-added products, starting with T-shirts, and moving up the scale of the textile and clothing sector. Each time a product threatened to flood the Community market and faced quantitative restrictions, Turkish industrialists were encouraged to move one rung up the scale so that, over the years, Turkey acquired one of the most competitive textile and clothing industries in the world and, for many years, its products constituted Turkey's chief exports to EC countries. It is doubtful that the same result could have been achieved in the absence of the Association as the Community would then have been free to impose tariffs.

By the mid-1980s, the import substitution policy, which had long been the mantra of Turkish politicians, bureaucrats and industrialists alike, began to be seriously questioned. It became clear that infant industries, such as the motor car industry, refused to grow up behind the high protective barriers that coddled them. Turkey had suffered several economic crises that had aggravated the political situation. In addition, it was clear that if the EC–Turkey Customs Union was not completed by 1 January 1995 as envisaged in the Additional Protocol, the preferential treatment accorded to Turkey would cease to exist and Turkish products would lose their tariff advantage in Community markets.

In addition, in April 1987 Turkey had made a fresh application to accede to the Communities. The response it received two years later was that first the Association should evolve as planned and the Customs Union be completed on schedule.

Despite the fact that little had been done to prepare Turkey over the previous 18 years, and the shortness of the remaining time available, the Turkish government accepted the Community proposal, and frantic efforts were made to complete the customs union on time. But it soon became clear that the Customs Union was not simply about eliminating tariffs on bilateral trade and aligning on the Common Customs Tariff. All sorts of things needed to be done to ensure that a level playing field was achieved between the two sides and that the terms of competition between them were equalized.

Turkey was required to adopt legislation to protect intellectual and industrial property. Prior to the completion of the customs union, intellectual property protection had been very weak, and had been based on outdated legislation going back to the 1880s. There was no functioning patent registration system, and Turkey was a paradise of counterfeit products of all kinds, ranging from branded clothing products to pharmaceutical products and mechanical parts of all sorts. From the EU perspective, it was imperative that discipline be introduced into this area since products manufactured in Turkey or imported from abroad into Turkey would thereafter be in free circulation inside the territory of the Customs Union, that is, Turkey and the member states of the European Union.

Similarly, and for the same reasons, Turkey was expected to adopt EU industrial standards and regulations in all of the so-called regulated sectors. As this required time, the certification of products manufactured in Turkey took effect gradually and, in those areas where conformity had not been certified, Turkey had to continue to allow its products to be checked for conformity assessment by the competent authorities in EU member states before they were allowed into the EU market. Suggestions for having different standards for products destined for the domestic market and exports had been voiced but were rejected as impractical.

Nevertheless, the EU–Turkey Customs Union was formally completed on 31 December 1995, a year later than required. However, no country, including among Turkey's trading partners, quibbled about the one-year delay. Parallel to it and shortly afterwards, Turkey concluded a separate free trade agreement with the European Coal and Steel Community (ECSC) which provided for the elimination of tariffs and quantitative restrictions on imports of coal, iron and steel products. (The conclusion of a separate agreement had been made necessary by the fact that the ECSC had not yet at the time been absorbed into the EU.)

At the time the EU–Turkey Customs Union was completed, the European Union still maintained a restrictive policy on imports of textiles and clothing from close to 30 developing countries, under the Multifibre Agreement (MFA) negotiated in the General Agreement on Tariffs and Trade (GATT). Turkey had relied for protection on the very high tariff that it had been applying prior to the completion of the Customs Union. As a result, it had hardly any imports from any of these countries, but now it was expected to adopt quotas similar to those of the European Union, since otherwise imports into the EU would have been diverted through Turkey and would have demolished the protective system built there. Of all the concerned countries, only India rejected the deals offered to them, which opened the Turkish market to their products, but not to the extent that would have prevailed in the absence of quotas. India made this issue into a matter of principle, claiming with some justification that these arrangements were incompatible with Article XXIV of the GATT, under which customs unions and free trade areas should not raise barriers to the trade of third countries. It took the issue to the World Trade Organization (as the GATT had by then become) and won the case. However, the MFA expired in 2005 and all quantitative restrictions on imports of textile and clothing products into the EU and Turkish markets were abolished as a result.

Under the Customs Union, Turkey is allowed to apply higher but not lower duties on imports from third countries than those provided for the EU's Common Customs Tariff. It was also expected to align on the European Union's preferential trade policy towards third countries. As regards elements such as the Generalized System of Preferences (GSP) applied to developing and least developed countries, Turkey was able to fulfil its obligations because the GSP is applied unilaterally and no reciprocity is required.

However, problems arose with the free trade agreements that the EU has concluded with a large number of countries in all regions of the world. Those countries are under no particular obligation to conclude similar agreements with Turkey, although they have been encouraged to do so by the European Union. Most have complied with the EU's request but some countries, such as Mexico and South Africa, have not, because they have concluded that the volume of their trade with Turkey did not justify such an agreement and that, in any case, when their exports to Turkey transited through an EU country they entered the Turkish market free of duty as there exist no rules of origin within the EU–Turkey Customs Union that would permit easy identification of the source of the product.

Thus, cars manufactured in Mexico by a German company entered the Turkish market through Germany, free of the customs duty that would have been payable if they had come directly from Mexico. When the Turkish authorities discovered that the particular model of car that was finding its way to Turkey was only manufactured in Mexico and not in Germany or any other EU member state, a waiver was sought and obtained from the European Commission for those cars to be subject to the duty payable for imports from Mexico, even though they continued to arrive from Germany.

Over the years, the functioning of the EU–Turkey Customs Union has been quite satisfactory. Contrary to widespread expectations, Turkish industry has not only survived but thrived since completion of the Customs Union. Whereas prophets of doom had predicted that the domestic car industry – which had been created exclusively for the domestic market – would collapse, the opposite has happened. The main manufacturers, themselves offshoots of European companies, have integrated their production patterns with those of foreign plants controlled abroad by those companies. Thus, certain models are produced in Turkey primarily for the export market, which means that they satisfy EU regulations. Moreover, Japanese and Korean manufacturers have been attracted to Turkey by the advantage that the Customs Union gave them in terms of access to the EU market. As a result, cars and other vehicles have displaced textiles and clothing as Turkey's biggest export product.

Nevertheless, several criticisms have been directed at the EU–Turkey Customs Union over the years. These can be grouped under two separate headings.

First, under the Customs Union, Turkey is expected to align with the EU's external trade policy, both preferential and non-preferential, and apply any changes to it that the EU may decide to implement. However, Turkey has no say in the elaboration of this policy, nor is it consulted when changes are considered and adopted. When the EU is negotiating agreements with third countries, such as free trade agreements, Turkey is not involved in the process. The EU encourages its partners to negotiate parallel agreements with Turkey, but there is no legally binding obligation for those countries to do so and at least two have resisted the pressure over the years, as seen above.

The other side of the coin is that Turkey faces constraints in the conduct of its trade policy with neighbouring countries or other countries that may not have bilateral agreements with the EU. Since Turkey is not allowed to apply a tariff on its imports lower than the Common External Tariff in order to avoid the risk of trade diversion, it cannot conclude preferential trade agreements with countries that do not have such agreements with the EU unless a waiver is granted by the Union, which has only happened very rarely since the Customs Union was completed. Waivers were sought and obtained in the past for the implementation of free trade agreements with Syria, Georgia and Macedonia, after the European Commission concluded that the risk of trade diversion from those countries was minimal.

The EU–Turkey Customs Union remains an incomplete work. Its structure was designed in the 1970s at a time when the European construction was at a relatively preliminary stage and the Single Market still far from the drawing board. As a result, the Customs Union did not cover policy areas such as services, government procurement, dispute settlement and others. An attempt was made after the completion of the Customs Union to complement it with a free trade agreement that would have covered services. Several rounds of negotiations were held in Brussels with the European Commission in 1999–2001 which could have led to the parallel opening of the respective procurement and services markets, but the negotiations foundered, essentially for two reasons: (1) the Turkish government of the day was not prepared to open professional and financial services, as well as the country's procurement market, to foreign competition; and (2) on the EU side, Austria and Germany principally, but perhaps other member states, were not prepared to envisage even the minimum degree of movement of physical persons that a free trade agreement on services would have required.

As a result of this, the effort at closing some of the gaps in the Customs Union were abandoned. Prior to this, a market access agreement for agricultural products had been concluded in 1998 between the two parties, but that was never fully implemented because animal health considerations and the powerful meat and dairy lobby in Turkey prevented successive governments from opening the meat market to imports.

THE CUSTOMS UNION: THE STEPPING STONE BECOMES THE OBJECTIVE?

The failure to make progress towards addressing the missing parts of the EU–Turkey Customs Union did not matter at first because the Customs Union was not expected to remain in effect as a separate instrument for a long time. Its completion coincided with the preparations for the "big bang" round of EU enlargement which began in earnest in 1997. Turkey was only accepted as a candidate for accession to the European Union two years later, and accession negotiations began in 2005. While there was never a precise timetable or target date for the conclusion of these negotiations, previous experience had indicated that they lasted around seven years on average. The timespan had tended to become longer with each enlargement but nevertheless, all accession negotiations had been completed successfully and Turkey had no reason to believe at the beginning of the exercise that its own accession process would have a different ending.

For that reason, the weaknesses of the Customs Union were not addressed immediately, despite early misgivings about them. However, a few years after the accession negotiations started, they began to confront serious obstacles which first slowed them down and then stopped them altogether. The perspective of accession began to fade away gradually, to the extent that it has now completely disappeared for all practical purposes.

As a result, attention has been drawn back to the EU–Turkey Customs Union and what needs to be done to fill in its gaps and deal with its weaknesses. The European Commission asked the World Bank to prepare an impartial report which was published in 2014 and made a number of suggestions to address these gaps and weaknesses.[3] This study remains to this day the only comprehensive analysis of the impact and potential benefits for both sides of modernizing the Customs Union. In broad terms, it concludes that both sides would benefit if current barriers on trade in agricultural products and services were removed and each side opened its procurement market to the other. It also found that an effective dispute settlement mechanism was needed, that road transport permits should be liberalized, a "green" visa system introduced for bona fide business people and a better consultation system put in place for dealing swiftly with "trade irritants": mainly measures that one of the parties accuses the other of taking in contravention of Customs Union rules.

The European Commission conducted its own impact assessment which concluded in December 2016 with a recommendation for a Council Decision "authorising the opening of negotiations with Turkey on an Agreement on the extension of the scope of the bilateral trade relationship and on the modernisation of the Customs Union".[4] However, this authorization has not been given so far, essentially for political reasons. The European Parliament, in a resolution adopted on 3 March 2019, recommended the suspension of accession negotiations but left the updating of the Customs Union as an option, "but only if there are concrete improvements in the field of democracy, human rights, fundamental freedoms and the rule of law".[5] On 18 June 2019, the Council of the European Union noted that, "Turkey continues to move further away from the European Union … no further work towards the modernisation of the EU–Turkey Customs Union is foreseen".[6] Despite occasional calls for modernization negotiations, this remains, for the time being, the last word on the topic.

It therefore looks as if the EU–Turkey Customs Union is likely neither to be replaced by accession nor modernized and extended to include all the missing sectors and topics. Despite this unhappy state of affairs, which is likely to continue for the foreseeable future, nobody in Turkey is suggesting that the Customs Union be terminated. The EU remains Turkey's biggest trading partner and source of foreign direct investment. Even in the absence of structural improvements to the relationship with the EU, Turkey does not have an alternative with which to replace it.

Having said that, it cannot be claimed that the EU–Turkey Customs Union can serve as a model for any other country. Indeed, other than Turkey and the micro-states Andorra and San Marino, there are no non-EU member countries that have entered into a customs union with the EU. As has been seen, the EU–Turkey Customs Union had been intended as a stepping stone for accession. However, that model has never been followed in any of the enlargements that have occurred since the EEC was created in 1958. No acceding country has been asked to complete a customs union with the EEC/EC/EU before accession. The burden in terms of the asymmetry of the relationship was simply too high to be countenanced by sovereign nations even for a temporary period until accession occurred. It would therefore be even more difficult to carry out for a departing nation such as the UK, which wouldn't even have accession as a goal.[7]

Notes for Chapter 5

1. Agreement establishing an Association between the European Economic Community and Turkey (signed at Ankara, 12 September 1963), *Official Journal of the European Communities*, 31.12.77, No. L 361/29.

2. Following the 1966 "Merger Treaty" the EEC, the ECSC and Euratom were merged into a single organization, the European Communities (EC). This became the European Union (EU) after the 1993 implementation of the Maastricht Treaty.

3. World Bank, 2014, Evaluation of the EU-Turkey customs union: http://documents. worldbank.org/curated/en/298151468308967367/Evaluation-of-the-EU-Turkey-customs-union.

4. European Commission Staff Working Document, Impact Assessment Accompanying the document, Recommendation for a Council Decision authorising the opening of negotiations with Turkey on an Agreement on the extension of the scope of the bilateral preferential trade relationship and on the modernisation of the Customs Union {COM(2016) 830 final} {SWD(2016) 476 final} Brussels, 21.12.2016 SWD(2016) 475 final.

5. European Parliament resolution of 13 March 2019 on the 2018 Commission Report on Turkey (2018/2150(INI)): https://www.europarl.europa.eu/doceo/document/TA-8-2019-0200_EN.html.

6. Council of the European Union, 18 June 2019, Council conclusions on enlargement and stabilisation and association process: https://www.consilium.europa.eu/en/press/press-releases/2019/06/18/council-conclusions-on-enlargement-and-stabilisation-and-association-process/.

7. F. Hakura, "EU-Turkey Customs Union: prospects of modernization and lessons for Brexit", Chatham House, December 2018.

6

UKRAINE: THE ASSOCIATION
AGREEMENT MODEL

Nazar Bobitski

The EU–Ukraine Association Agreement famously featured as one of the available models in the EU chief Brexit negotiator Michel Barnier's scale of options for the UK–EU post-Brexit future relationship, sandwiched between the EU–Swiss system of bilateral agreements and the EU–Turkey Customs Union.[1] It was selected by the European Commission in view of its comprehensive scope, covering political dialogue and coordination of foreign policy, justice and home affairs, trade, economic and social matters, as well as a considerable depth of legal commitments which, if sufficiently implemented, would offer significant opportunities to access the EU internal market. As was stated by the then European Council president, Herman Van Rompuy, at the time of its inception the EU–Ukraine Association represented the most advanced framework of relationships ever concluded between the EU and a third country.[2]

Yet the Agreement's origins and its evolution were taking place in a markedly different political context compared with the EU enlargement history from 1973 onwards. First, from the political perspective, the EU was placing its relationship with Ukraine and other countries of the former Soviet Union on a different conceptual premise as compared with the EU pre-2004 neighbours in Central Europe, avoiding a political commitment towards their EU membership perspective, as well as taking a cautious approach towards closer trade ties and economic cooperation in the first generation of bilateral agreements, known as Partnership and Cooperation Agreements (PCAs). Only after the 2004 EU enlargement, as the success of transformations in the candidate countries was attributed to the transformative power of the pre-accession processes, did the EU start to contemplate ways of replicating the winning formula without the apparently high political, institutional and economic costs of continued expansion. The European Neighbourhood Policy (ENP) sought to substitute the membership perspective instrument by a carefully calibrated idea of a "stake in

the EU Internal Market" achievable through consistent, enforceable and verifiable processes of legislative approximation to the EU's *acquis communautaire*
and accompanying institutional reforms in the partner countries.

Second, the relationship evolved in a much more complicated and conflict-
ridden geopolitical landscape across the former Soviet territories. Some of the
European post-Soviet states,[3] led by Ukraine, openly sought to emulate the successful transition of their western neighbours by locking their recognition "as
European nations, with a perspective, one day, to become members of the EU
club" into the political and legal framework of their relations with the EU.[4] Their
aspirations were too often sabotaged from within by the slow and often revers-
ible pace of economic reforms, endemic corruption and lack of political will.
From without, the pace and depth of rapprochement of these countries with the
EU was actively opposed by a resurgent Russia, which under President Vladimir
Putin was aggressively denying its European neighbours their European choice
by imposing an alternative vision of a Moscow-centred common economic
space. Russia's revenge for the Euromaidan revolution in Ukraine in 2013–14,
through the covert annexation of Crimea and the hybrid warfare in eastern
Ukraine, provided the powerful political impetus towards the conclusion and
initial implementation of the Association Agreement and, at the same time, significantly impaired the ability of the Ukrainian state to implement it by divert-
ing attention and resources towards a protracted war in the east.

Under the influence of these factors, the EU–Ukraine Association Agreement
emerged as a distinctly new model of the relationship between the EU and
a third country, with a clear legal basis in Treaty on European Union (TEU)
Article 8, as amended by the Treaty of Lisbon, offering a new type of integration
without membership[5] and characterized by comprehensiveness, complexity and
conditionality.[6]

This chapter will look at the political context of the EU's relations with its
current neighbours which shaped the legal and institutional framework of the
Association Agreement, the Agreement's legal and institutional scope, as well
as the achievements and shortfalls of the first five years of its implementation.

THE CONTEXT

The Association Agreement is a brainchild of the landmark EU foreign policy
framework, developed and launched in the aftermath of the 2004 enlargement:
the ENP. The 2004 "Big Bang" enlargement drastically expanded the political
geography at the EU's external borders, sparking a debate about the limits of
Europe, as well as about the right policy approach towards the next ring of the
EU's neighbours from the Maghreb and the Levant to the newly independent

states of the former Soviet Union in Eastern Europe and the South Caucasus. Responding to this new reality, the then president of the European Commission, Romano Prodi (1999–2004), said, "[a]ccession is not the only game in town … enlargement does not benefit only present and future members. Future neighbours will benefit too."[7] The first ENP policy concept by the European Commission saw the light in May 2003[8] and was subsequently refined in a European Commission ENP Strategy Paper in 2004.[9]

The key policy tenet of the ENP was an offer of an advanced comprehensive relationship with the EU, which is different from the possibilities available under the accession paradigm offered by TEU Article 49.[10] In other words, the ENP was to provide a solution to the EU's looming post-2004 enlargement foreign policy dilemma: namely, how to maintain a stabilizing and transformative influence on its neighbours in a way similar to the pre-accession process without a corresponding commitment to absorb new members.

The ENP policy toolbox offered solutions remarkable in their flexibility as to their end result. The offer on the table included "a stake in the EU internal market", gradually achievable in line with progress, with legislative approximation, close collaboration and alignment in foreign and security policy, and an enhanced technical assistance commitment. As was remarked by Romano Prodi in 2004, the eventual deliverable of the ENP would be a relationship between the EU and its neighbours which would "share everything but the institutions".[11] The ENP methodology would closely mirror that of the pre-accession negotiations, where the EU and the partner countries would engage in a regular, comprehensive political dialogue in the framework of the ENP "Action Plans", legally non-binding bilateral agendas for legislative approximation and institutional and political reforms, supported by EU assistance. As with the pre-accession process, the lion's share of commitments would fall upon the partner countries. However, the key political stimulus that mobilized the political will and broad public support in the candidate countries for pre-accession reforms, "the EU membership perspective", was firmly taken off the table.

Initially the EU also left untouched the existing treaty framework of relations with neighbours concluded in the course of the 1980s and 1990s, the PCAs in the east and the Association Agreements in the south, despite their increasing obsolescence. Instead, the Action Plans were positioned to plug those legal and institutional gaps while avoiding potentially far-reaching legal commitments. In short, the ENP hoped to deliver the similar transformational effect as that of the pre-accession process, but at a considerably lower political, institutional and financial cost to the EU.

However, the unified ENP approach quickly fragmented under the pressure of the economic, social and political realities of the southern and eastern neighbours, as well as the different levels of their governments' political aspirations vis-à-vis the EU. First, geography played an obvious role: southern neighbours' non-European location established a clear objective limit to the extent of their aspirations, while the eastern neighbours led by Ukraine, and with the exception of Armenia and Azerbaijan, were quick to press for a more ambitious agenda, including recognition of their potential EU membership.

Second, that drive was received sympathetically and even encouraged from within, by the eastern and southern EU member states, keen on mobilizing the political impetus and resources of the ENP for the neighbouring countries on their doorstep. As France, under the leadership of President Nicolas Sarkozy, launched an ambitious initiative of the Union for the Mediterranean to focus the EU's attention on the challenges in the south, the eastern member states were looking to raise a comparable level of the EU's engagement with the successor states of the former Soviet Union. One could say that President's Sarkozy dashing geopolitical move to the south eventually opened a window of opportunity to move towards the east.

The Swedish–Polish initiative of the Eastern Partnership (EaP) was unveiled in May 2008 by Foreign Ministers Carl Bildt and Radosław Sikorski with the purpose of offering the EU's neighbours in the east something more than just a good-neighbourly relationship. In Sikorski's words,[12] the EaP was about offering the EU's "European Neighbours" a more enhanced menu for choice in the relationship where a membership perspective was not ruled out. In the aftermath of the August 2008 Russia–Georgia war, which shed a stark light on the vulnerabilities of the newly independent post-Soviet states facing an increasingly aggressive former capital, the need for a beefed-up ENP eastern dimension quickly gained ground, culminating in the launch of the first EU Eastern Partnership Summit in Prague in May 2009.[13]

Against the background of these political developments, the ENP toolbox continued to evolve. The Action Plans proved their ineffectiveness as "soft law" political instruments unable to enforce commitments by the partner countries to legislative approximation reforms. As delivery on the promise of a "stake in the EU internal market" depended on hard, verifiable compliance with the relevant EU *acquis*, a different approach was needed, with firm anchors in legally binding commitments.

The vision of a strengthened European Neighbourhood Policy, rolled out by the European Commission in December 2006,[14] was centred on the argument for a new generation of "deep and comprehensive free trade agreements" with the ENP partner countries. These agreements would constitute a significant step forwards from existing Association Agreements between the EU and the south Mediterranean neighbours as well as the PCAs with the neighbours in the east of the continent. The negotiations towards the first "new enhanced agreement" with Ukraine were launched in 2007, and initially focused on chapters for political dialogue and cooperation in foreign policy, security policy, justice and home affairs. After Ukraine's accession to the World Trade Organization (WTO) in 2008, the negotiations were expanded to include provisions on a "deep and comprehensive free trade area" (DCFTA) and a long list of economic and sectoral chapters. At the EU–Ukraine Summit in Paris on 9 September 2008, the EU, under the French presidency, and Ukraine agreed to name the new enhanced agreement the Association Agreement, to craft a careful language about "leaving open the way for further progressive developments in EU–Ukraine relations" and to introduce a core principle of the renewed relationship as "political association and economic integration".[15] Subsequently, the Treaty of Lisbon provided the firm legal basis for this new type of EU agreement, introducing the EU's "special relationship with neighbouring countries, aiming to establish an area of prosperity and good neighbourliness, founded on the values of the Union and characterised by close and peaceful relations based on cooperation".[16]

Following an aborted attempt to sign the Association Agreement at the Eastern Partnership Summit in Vilnius in November 2013, the ensuing Euromaidan revolution in Ukraine and the change of government, followed by the tragedy of Russia's hybrid revenge, the Association Agreement was signed by the parties in two successive stages. Reflecting the hesitancy of some EU member states to conclude the agreement with a country under interim leadership, the parties agreed to sign the political part on 21 March 2014, pending early presidential elections in Ukraine, followed by the signing of the trade and economic part with the newly elected Ukrainian president on 27 June 2014. The Agreement entered into force on 1 September 2017 following ratification by all EU member states, while the DCFTA segment of the Agreement was provisionally applied by the EU from 1 January 2016.[17]

THE FRAMEWORK

The EU–Ukraine Association Agreement is a framework agreement covering almost the entire extent of EU–Ukraine relations. Its 2,140 pages comprise seven titles, include 46 annexes, three protocols and one declaration.[18] The reliance on the Association Agreement option in the EU treaties prior to the Lisbon Treaty allowed the EU to design a remarkable legal framework that transformed the opportunities and attractions of a preferential trade arrangement into a sophisticated foreign policy tool capable of addressing multiple objectives in the EU's relations.

The EU–Ukraine Association Agreement's objectives provide a clear picture of the incentives that justify the obligations of the parties. In the absence of the promise of EU membership, they also accurately reflect the limits, imposed by the EU treaties, of what the EU can offer to a third country. Article 1 of the Agreement envisages "enhanced political dialogue in all areas of mutual interest", cooperation to "promote, preserve and strengthen peace and stability in the regional and international dimensions" in accordance with internationally recognized principles, establishment of conditions for "enhanced economic and trade relations leading towards Ukraine's gradual integration into the EU internal market, including through setting up a [DCFTA]", "to enhance cooperation in the area of justice, freedom and security" and, last but not least, to "establish conditions for increasingly close cooperation in other areas of mutual interest". As we can see, gradual integration into the EU internal market is the most far-reaching offer, derived from the EU's exclusive competence in the area of trade policy, while in other areas cooperation and dialogue are the only available options.

Indeed, the backbone of the EU–Ukraine Association are provisions that establish a DCFTA between the EU and Ukraine. The DCFTA provisions for the liberalization of trade in goods comply with the criteria of GATT Article XXIV for a "preferential trade arrangement", covering immediate or gradual removal of tariffs for "substantially all trade" between the parties in terms of trade liberalization for 97 per cent of tariff lines. The DCFTA allows for relatively limited derogations from the free trade principle, either in the form of asymmetrical mutual opening of the markets favouring Ukrainian exports but with clear phasing-out schedules, or a range of limited tariff rate quotas (TRQs) for 36 product categories of mostly agricultural commodities, and certain semi-processed agricultural and industrial goods. The tariff liberalization under the DCFTA is complemented by reaffirmation of key GATT principles such as the most favoured nation clause, the national treatment, objective and impartial execution of licensing and other administrative regulations of trade, and so on.

However, the design of the Agreement's DCFTA segment goes far beyond the model of classical free trade agreements with their typical focus on goods. For trade in goods it also tackles the problem of non-tariff barriers through harmonization of technical regulations and standards for industrial products, alignment of sanitary and phytosanitary (SPS) measures for foodstuffs, as well as coordination of trade defence instruments. It covers areas hitherto difficult to regulate by means of classical free trade agreements, such as liberalization of trade in services, including right of establishment, cross-border trade in services and e-commerce, access to public procurement and the liberalization of the movement of capital, including freedom of payments. The DCFTA's greatest added value is a clearly defined Ukrainian commitment to approximate its legislation to that of the EU in those economic areas where a level playing field would facilitate mutual market access, delivering de facto integration of Ukraine into specific segments of the EU internal market. The approximation mechanism is organized by means of adding annexes to respective economic and sectoral chapters which spell out the relevant EU *acquis*, the timetables for approximation and the powers of joint association bodies to steer, monitor and adjust the approximation effort in line with the continuous evolution of the EU *acquis*.

BOX 1. TWO EXAMPLES OF HOW THE AGREEMENT WORKS

Example 1: Harmonization of Technical Regulations and Standards

In the area of technical regulations and standards for industrial products, the Association Agreement establishes a comprehensive mechanism for mutual recognition of applicable regulations and standards. It takes a distinct approach compared to the existing bilateral sectoral mutual recognition agreements[19] between the EU and the USA, Canada, Japan, New Zealand and Switzerland, which confer mutual recognition of assessments of conformity of industrial products on the assumption of equivalence of relevant national legislation. The Association Agreement approaches the subject from the premise that recognition of conformity assessment can be possible only on the basis of prior comprehensive approximation by Ukraine of the EU rule book on technical regulations, standardization, conformity assessment procedures, general product safety, marketing of products, product liability, units of measurement and the market surveillance system (horizontal or framework legislation).[20] Ukraine further undertakes to gradually transpose the corpus of the European standards ("EN" – a key component of the European Single Market). Annex III of the Agreement establishes the list of 27 priority sectors or product categories to be the focus of Ukraine's approximation efforts (vertical or product-focused legislation). The completion of the approximation process would be accompanied by the verifiable establishment of institutions and administrative procedures needed to enforce the transposed rule book.

Once the EU verification of a sufficient level of alignment has been achieved, a separate agreement on conformity assessment and acceptance of industrial products (ACAA) will be concluded by the parties as an annex to the Association Agreement.[21] The conclusion of the ACAA would serve as certification that trade between the parties in goods in the sectors under its coverage takes place under the same conditions as those applying to trade in such goods between the member states of the European Union.

Example 2: Liberalization of Trade in Services, with Focus on Banking and Finance

Liberalization of the trade in services under the Agreement, particularly for the banking and financial sector, rests on three pillars.

First, Chapter 6 of the Agreement introduces principles of non-discrimination in market access and national treatment for company establishment[22] and the cross-border supply of services.[23] The Agreement also spells out the objectives of cooperation in the financial sector, such as the need to reinforce the functioning open market economy, protection of investors and other consumers of financial services, the stability and integrity of the financial system and ensuring independent and effective supervision.[24]

Second, the parties circumscribe the extent of their mutual concessions on delivery of cross-border financial services as per the type of service. Annex XVI-B, Part 7 spells out the exceptions and reservations of individual member states with regard to liberalization of cross-border financial services, while Annex XVI-E, Part 7 spells out those of Ukraine.

Third, Annex XVII of the Agreement introduces the mechanism of comprehensive legislative approximation by Ukraine of the EU *acquis* relevant to, *inter alia*, financial services, which, when completed by Ukraine, would lead to the ultimate prize: granting Ukraine the "full internal market treatment" for the sector in question.[25] The mechanism includes (1) general principles and obligations applicable to Ukraine in the approximation process, including the procedure of transposing the EU rules depending on the type of EU legislative act; (2) commitment to regular consultations and assistance to ensure smooth and effective legislative approximation; (3) a procedure leading towards full internal market treatment, which includes the EU comprehensive assessment of the state of approximation[26] guided by specially defined assessment principles,[27] and approval of the assessment by a joint association body giving the green light for the granting of full internal market treatment;[28] (4) a procedure for Ukraine to keep up with the evolution of the relevant EU *acquis* after receiving full internal market treatment;[29] (5) provisions for resolution of disputes related to interpretation and implementation of the Annex, including the use of the dispute settlement mechanism (DSM); (6) recognition of the right by the parties to apply prudential oversight measures with regard to financial services in line with principles of the WTO General Agreement on Trade in Services Annex on financial services ("prudential carve-out").

Appendix XVII-2 to Annex XVII outlines the select list of the EU horizontal legislation regulating the financial sector to be transposed by Ukraine, including banking, insurance, securities trading, financial markets infrastructure, free movement of capital and payments (implementation of relevant articles of the EU treaties) and investment funds management.

An important part of the DCFTA segment of the Agreement is a Dispute Settlement Mechanism (DSM). The Association Agreement DSM focuses on disputes related to the interpretation and implementation of the Agreement, with a special focus on trade matters, with exclusion of measures like trade remedies, anti-trust and mergers, and measures in the area of trade and sustainable development.[30] In the area of approximation and implementation of EU legislation in the Ukrainian body of law, the DSM envisages a clearly defined scope for the jurisdiction of the European Court of Justice (ECJ). Where a dispute concerns the interpretation and application of the Agreement's provisions covering regulatory approximation, the DSM panel of arbitrators does not issue a ruling but requests the ECJ to give a ruling on the matter. The ECJ ruling becomes binding on the arbitration panel. In this way, the limited jurisdiction of the ECJ over the EU–Ukraine relationship of association ensures a uniform application of the EU rules, thus reinforcing Ukraine's integration into the EU Single Market.

IMPLEMENTATION AND MONITORING

Provisions of the Association Agreement do not have a direct effect in the Ukrainian legal system and are not directly enforceable in the domestic courts. Therefore, realization of the eventual rights and obligations that may arise out of the Association's provisions will depend upon the effective process and the toolbox of transposition of the Agreement's provisions within the Ukrainian constitutional order.[31]

In this context, one should consider that the quality of the implementation of the Agreement by the Ukrainian side, in particular its trade and economic segments, depends on the effective legislative toolbox, as well as the correct application of the implemented rules by the national courts. It is argued that one of the challenges is the lack of a single, special, implementing legislative act which would clarify existing, and prevent future, conflicts of the Agreement's provisions with Ukrainian legislation.[32] With the lack thereof, a single toolbox for legislative approximation is provided at the level of the secondary legislation at the level of the Cabinet of Ministers of Ukraine.[33] However, the function of the act is only to introduce the scope and timetable of transposition of the EU legislation listed in the annexes to the Agreement which accompany provisions on trade, economic and sectoral cooperation.[34] The main disadvantage of this approach is that no integrated legal and procedural framework is established to offer minimal guarantees of compliance with the Agreement's obligations during the parliamentary approval stage of the process.

Another serious challenge arising in the process of approximation is reluctance and a low level of effectiveness within the judiciary branch to apply and effectively implement international law sources in their own judgments. Specifically, it is pointed out that the correct application of international agreements is not guaranteed owing to an as yet insufficient level of understanding of international law sources as well as applicable foreign court judgments by national judges.[35]

An implementation compliance mechanism is embedded in the concept of conditionality that cuts across the Agreement. In accordance with the Agreement's objectives, Ukraine's gradual integration into the EU internal market by means of setting up the DCFTA is to be achieved through the progressive approximation of Ukrainian legislation to that of the EU.[36] The Agreement further establishes a general obligation of Ukraine, in line with the Agreement's objectives, to carry out gradual approximation of its legislation to EU law as referred to in the respective annexes, without prejudice to any specific principles and obligations on regulatory approximation for the Agreement's trade segment.[37] The process of verification of the approximation effort is best exemplified in the Agreement's provisions related to non-tariff trade measures (technical regulations and standards, SPS measures) or liberalization of trade in services, as described above.

Furthermore, important implementation verification functions are entrusted to the joint bodies of the Association.[38] Specifically, policy dialogue, supervision and monitoring of the application and implementation of the Agreement,[39] as well as a function of a forum for the exchange of information on the EU and Ukrainian legislative acts, are entrusted to the Association Council, which is convened on a periodical basis at the ministerial level. Importantly, in the case of disputes between the parties as regards interpretation, application and implementation of the Agreement with the exception of its trade-related segment (competence of a separate DSM), the Association Council has the power to resolve the dispute by means of negotiations and a subsequent decision. The Association Council is also empowered to update the annexes with the EU *acquis* in order to keep pace with the evolution of EU law. The decisions of the Association Council have binding force where explicitly established by the Agreement, in particular as regards the update of the legislative approximation annexes.[40]

The 2019 Association Implementation Report on Ukraine by the European Commission noted progress in attaining some key legislative approximation targets, such as horizontal legislation for technical regulations and market surveillance, the system of SPS oversight, reform of the public procurement system, and the energy sector.[41] Lack of progress has been found in areas like trade in postal services and electronic communications, transport services and infrastructure, financial services and the protection of intellectual property rights.

The 2019 Association Agreement Implementation Report[42] published by the Ukrainian government provides a more detailed picture, assessing overall progress with attainment of the Agreement's overall legislative approximation targets at 43 per cent. This aggregate figure hides uneven progress in reaching approximation targets across segments of the Agreement as well as in the competence of the legislating authority. While significant progress has been achieved in areas such as justice, freedom, security and human rights (82 per cent), public procurement (79 per cent) and technical barriers to trade (76 per cent), other areas such as transport, transport infrastructure, postal and courier services (22 per cent) and the financial sector (29 per cent) have been lagging behind. The report also acknowledged particularly low progress in implementing primary legislative acts at the Parliament level (34 per cent of approximation targets) as compared with the secondary legislation at the Cabinet of Ministers level (46 per cent).

WHAT IS NEXT?

The EU–Ukraine relationship underwent profound changes in the course of the five years that followed the signing of the Association Agreement in 2014. In the wake of the Russian aggression in 2014, Ukrainian producers were desperate to diversify from the suddenly unavailable Russian market. The EU market with its logistical proximity, enormous size, transparency and the rule of law provided an alternative that served as a lifeline to the Ukrainian economy. To a considerable extent, the DCFTA preferential tariff regime for trade in goods was an encouraging factor in the diversification effort. However, the full potential of liberalization of trade in goods is hampered by limited TRQs for a range of Ukrainian products which are deemed sensitive for the EU agricultural sector. In addition, lack of progress with approximation of technical regulations and standards for industrial goods, and SPS requirements for several other categories of foodstuffs, denies access to those low-hanging fruits of opportunities that can be available to exporters in the short to medium term.

Most importantly there has not yet been a single positive precedent of a successful and verifiable completion of the approximation process within a particular sector of the Agreement, that is, on non-tariff barriers to trade in goods or on trade in services, which would have culminated in an EU decision to expand access to the EU internal market for goods or "to grant full internal market treatment" for services. As a result, in overall terms implementation of the Association Agreement remains very much a work in progress, with the key objectives of the Association and the tools for attaining them retaining their relevance and appeal to the Ukrainian government and society at large to continue needed reforms.

For the EU, the Association Agreement with Ukraine remains a valuable first case of the practical embodiment of the policy of the special relationship with its neighbours as mandated by TEU Article 8. The Agreement also continues to function as the most effective tool available to realize the objective of this policy vis-à-vis Ukraine, that is, to advance the area of prosperity and good neighbourliness with the country, founded on the EU's values and characterized by close and peaceful cooperative relations.

For the UK, the lessons are mixed. Ukraine's preferred direction of travel towards the EU is the opposite of the UK's declared preference since 2016. Where Ukraine seeks more convergence as a means to access, the newly free-trading UK seeks acknowledgement of the possibility of divergence. Yet, in the detailed mechanics of the Association Agreement there may be much to inspire the negotiators on both sides.

Notes for Chapter 6

1. See https://ec.europa.eu/commission/sites/beta-political/files/slide_presented_by_barnier_at_euco_15-12-2017.pdf.

2. Remarks by Herman van Rompuy at the EU-Ukraine Summit, 25 February 2013, https://ec.europa.eu/commission/presscorner/detail/en/PRES_13_74.

3. Georgia, Moldova, Ukraine and Armenia until 2013.

4. K. Yelisieiev, foreword in P. van Elsuwege & R. Petrov (eds), *Legislative Approximation and Application of EU Law in the Eastern Neighbourhood of the European Union: Toward a Common Regulatory Space?* (Abingdon: Routledge, 2013).

5. A. Łazowski, "Enhanced multilateralism and enhanced bilateralism: integration without membership in the European Union", *Common Market Law Review* 45:5 (2008).

6. R. Petrov, G. van der Loo & P. van Elsuwege, "The EU-Ukraine Association Agreement: a new legal instrument of integration without membership?", *Kyiv-Mohyla Law and Politics Journal* 1 (2015).

7. Speech by the Commission President Romano Prodi "Wider Europe – a Proximity Policy as the key to stability", 5–6 December 2002; https://ec.europa.eu/commission/presscorner/detail/en/SPEECH_02_619.

8. Commission Communication "Wider Europe – Neighbourhood: a new framework for relations with our Southern and Eastern Neighbours", COM 2003.104.22.03.2003.

9. Commission Communication, "European Neighbourhood Policy: Strategy Paper", COM (2004)373.12.05.2004.

10. European Neighbourhood Policy, Strategy Paper, COM (2004), 373 final, 3.

11. See https://ec.europa.eu/commission/presscorner/detail/en/SPEECH_04_463.

12. See https://www.politico.eu/article/plans-for-eastern-partnership-unveiled/.

13. "EU pact challenges Russian influence in the east", *The Guardian*, 7 May 2009, https://www.theguardian.com/world/2009/may/07/russia-eu-europe-partnership-deal.

14. See https://eur-lex.europa.eu/legal-content/EN/TXT/PDF/?uri=CELEX:52006DC0726&from=en.

15. Joint Statement, the EU-Ukraine Summit, https://library.euneighbours.eu/content/joint-statement-eu-ukraine-summit-2008.

16. Article 8 of the Treaty of the European Union, as amended by the Treaty of Lisbon.

17. The long and convoluted path toward the Agreement's entry into force was in no small way attributed to the active political and military pressure put on Ukraine by Russia. In particular, in the framework of the first Minsk accords in September 2014, Moscow managed to secure a delay in the start of provisional application of the DCFTA segment of the Agreement until 1 January 2016, pending trilateral EU–Ukraine–Russia consultations on perceived DCFTA risks to the Russian economy that were completed without a result by the end of 2015.

18. Petrov, van der Loo & van Elsuwege, "The EU-Ukraine Association Agreement".

19. See https://ec.europa.eu/growth/single-market/goods/international-aspects/mutual-recognition-agreements_en.

20. Article 56 of the Association Agreement.

21. Article 57 of the Association Agreement.

22. Article 88 of the Association Agreement.

23. *Ibid.*, Articles 93–4.

24. *Ibid.*, Article 383.

25. Article 3, Annex XVII.

26. *Ibid.*, Article 4.

27. *Ibid.*, Appendix XVII-6 to Annex XVII.

28. Association Committee in Trade Configuration, Article 465, Article 4, Annex XVII of the Association Agreement.

29. Article 5, Annex XVII.

30. Y. Rudyuk, "How the trade disputes between the EU and Ukraine will be settled under the EU-Ukraine Association Agreement", *Lex Portus* 2 (2017), https://lexportus.net.ua/zhurnal-4/159-rudyuk-yu-how-the-trade-disputes-between-eu-and-ukraine-will-be-settled-under-the-eu-ukraine-association-agreement.

31. A footnote to Chapter 14 of the Association Agreement, which is concerned with DCFTA dispute settlement procedure, explicitly states that the DCFTA segment of the Agreement cannot be construed as conferring rights and obligations to be directly invoked before the domestic courts of the parties.

32. R. Petrov & P. van Elsuwege, "What does the Association Agreement mean for Ukraine, the EU and its member states?" in A. Heringa (ed.) *Het eerste raadgevend referendum: Het EU-Oekraine Associatieakkoord* (Den Haag: Montesquieu Institute, 2016). For more on judicial activism and voluntary application of the EU *acquis* in the eastern neighbouring countries, see Van Elsuwege & Petrov, *Legal Approximation of EU Law in the Eastern Neighbourhood of the EU*.

33. Resolution of the Cabinet of Ministers of Ukraine Nr. 1106 from 25.10.2017.

34. Titles IV, V, VI of the Association Agreement.

35. Petrov & van Elsuwege, "What does the Association Agreement mean for Ukraine, the EU and its member states?"

36. Article 1 (2b) of the Association Agreement.

37. Article 474 of the Association Agreement.

38. Title VII, Chapter 1, Institutional Framework of the Association Agreement.

39. Article 461 of the Agreement.

40. Article 463 of the Agreement.

41. See https://eeas.europa.eu/headquarters/headquarters-homepage/72011/association-implementation-report-ukraine-2019_en.

42. See http://eu-ua.org/sites/default/files/inline/files/ar_aa_implementation-2019-4_eng_0.pdf.

7

CANADA AND THE COMPREHENSIVE AND ECONOMIC TRADE AGREEMENT

Kurt Hübner

For a while, the Comprehensive and Economic Trade Agreement (CETA) between Canada and the European Union, which provisionally entered into force on 21 September 2017, seemed to be the preferred post-Brexit default option for the United Kingdom, at least in the eyes of the prime minister, Boris Johnson, who on 3 February 2020 declared, "We want a comprehensive free trade agreement, similar to Canada's."[1] But the initial suggestion of aiming for an ambitious "CETA+" soon lost steam and the Conservative government started instead to talk about a more basic CETA-like agreement that would allow the UK to escape key EU regulations and to align with the EU's regulatory regime at the lowest level possible. And then, when negotiations between the EU and the UK officially started, the UK turned even further away from the CETA template by stressing the goal of regulatory independence.

From an analytical perspective, the idea that the CETA could be a model for the UK seemed a little far-fetched from the outset, for three reasons. First, the UK's economy (2019 gross domestic product (GDP) = $2,910 billion), is much larger than Canada's economy (2019 GDP = $1,730 billion)[2] and, usually, size counts when it comes to the scope of trade agreements. Second, the UK is much more relevant, in terms of exports and imports, to EU economies than it is to Canada. This observation holds particularly for financial services, where, as will be seen below, the CETA does not even go beyond existing World Trade Organization (WTO) practices. Third, the gravity model shows that distance is critical in regard to trade volumes.[3] The CETA is an agreement between faraway entities and can't be easily used as a model for neighbouring economies.

However, analytical considerations often do not square with political considerations, and so CETA might yet become an option for the UK–EU negotiators if the Johnson government's "hard Brexit" option does not materialize. But given that, as matters currently stand, the transition period ends on 31 December

2020, it would be an illusion to expect that a CETA-style agreement could be negotiated in the few months left before then, especially given that the Covid-19 pandemic has interrupted and badly delayed talks between the parties. Whether or not a CETA path materializes will depend not least on the willingness to compromise on the side of the UK and of the EU, as well as – probably equally critically – on domestic economic policy decisions about the UK's future economic model. The more the post-Brexit model diverges from the status quo, the less the chances that the CETA will be replicated for EU–UK relations, and vice versa.

WHAT IS CETA ALL ABOUT, AND WHAT IS IT NOT ABOUT?

The CETA is a trade agreement which delivers what its title suggests. In the seven years after ratification, common tariff lines for 99 per cent of goods will be eliminated. This duty-free access will not amount to "free trade" as restrictions and quotas will still be in place. For the automotive industry, for example, CETA foresees duty-free exports of Canadian cars, defined as cars with a minimum of 30 per cent value-added in Canada, of 100,000 units per year. One can argue that the elimination of tariff lines is a big step, and indeed that is the case. But then it should also be noted that the removal of tariffs is a low-hanging fruit in trade negotiations, as the average tariff before the CETA was negotiated was already rather small. There are exemptions. And a reduction, or even elimination, of tariffs will be particularly beneficial for sectors where above-average tariffs were in place before the CETA.

The CETA is no template for "free trade", if the latter stands for unrestricted trade. When it comes to agriculture, for example, quotas and rules of origin for products such as beef, pork, sweetcorn and bison are an integral and essential part of the CETA. Products that contain genetically modified elements need to be labelled accordingly and will need to pass EU regulations. Some agricultural products will benefit from the agreement, mostly within clearly defined quotas, but the CETA does not at all offer unrestricted trade on agricultural goods. A whole chapter in the CETA (Chapter 15) is devoted to financial services, but this sector will nevertheless not receive the same preferential treatment as industry and agriculture. Instead, the terms of business are equivalent to the WTO terms for services.[4] Canadian financial institutions do not enjoy automatic free "passporting", and thus can only be relevant financial institutions if they locate inside the EU.

Regarding technical and sanitary regulations, the CETA comes with a mutual recognition mechanism but still also entails a forum of regulatory cooperation where both sides are to work out how to reconcile potential differences. The idea is to minimize costs related to regulatory differences. When it comes to foreign direct investment, the CETA – after quite a struggle – includes a new dispute mechanism that installs a revamped court system. Even if this chapter of the CETA may never be ratified in its existing form, as some European countries' governments have run into insurmountable domestic resistance, it indicates how difficult it has become to establish a proper procedure for dealing with conflicting issues. To develop mechanisms and methods of dispute settlement will become more relevant if the EU eventually moves its ambitious climate policy project forwards. In that case, one can expect that some companies may try hard to escape stricter regulations and to use any transnational status to avoid EU rules and regulations. (In the agreement, the EU established as a clear principle that the European Court of Justice has the last say when it comes to the interpretation of EU laws and regulations.)

The CETA is also the EU's first agreement with an Organisation for Economic Co-operation and Development economy where the opening of public procurement became an essential consideration in the negotiations. Given the enormous size of public procurement markets in both entities, this liberalization gives mutual market access to so far untapped opportunities. For EU–UK relations, a CETA template would have to include provision for public procurement markets to be kept open after 1 January 2021.

It goes without saying that the CETA is an ambitious agreement, due also to its dynamic character. Both sides established a mechanism of committees and meetings at various levels to deal with the ongoing business of different chapters of the CETA. However, despite all the ambitions it should be stressed that the CETA does not create a customs union but, rather, a preferential trade agreement, although one comprehensive in its scope. The agreement reflects the fact that mutual trade between both entities is not as strong as could be expected. Overcoming this "undertrading" was a driving force for the CETA from the very start. However, when it comes to an EU–UK agreement, the driving force is not to overcome "undertrading". Rather, such an agreement will have to find a mechanism to minimize the unavoidable reduction in economic exchanges between both entities.

SOVEREIGNTY AND TAKING BACK CONTROL

The Boris Johnson administration is a very different beast from the preceding government of Theresa May. The latter's basic vision was to leave the European Union while simultaneously keeping the UK as close as possible to it. Under the Johnson government, the UK has left the EU and it now wants to maximize its policy-making sovereignty. Rather than seeking a close alignment with EU regulations and laws, the UK wants to set its own rules and regulations. In many ways, this is a logical policy conclusion of the initial Brexit decision. From an EU perspective, this might be seen as unfortunate but also as a legitimate policy decision. If this assessment is correct, then the CETA is an agreement that is closer to Theresa May's intentions then to the ambitions of the current Johnson government.

The latter strategy implies trading and access costs, as the European Union needs to make sure that EU membership comes with a robust positive premium: only members who follow the obligations of the common market and, for that purpose, also the Customs Union, may share the benefits of integrated markets. Defending the integrity of the Single Market became the core principle for all Brexit-related negotiations with the UK. To some degree this reflected a weakness on the EU's side. The Union is potentially vulnerable, and any sign that a country can leave and continue enjoying the benefits might encourage others to follow the UK's example. At the same time, defending the core of the Single Market is critical to maximizing the benefits of its members.

Using the CETA as a template could still make sense when it comes to securing sovereignty and to taking back – partial – control of borders. Both are the foremost political goals that stress the centrality of the nation state for identity and coherence, even under conditions of "free" trade. As is well known, the political aim of safeguarding sovereignty is not fully compatible with an open economy, as the latter necessarily implies influence from the "outside". What is gained in political terms does not automatically translate into economic benefits (if at all), nor does the sovereign control of borders allow for full engagement with a common market organization such as the EU, since the latter implies a partial transfer of national sovereignty to a supranational entity.

Like any free trade agreement, the CETA does not require any transfer of sovereignty to a supranational body, as membership of the European Union does, and nor does it open up borders in an uncontrolled way. Canada continues to be a sovereign nation state, and yet the CETA requires both sides of the agreement to accept mutually agreed principles, norms and regulations. Liberalization is mainly restricted to the flow of goods, which can cross borders without any additional duty costs. There may still be quantitative restrictions in the form of quotas but, as a general rule, such an agreement does not generate prohibitive additional trade costs. When it comes to the regulatory aspect of cross-border trade, the picture is more complicated.

As seen above, in the case of EU–UK exports the "undertrading" argument does not hold. Trade between both entities follows very much what should be expected of geographically close neighbours, as suggested by gravity model predictions. In particular, until now trade volume and trade pattern have been driven by an integrated market which facilitates and encourages strong intra-community trade. A recent modelling exercise estimated the net benefits of EU membership for the UK to be 8.6 per cent of GDP over ten years:[5] if the UK had not joined the (then) European Economic Community in 1973 its economy would have stayed on a significantly lower growth trajectory. Another study found that, "the increase in domestic value-added in gross exports from the UK is driven by stronger global value chain links: the UK's 'forward linkages' increased by about 30% due to deepening integration, while its 'backward linkages' increased by almost 40% thanks to EU membership".[6] The study furthermore found that the UK benefitted disproportionately from EU membership in terms of services exports to new EU member states.

Brexit, as it has now evolved, means that the UK will be leaving this integrated market, resulting in a lower volume of trade and higher trade costs for both sides. (Almost) all econometric Brexit modelling exercises conclude that exiting the EU will lead to negative GDP effects.[7] The goal of taking back sovereignty and control of national borders conflicts with the goal of maximizing economic growth under conditions of openness. Brexit is a decision to maintain or return national sovereignty and to give up unlimited access to the UK's primary export market, and this decision will almost certainly come with adverse growth effects. The question is how to mitigate those negative effects. In particular, could some variant of a CETA help mitigate those effects?

POTENTIAL OPPORTUNITIES AND CHALLENGES
OF A CETA-LIKE AGREEMENT

Were the UK and the EU to wish to avoid a WTO rules scenario (see Chapter 8), a common landing zone would have to be identified. The CETA could be a model for such a landing zone. What the CETA delivers is a quasi-tariff-free flow of goods within quota restrictions for some items.

The EU is the UK's largest trading partner, even though the EU share in British exports of goods services decreased from 55 per cent in 2006 to 45 per cent in 2018. The share of imports from the EU also decreased, from 58 per cent in 2001 to 53 per cent in 2018. The trade balance for the UK with the EU is negative, with a deficit of £66 billion in 2018. This deficit reflects the deficit in the trade in goods which amounted to £94 billion in 2018. When it comes to services, the UK had a surplus of £28 billion in the same year. As a matter of fact, the UK had an overall trade balance deficit with the EU in every year between 1999 and 2018, always with the split of a surplus for services and a deficit for goods.

There is no reason to suppose this structural relationship would change in the case of a CETA-like agreement. Then, as now, goods would flow without customs duties and thus without any additional trade costs. This would not be the case for services though. Given that the bulk of the service surplus stems from financial services, any agreement between the EU and UK would need to include a financial service chapter that mimicked the current situation. In that case the CETA alone could not be a model for such a section since, as was seen above, it offers only WTO access rules and no preferential treatment at all. The UK would ideally need a passporting clause that would give certainty to its financial industry as it sought to continue to do business within the EU. Neither a "hard" Brexit (obviously), nor also the basic CETA model could provide British financial institutions with the "passport" they would need to conduct business across the EU-27. A UK–EU agreement that accommodated the interests of the British financial industry would need to go beyond the CETA rules. Alternatively, British financial institutions could circumvent any stalemate by opening subsidiaries within the EU-27 through which they could operate their business. Or the UK could, in parallel, negotiate equivalence rights with the EU: the EU would recognize British rules of financial markets as equivalent to EU rules. Precisely this principle guided for some time relations between the EU and Switzerland regarding financial services. But, as Chapter 4 relates, the Switzerland example shows the downside of such a practice: when Switzerland violated agreements with the EU, the European Commission decided to use the equivalence practice as a political lever by threatening to allow the equivalence practice to lapse, as indeed it did after 30 June 2019.

Similarly, the CETA chapter on agriculture does not offer a good model for the UK. The CETA provides Canadian agricultural and fishery products much-improved access to the EU's markets. Nevertheless, quotas stay in place and so do trade distortions created by the differing agricultural policy practices in the two entities. The CETA removed tariffs on 91 per cent of agricultural and food products, but imports of beef and pork from Canada and EU exports of dairy products are subject to quotas, while poultry and eggs are not included in the agreement. Furthermore, all imports from Canada must meet EU rules and regulations relating to production standards, food safety, animal or plant health and environmental protection. As seen above, a UK–EU agreement would be not so much about increasing mutual trade in agricultural products as about limiting the negative effects of Brexit. Currently, agricultural products make up 11 per cent of the bilateral trade flows between the UK and the EU-27. In 2018, the EU-27 had a positive trade balance with the UK: US$47 billion worth of agricultural goods were exported to the UK, compared to US$18 billion worth of agricultural imports. Clearly, a reduction in the trade volume would hurt both the EU and the UK.

The CETA template would not be very useful as a way of enhancing trade in this sector post-Brexit. Due to the UK's longstanding participation in the EU's agricultural regime, many preconditions for entering the European markets have been fulfilled, but the UK is now about to move to third-country status, for which particular access quotas would need to be negotiated. Given the size of export and import relations between both entities, quotas for agricultural products would have to be higher than in the CETA case. At the same time, the EU would surely insist that its regulations be recognized, particularly relating to food safety. This could well put downward pressure on actual UK exports, were the Johnson government to violate those benchmarks by negotiating trade agreements with other countries. Current discussions between Canada and the EU about the allocation of import licences for Canadian producers suggest that the devil is in the detail, and that there is considerable room for non-tariff trade barriers.[8] Recent UNCTAD (United Nations Conference on Trade and Development) research confirms that there is not only a substantial economic membership effect resulting in strong bilateral trade, but also that non-tariff barriers (NTBs) are significant, even in the presence of trade agreements.[9] The CETA offers institutional mechanisms to deal with the complaints of both parties. Any CETA-like agreement between the UK and the EU would need to have firm mechanisms in place, as NTBs would potentially be high. The governance structure of the CETA is not very complex, but it is definitely rather cumbersome due to the many committees involved.[10]

Not all regulations included in the CETA are NTBs. When it comes to fish, for example, the CETA will bring existing tariffs down to close to zero over a period of eight years, as long as fish are caught by Canadians fishing in Canadian waters, or caught in the Canadian/European Exclusive Economic Zones (EEZs), in the high seas or in the EEZs of other countries by licensed Canadians using registered vessels that are entitled to fly the Canadian flag. The fisheries agreement in the CETA, however, may also not be the best template for an EU–UK agreement since, rather than seeking to open up markets, as in the CETA, the UK's position is all about reducing access, in this case for EU fisheries, as it asserts full sovereignty of its waters after Brexit.

The possibility of using the CETA as a template for a future EU–UK agreement would in any case conflict with the current legally given time envelope for such negotiations. Rather than making use of the expansion clause in the Withdrawal Agreement, the Johnson government insisted on enshrining in law the fact that the UK will leave the EU at midnight on 31 December 2020. Put another way, the British government does not currently envisage extending the transitional period to allow additional time for negotiation. But a CETA-like agreement, let alone a CETA+ agreement, could not possibly be negotiated in such a short time. Whether the CETA could be used as a template for a further round of negotiations after a hard Brexit would depend on several factors. First and foremost, the negotiation of a CETA-like agreement would require mutual trust and a strong desire to optimize potential mutual benefits. Second, such an agreement would need both sides to recognize that even the best possible version would still be second best compared to the status quo ante. Both sides would have to compromise on that basis if an agreement were to be achieved and implemented. Third, the landing zone and thus the zone of compromise would depend very much on the future path of the UK economy. In particular, the more the Johnson government moves towards an interventionist industrial policy, the less the chances will be that the EU will grant market access without alignment guarantees.

KEEPING RELATIONS CLOSE?

Modelling exercises of various Brexit scenarios all conclude that a "WTO rules" scenario would cause severe economic costs for both sides, although more so for the UK. A simulation of various scenarios by Rand,[11] for example, shows that leaving the EU with no deal and simply applying WTO tariffs would reduce future GDP by around 5 per cent over a period of ten years, or $140 billion, compared with a growth path as a member of the EU. Other studies arrive at similar results.[12] As the contributions to this book explore, Brexit poses the question as to whether and how trade costs might be minimized by either trade diversion towards other regions of the global economy and/or by designing trade agreements that at least partially compensate the losses incurred by leaving the European Union's Single Market.

The concept of comparative advantage is one of the few economic principles that is almost universally recognized as meaningful and also as a valid general guide for political decisions: trading across national borders generates macroeconomic welfare benefits (although the internal redistribution of those benefits is another matter). In the real world, trade agreements are the political tools used to translate this insight into meaningful rules and norms. Today, trade negotiations are no longer predominantly about tariffs, but increasingly about NTBs, regulatory practices and standards, environmental and labour laws, service sector issues and foreign direct investment procedures. What used to be relatively straightforward agreements, during the early trade negotiation rounds within the General Agreement on Tariffs and Trade/WTO, have today become comprehensive negotiations that result in voluminous tombs of legalese that eventually frame economic exchanges. This also holds for the CETA. Getting rid of tariffs is a helpful way to advertise the agreement; but direct trade effects because of the abolishment of tariffs are actually rather small. What the CETA potentially accomplishes is to provide a more level playing field that can lead to deepening and widening market access. This will be achieved by implementing the text of the agreement and, even more critically, by continuing cooperation to optimize the effects of the agreement. The CETA comes with the launch of a "CETA Joint Committee" and no less than 13 specialized committees together with six bilateral dialogues. All those groups have regular meetings to discuss upcoming issues and to develop concrete accommodations and interpretations of the agreement. Obviously, these meetings are not about tariffs but about all kind of regulatory issues that emerge in "real life".

Experience with the CETA to date shows that – at least in its first phase – the party with a history of a surplus tends initially to benefit most from the new agreement. Even though Canada saw a slight increase in its exports to the EU, its imports grew much stronger, resulting in an increasing surplus with the new EU in trade in goods.[13] Whether this outcome only stresses a longer trend or indicates that European exporters are better equipped to conquer the markets than their Canadian counterparts is difficult to assess. The UK is currently running a structural deficit with the EU's economies in terms of trade in goods. As seen above, the UK has had a trade deficit with the EU every year since 1999 which has never been balanced by its surplus in trade in services.[14] Brexit may change the UK's import and export relations in quantitative terms, but it should not come as a surprise if, even under WTO rules, the UK's trade deficit continues.

The CETA could only ever be a template for future EU–UK relations if both sides were to have the political appetite to bring both economies and regulatory regimes closer. As the CETA shows, that does not mean that one party has to abandon national sovereignty. What is required, though, is an agreement on common norms and practices for cross-border economic transactions. As matters stand, the EU is a more powerful regulatory actor than a stand-alone economy such as the UK. Realistically, this requires relatively more compromise on the UK side. The brief period since the launch of the CETA indicates that compromises can be managed within the political structures of the agreement, where regular meetings of numerous subcommittees are held to work out solutions for practical problems. But this sort of consensual accommodation seems a far cry from the political declarations of the Johnson government.

Matters are even more complicated when it comes to the UK's key services industry, where the EU and the UK would have to go far beyond the CETA chapter to provide security and certainty for the UK's financial services. Keeping the UK close to the EU would come with a price which simply may be too high in political terms. How high such a price will be depends on the trade policy approach of the EU. If – and this is a big if in times of a global pandemic – the EU moves in strict ways towards its proposed "European Green Deal", then the maintenance of a level playing field will become more pre-eminent. The proposed carbon border adjustment tax, for example, is only one indication of such a trade policy reinforcement. Trade partners who do not keep up with EU regulations and thus get a price competitiveness advantage may not get unrestricted tariff- and quota-free access. The CETA is an example of partial alignment with the regulatory system of the EU. The political question is whether the UK is willing to pay such a price for accessing EU markets.

Notes for Chapter 7

1. See "Johnson says UK doesn't need EU rules for a post-Brexit trade deal", Reuters, 3 February 2020, https://www.reuters.com/article/britain-eu-johnson/highlights-johnson-says-uk-doesnt-need-eu-rules-for-a-post-brexit-trade-deal-idUSL8N2A3374.

2. International Monetary Fund figures.

3. See, for example, C. Carrère, M. Mrázová & J. Neary, "Gravity without apology: the science of elasticities, distance, and trade", *Economic Journal*, ueaa034, 2 April 2020, https://doi.org/10.1093/ej/ueaa034.

4. P. Leblond, "CETA and financial services: what to expect?", CIGI PAPERS 91 (2016).

5. N. Campos, F. Coricelli & L. Moretti, "Institutional Integration and Economic Growth in Europe," *Journal of Monetary Economics* (2019), https://doi.org/10.1016/j.jmoneco.2018.08.001.

6. A. Mulabdic, A. Osnago & M. Ruta, "Deep integration and UK–EU trade relations", World Bank Policy Research Working Paper 7947 (2017).

7. See, "Examining economic outcomes: after Brexit", Rand Europe, https://www.rand.org/randeurope/research/projects/brexit-economic-implications.html; C. Mathieu, "Brexit: what economic impacts does the literature anticipate?", *Revue de l'OFCE*, 167 (2020/3).

8. See https://eur-lex.europa.eu/legal-content/EN/TXT/PDF/?uri=CELEX:02006R1301-20130701&qid=1505124447177&from=FR.

9. UNCTAD, "Brexit beyond tariffs: the role of non-tariff measures and the impact on developing countries", UNCTAD Research Paper No. 42, (February 2020), https://unctad.org/en/PublicationsLibrary/ser-rp-2020d1_en.pdf.

10. See https://www.international.gc.ca/trade-commerce/trade-agreements-accords-commerciaux/agr-acc/ceta-aecg/committees-comites.aspx?lang=eng.

11. See, "Examining economic outcomes: after Brexit", Rand Europe.

12. Mathieu, "Brexit: what economic impacts does the literature anticipate?"

13. See https://ec.europa.eu/eurostat/statistics-explained/index.php/Canada-EU_-_international_trade_in_goods_statistics.

14. M. Ward, "Statistics on UK–EU trade", House of Commons Library, Briefing Paper No. 7851 (2019).

8

THE WORLD TRADE ORGANIZATION MODEL

L. Alan Winters

For over 7.5 billion people in the world, "the World Trade Organization (WTO) model", if it means anything at all, signifies the set of rules overseen by the WTO that have largely governed world trade since the Second World War.[1] To 60 million people in the United Kingdom, on the other hand, it means what happens if their government fails to reach a trade agreement with the European Union by the end of the transitional period foreseen in the Withdrawal Agreement, and their mutual trade is governed by WTO rules alone. Such an outcome is also often known as "no deal" and this chapter is mostly about the implications and consequences of that outcome. I start, however, by outlining what WTO rules in general mean.

THE WTO

The WTO came into operation on 1 January 1995, following the conclusion of the 1986–94 Uruguay Round of trade talks held under the auspices of the the General Agreement on Tariffs and Trade (GATT). It is an international organization with 164 members and codifies the rules for international trade in goods (the GATT), services (the General Agreement on Trade in Services, GATS) and intellectual property (Agreement on Trade-Related Aspects of Intellectual Property Rights, TRIPS), and supports a dispute settlement procedure and a monitoring function. In addition, it has a number of side agreements such as the Trade Facilitation Agreement and the Government Procurement Agreement.

The GATT, the WTO's intellectual and operational forerunner, arose in 1947 as a means to achieve trade liberalization following the Second World War. Recognizing that the protectionism and competitive devaluations of the 1920s and 1930s had exacerbated the slump and that trade tensions had contributed to the war itself, the USA led 21 other countries to a more liberal but rules-based system than had pertained previously. There had initially been hopes for an

International Trade Organization (ITO) which would have had extensive and far-reaching powers to manage world commerce, but the Americans eventually felt this a bridge too far and let plans for the ITO fail. The GATT was a temporary agreement (a treaty, not an international organization, as were the International Monetary Fund and the World Bank) designed just to let desired levels of trade liberalization proceed with sufficient international oversight to make them credible.

The basic structure and philosophy of the GATT 1947 continued into the (revised) GATT 1994 and the GATS. Its fundamental principle is non-discrimination: treating all suppliers of imports equally and, once they have paid any import duties, treating imports and domestic supplies equally. The former is known as the "most favoured nation" (MFN) principle (everyone is treated as well as the most favoured partner) and the latter as "national treatment". There are various commitments to prevent protection from slipping in the back door via, say, import-processing fees, unreasonable customs valuations or quantitative import restrictions (quotas), and so on, and some weak rules on export restrictions. There are then a series of articles authorizing countries to restrict imports, but only via certain procedures, and also a string of operational requirements to facilitate trade. The GATT itself has a rudimentary, and essentially diplomatic, dispute settlement process, which was considerably enhanced and extended to the GATS and the TRIPS in the WTO Agreement.

Interestingly, the largest exception to the MFN rule slipped in almost unannounced via a technical definition. Strictly, the GATT pertains to the policies of a "customs territory" and, in defining the latter, the GATT permitted countries to sign agreements which granted each other better treatment than their MFN commitments, subject to a series of conditions. This is what underpins the around 400 free trade agreements (FTAs) and customs unions that operate among WTO members today. The most important conditions are that FTAs must cover "substantially all trade" (goods) or have "substantial sectoral coverage" (services) and that tariffs within them must be cut to zero.

The GATT (and hence the WTO) had two important operational features that reduced its trade-liberalizing power, but which rendered it consistent with national sovereignty in the hugely sensitive area of relationships between separate nations.

First, the GATT does not oblige members to liberalize their trade. It encourages them to do so and facilitates negotiations among them to reach mutually agreeable outcomes that do so. When the latter are concluded, the Secretariat records the outcome (it refers to them as "concessions", recognizing that most politicians want to maintain their own trade restrictions while eliminating those of others) and tries to hold countries to what they have agreed. It has no enforcement power itself but can authorize a country that is adversely affected by another's failure to adhere to an agreement to withdraw some of its conces-sions to "rebalance" the agreement.

The second feature is that, by convention, all decisions are taken by consen-sus (strictly, the absence of dissent). This makes change very difficult and has precluded reaching any serious agreement on new or different rules since 1995.

WHAT IS THE POINT OF WTO RULES?

The previous section should have left the reader with an impression of the lim-itations of WTO rules. That is correct, but the rules were still an immeasurable improvement on what preceded them, and on what will succeed them if we allow them to fail.[2] Given its origins, the GATT could only ever achieve the lowest common denominator of discipline on policy. It stems from a period of prolonged severe fighting to preserve national sovereignty, at a point at which governments were supreme (having managed every aspect of life for six years during the war), and intervention in commerce the norm. By 2020, the WTO now has 164 members at all levels of development, some of whom have been at declared or undeclared war with each other. That there are any effective rules is something of a miracle. But it is not surprising that they fall short of what can be agreed by smaller groups of more similar countries.

The European Union and its precursors were created precisely to achieve higher degrees of coordination and cooperation than was possible on WTO rules. The initial impetus – the European Coal and Steel Community (1951) – was conceived to make European war "not merely unthinkable, but materi-ally impossible",[3] by pooling resources and responsibility between members. Subsequently, having failed to create European defence and political unions, attention turned to further deepening economic ties supported by strong cen-tral institutions. It is the latter, of course, that advocates of Brexit objected to, but to move from the strongest integration ever achieved between sovereign nations to the lowest common denominator rules agreeable to 164 diverse countries inevitably involves some pretty dramatic changes in economic management. These are the subject matter of the rest of this chapter.

TRADE IN GOODS

The main consequence of trading with the EU on "WTO terms" is that each side *must* charge its MFN tariff on imports from the other. However, there are also serious consequences so far as the management of trade and regulations of goods are concerned.

Tariffs

The UK has always been a full member of the WTO, but through membership of the EU Customs Union and Single Market, it constrained its policies on almost all aspects of trade in goods to be the same as those of other member states.[4] These policies were notified to the WTO by the EU on behalf of members. On exit, the UK needed to relabel them as UK commitments in the WTO, and it used a procedure termed "rectification", which is used to record (and agree) technical changes to obligations that do not change their essence. It proposed no changes to tariff rates as committed (bound) in the WTO and thus it effectively adopted the EU's MFN tariff as national policy.

Relabelling the tariff binding from EU to UK caused no substantive problem, but in two areas the rectification was not straightforward because commitments made in the GATT applied to the EU in aggregate and had to be broken up into UK and EU-27 components. The first was the cap on the amount paid in subsidies to agriculture, but since this cap was far from binding over the 2010s it caused little difficulty.

The second complication was so-called tariff rate quotas (TRQs) on around a hundred agricultural products. These committed the EU to import a certain volume of these products tariff free (or at low tariffs), with the (generally high) MFN tariffs applying only over that cap. The EU and UK proposed to their partners that these TRQs should be split according to trade over the few years before the UK referendum, but several of them objected. They argued (reasonably) that the right to sell, say, 18,500 tons of sheep meat across the whole of the EU was worth more than the right to sell 12,000 to the UK and 6,500 to the EU-27, because the former allowed more flexibility over destinations. They objected and as a result rectification was escalated into a negotiation which is ongoing, and which until concluded prevents the new tariff policy being certified (essentially agreed) by the WTO members. Ironically, however, it makes no difference to tariff rates.[5] Until the rectification is agreed, the UK cannot change its bound MFN tariff, but it never wanted to anyway!

If the UK actually charges the EU MFN tariff on goods after the transition period ends, tariffs on the 53 per cent of UK imports that come from the EU-27 will change from zero to the MFN rates. About 33 per cent of such imports face zero MFN tariffs (that is, everyone faces zero, e.g. on medicines), so that around 35 per cent of UK imports face a change from zero to a positive value. Table 8.1 gives a breakdown of the tariff by tariff band. About an eighth of the increases will exceed 10 per cent.

What are these tariffs levied on? Table 8.2 shows the products facing the highest tariffs in the EU MFN tariff schedule at the Chapter level of the Harmonised System Trade Classification (there are 98 Chapters).[6] The highest rates are for

Table 8.1. The distribution of UK imports from the EU across tariff bands

EU MFN tariff bracket (%)	Simple average (%)	Weighted average (%)	Imports EU-27 (£bn)	Share of UK imports from EU-27 (%)
0	0.0	0.0	80.0	33.0
>0–2.5	1.7	1.6	27.0	11.1
>2.5–5	3.6	3.6	45.1	18.6
>5–7.5	6.2	6.5	24.1	10.0
>7.5–10	8.4	9.8	37.5	15.5
>10–12.5	11.7	11.8	7.6	3.1
>12.5–15	14.1	13.8	4.1	1.7
>15–17.5	16.2	16.5	3.3	1.4
>17.5–20	18.6	18.2	1.6	0.7
>20–50	30.6	29.8	9.2	3.8
>50	93.8	67.3	3.1	1.3
Total	7.6	5.9	242.5	100.0

Note: Based on tariff and trade data for 2018 at the CN eight-digit level of aggregation. Tariff data from UNCTAD TRAINS and trade data from HMRC Overseas Trade Statistics. Excludes any trade values for which tariff rates are missing (less than 1 per cent).

food and agriculture, followed by clothing and footwear; only a few other manufacturing sectors fall in the 20 most protected chapters, most notably vehicles (cars, part of this Chapter, face a tariff of 10 per cent). Note in agriculture how high the highest rates are in each Chapter.

Tariffs of this magnitude on a third of imports will have significant effects on the cost of living in the UK. Clarke et al.[7] estimate that the price of clothing will rise by 2.4 per cent, and the price of transport vehicles will rise by 5.5 per cent while prices for dairy goods will rise by an average of 8.1 per cent and by 5.8 per cent for meat products. These price rises will have a significant impact on the cost of living. A family's weekly shop on the final consumption goods for which Clarke et al. estimate tariff changes would rise by 2.7 per cent, pushing up annual spending by around £260. However, this is just an average effect. Some

Table 8.2. Illustrative tariff rates from EU (UK) MFN tariff

Rank	HS 2 code	Product name	Weighted Ave %	Minimum Rate %	Maximum Rate %
		Food and agriculture			
1	2	Meat and edible meat offal	47.8	0.0	146.5
2	17	Sugars and sugar confectionery	43.1	0.1	141.8
3	4	Dairy produce, birds' eggs, natural honey, etc.	33.0	0.0	247.5
		Clothing and footwear			
8	64	Footwear, gaiters and the like; parts of	12.7	3.0	17.0
9	61	Articles of apparel and clothing accessories	11.8	8.0	12.0
10	62	Articles of apparel and clothing accessories, nes	11.6	6.3	12.0
		Other manufacturing			
16	87	Vehicles, not railway or tramway rolling stock	8.0	0.0	22.0
19	57	Carpets and other textile floor coverings	7.7	3.0	8.0

Note: Tariff averages calculated for two-digit Chapters of the Harmonised System; weighted averages of HS six-digit data, EU trade 2018.

households would experience more significant price rises, with approximately 3.2 million households facing additional costs of £500 or more. The negative impact on households near the bottom of the income distribution (in the bottom 20 per cent) will be a third greater than for those near the top (in the top 20 per cent) and that on households in Northern Ireland will, on average, be a third greater than for those in London.

Of course, UK exports to the EU will face the same increases in tariffs as in Table 8.2. These will affect UK competitiveness and sales in the EU which will only partly be offset by the fact that UK sales may replace some EU sales within the UK. I will come to estimates of the effect after I deal with two other aspects of "no deal" on trade in goods. First, membership of the EU Single Market has brought industrial standards and practices almost perfectly into line across the EU, and second, the combination of the Single Market and the Customs Union have dramatically reduced the costs of doing trade with Europe and produced almost perfectly frictionless borders.[8]

Regulations and Borders

The Single Market is virtually complete in the area of goods. Until now, trading from Manchester to Milan has barely been any more complicated than trading from Manchester to Minehead. The Single Market guarantees that goods legally put onto the market in the UK (that is, meeting required standards) can also be put onto the market in any other member state. In the vast majority of products there is no need to have different products for different markets (exceptions include the side of the steering wheel in a car and UK electric plugs) and no need at all for any inspection of goods moving between countries. In addition, all international trade is governed by the Union Customs Code so that goods entering the EU are treated equally no matter where they land, and there is no need for any subsequent inspection or control as they move about the Union. The whole system is underpinned by a single legal structure which ensures that rules are applied (more or less) evenly and disputes settled even-handedly.

All these things create certainty for business and reduce transaction costs, allowing markets to be more competitive and efficient. Estimates of the economic benefits of the Single Market vary but they are considerable. Of course, they come at the cost of short-term constraints on government behaviour. The decision-making process allows member states – particularly the large ones like the UK used to be – considerable influence over the rules, but they do involve compromise and once they are fixed they are unavoidable and slow to change.

The UK government hopes to negotiate many side deals with the EU after Brexit which will allow the UK to benefit de facto from pseudo-membership of the Single Market. This is almost certainly a delusion even if there is an FTA but will be doubly difficult if there is none, as in "no deal". The UK view is that since the UK and the EU start off from perfect alignment in regulations, if the UK does not change these, or if it achieves equivalent outcomes by different means, there are no rational grounds for the EU to reject or even to test rigorously goods arriving from the UK.

This is unrealistic because the EU fears that the UK will gain a competitive advantage by picking and choosing between regulations, which would undermine the careful compromises that underpin the whole Single Market edifice, and they also fear that the UK may not be attentive in enforcing rules that it does not like. The UK also ignores the fact that in the absence of a common legal structure, the current sets of redress if something goes wrong will no longer be possible.

The upshot of this discussion is that UK–EU trade under WTO rules will be costly as there will be a good deal of testing and paperwork to carry out. Unfortunately, we do not have much idea of how large a burden this will be, but in a number of exercises UK Trade Policy Observatory (UKTPO) researchers have assumed it conservatively to be equivalent to a tariff of 3.5 per cent on average. This may sound small, but quite a lot of standard manufacturing sectors operate on profit margins not much larger than this, so it could actually be a very significant burden on industry.

Moreover, the burden will be greater if the UK does diverge from the EU in its standards. Manufacturing involves a good deal of trade in parts and this is substantially regionalized – that is, European – for reasons of geography as well as regulation. If a European producer needs a small part which is produced in Britain but on a different regulatory basis than that in the EU, they run the risk of losing accreditation for the whole of their product if they stick with UK supplies. The solution for the manufacturer is obvious.

In a survey of UK industrial product suppliers covered by the Single Market, UKTPO research found, for example, that 82 per cent of respondents import intermediate products from the EU (for use in the manufacturing process), 52 per cent of respondents stated that over half their sales were intermediate inputs for other companies and imports account for more than half of total costs for 44 per cent of companies.[9] The overwhelming majority of firms wished the government to keep regulations in manufacturing explicitly aligned with the EU's.

One irony of the situation over regulations and borders is that the Brexit that was hoped to free Britons from bureaucracy, stimulate innovation and rebalance the economy away from the City will have the opposite effect. The staffing of the UK-specific regulatory bodies (for example, in medicines and aircraft safety), the enforcement of their regulations on the border and elsewhere, and the private sector counterparts to that enforcement will absorb hundreds of thousands of relatively skilled workers. For example, for customs alone the government confirmed that even for a Canada-style FTA 50,000 customs agents will be needed as the number of declarations per year will increase from 50 million to 200 million.[10]

What is the Cost of Disrupting Trade in Goods?

The EU accounts for the bulk of UK trade – 49 per cent of exports and 55 per cent of imports (2017–18) – with a further 14 per cent of each being conducted under the auspices of EU free trade agreements with third countries. Changing the basis of these trades will be a major shock. There are several estimates, of which I detail two. Both assume not only that the UK fails to agree an FTA with the EU but that it also fails to agree them with the 70 countries that currently have trade agreements with the EU (and hence with the UK). In fact, the UK government has now agreed "continuity trade agreements" with 49 of these countries covering a little over 8 per cent of UK trade so these results are slightly pessimistic. The studies also assume that the new border frictions will be equivalent to a tariff of 3.5 per cent on UK–EU trade.

Gasiorek *et al.*[11] provide a detailed study of UK manufacturing (122 sectors) suggesting some very large costs: output of textiles and clothing is predicted to decline by 28.4 per cent and that in chemicals by 18.8 per cent. These are sectors heavily dependent on EU markets and in the latter case on conformity with EU regulations. The authors suggest that the burden will fall mainly on "medium-high R&D" industries (that is, relatively sophisticated ones) and that indeed the least sophisticated sectors, notably in food and agriculture, may actually increase their output as supplies from the EU (currently the vast majority of such imports) will face high tariffs after Brexit.

A second exercise, Fusacchia *et al.*,[12] covers the whole economy but considers only changes in policies pertaining to trade in goods. It focuses on value chains and so captures the damage done by tariffs on intermediate inputs traded between the UK and the EU. It estimates that the "no deal" changes in goods trade alone will cut UK GDP by around 4 per cent.

Do They Mean It?

When "no deal" looked like a serious possibility in March 2019, the government rushed out a proposal that its applied MFN tariff (as opposed to its bound tariff in WTO) would be substantially liberalized. Around 95 per cent of trade headings would have zero tariffs and the remainder (for example, on vehicles and dairy products) would remain at or a little below the bound rates. The proposal was modified in October 2019 to retain tariffs on more goods,[13] and in February 2020 the government initiated a public consultation suggesting only minor deviations from bound rates.[14] The latter was (perhaps) predicated on there being an FTA between the UK and the EU, but the upshot of all these changes is uncertainty and confusion. We really do not know yet what the UK tariff will be if the UK trades with the EU under "WTO rules" from January 2021.

TRADE IN SERVICES

The WTO also applies to trade in services through the GATS. Services transactions are typically managed via regulation rather than tariffs, but the same basic ideas of non-discrimination and of negotiating trade restrictions and then scheduling them, apply here too. Services have been covered by the multilateral trade rules only since 1995 and trade liberalization has been much less far reaching than in goods. There are several reasons for this:

- it has been going on for less time;
- regulations are necessary in many services markets even domestically because the product cannot be tested before it is purchased (unlicensed doctors, anyone?);
- for the same reason, one needs strong systems of redress if something goes wrong, and these are hard to guarantee internationally;
- it is difficult to estimate the degree of trade restriction in a regulation, and thus to trade it off against legitimate regulatory concerns; and
- regulations are typically "owned" bureaucratically by national regulating authorities whose briefs are safety, not opening markets, as is the Trade Ministry's.
- Finally, services trade is complex, with four different ways of delivering services, referred to as "Modes" in the GATS. These are: (1) cross-border trade (for example, streaming a video from abroad); (2) consumption abroad (for example, moving for medical treatment); (3) commercial presence (foreign direct investment); and (4) presence of natural persons. In any sector, each mode could be regulated in a different fashion and the effects of the regulations are not simply additive. For example, you may be able to establish a firm to provide services in a country, but if you cannot get your skilled workers in, say, to repair equipment or solve complaints, you may not be able to provide a decent service experience and so not bother.

For all these reasons, the GATS has not been very successful, and while there are disciplines on services trade they are weak and have offered little assurance of market access. In fact, there has been just one example of significant and extensive trade liberalization in services: the EU's Single Market.

The Single Market in services is far from complete and a significant number of services regulations differ across member states. For many years there was a Brexit narrative that services were no more liberal within the EU than between it and third countries.[15] However, in early 2019 the Organisation for Economic Co-operation and Development (OECD) published the definitive rebuttal of this view.[16]

The OECD's Services Trade Restrictiveness Index (STRI) is the definitive source for measuring restrictions on services trade for advanced economies. Its database on services trade policies vis-à-vis third countries, the so-called MFN regulatory regime, covers 22 sectors across 45 countries. Benz and Gonzales[17] extend the inventory to consider the regulatory regimes that govern trade between 25 European Economic Area countries (23 larger European Union member states, Iceland and Norway), which are appreciably different from the policies faced by service suppliers from third countries.

The OECD uses publicly available information from legal databases and government gazettes, and while there is some debate about exactly how they have combined all the various regulations into simple indices, it is widely accepted that it is not highly misleading. Benz and Gonzales[18] use identical methods for the MFN and the intra-European Economic Area (EEA) calculations and in both cases the resulting indices range from 0 (totally open) to 1 (totally closed). Their results are stark:

- intra-EEA trade is significantly freer on average than MFN services trade: an index of 0.06 compared with 0.22 for MFN trade;
- the wedge between intra-EEA and MFN regimes is particularly large for sectors outside the realm of the multilateral trading system (air transport) or in regulation-intensive sectors, notably legal services but also such sectors as engineering, architecture or computing services, high-skilled professional business services, in which the UK is very competitive;
- there is less variance between sectors within the EEA than in the MFN regime, which reduces the economic costs induced by policy; and
- as well as reducing barriers within the EEA, the Single Market has also harmonized regulations across member states, greatly reducing the costs of trading.

Figure 8.1 illustrates the magnitude of the impending change: the left-hand side refers to the mean internal and external STRI indices across EEA countries – that is, the change in what UK exporters will face – and the right-hand side to the internal and external STRIs for the UK. The latter is important because UK firms and consumers gain from cheaper services trade with the EEA and the competition that this provides to local providers.[19]

The EU accounts for 40 per cent of UK services exports and 49 per cent of services imports, so again, adopting the "WTO model" will disrupt around half of the relevant UK trade.[20] Coupled with the inevitable conclusion that UK services businesses will face massive disadvantages when the UK leaves the Single Market, there are bound to be major costs. Moreover, even if the government seeks to negotiate special sectoral deals (not unheard of in services trade), the fact that services trade policies vary by member state will make doing so costly and time-consuming.

THE BOTTOM LINE

WTO rules – "no deal" – represents a massive shock to UK trade and trading firms and a major cost to UK consumers. It is impossible to quantify the hit with

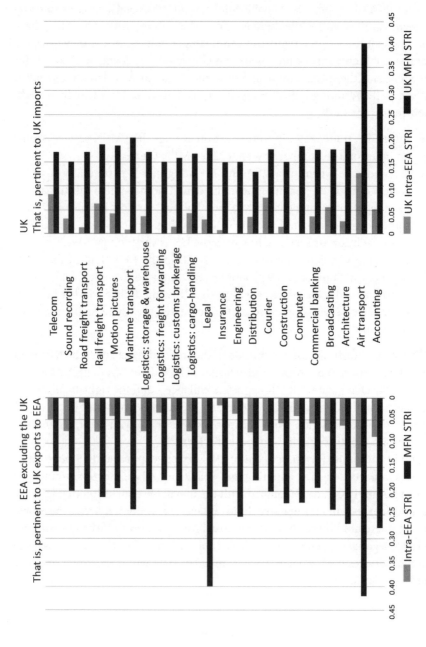

Figure 8.1. Intra-EEA and MFN services trade restrictions for the UK and EEA excluding the UK

any accuracy, but the UK government's own estimates are representative of what the economics profession, almost without exception, thinks the cost will be. The UK government[21] estimates that, relative to the status quo, "no deal" will cut GDP by 7.7 per cent, rising to 9.3 per cent if one factors in the elimination of net immigration of EU workers. These estimates are old, but the last 18 months have generated nothing to change their conclusion substantially.

Arguably the thing that has been most dramatically clarified since the estimates were made is the sickness of the WTO itself. The USA under President Trump has identified a number of failings in the WTO, which are not entirely disputed by other members, but it has then used these as an excuse to mount a massive challenge to the organization that makes its future ability to discipline world trade very doubtful. President Trump has unilaterally imposed tariffs on $30 billion of steel and aluminium imports, ostensibly on the grounds of "national security", and is threatening to raise tariffs on $350 billion worth of imported cars, trucks and auto parts on similarly dubious grounds. He has initiated a trade war with China by imposing tariffs on $360 billion of goods imported from China and threatened to impose further tariffs on all $520 billion of Chinese imports. He has coerced – including the threat of trade sanctions or withdrawal from trade agreements – other countries into renegotiating their trade agreements with the USA and making one-sided concessions, for example in the North American Free Trade Agreement and the Korea–US FTA. Finally, he has blocked appointments to the Appellate Body of the WTO's dispute settlement mechanism preventing it from hearing appeals and thus undermining the effectiveness of the whole system.

In other words, even if trading on WTO terms was a reasonable price for "taking back control" in 2016 (it was not, in my opinion), it may well not be so now.

Notes for Chapter 8

1. I am grateful to Julia Magntorn Garrett, Research Officer in the UK Trade Policy Observatory at the University of Sussex, for help in preparing some of the statistics used in this chapter.

2. That the latter is possible is illustrated by the aggressive unilateralism of the Trump White House, which has led the USA to impose tariffs on steel and aluminium trade on China on the flimsiest of justifications and blocked the appointment of judges to the WTO Appellate Body such that the WTO's Dispute Settlement Procedure is effectively moribund. The rules were designed to counter power-politics, which once suited the USA (to give other countries confidence that they could rely on the USA to trade fairly) but no longer do so.

3. The Schuman Declaration, 9 May 1950, https://www.robert-schuman.eu/en/doc/questions-d-europe/qe-204-en.pdf.

4. Despite comments to the contrary, this so-called common commercial policy was not imposed on the UK, but was negotiated between members and then agreed.

5. It does matter for the TRQs, however, and here one can expect a drawn-out process that results in a small enlargement of many of the quotas.

6. The basic data are for the approximately 5,300 products defined at the six-digit level and are weighted together to Chapter level by EU imports in 2018.

7. S. Clarke, I. Serwicka & L. A. Winters, "Changing lanes: the impact of different post-Brexit trading policies on the cost of living", UKTPO/Resolution Foundation, October 2017, https://blogs.sussex.ac.uk/uktpo/files/2017/10/Changing-Lanes.pdf.

8. It is worth noting that each of these will also apply if the UK and the EU sign a free trade agreement as foreseen by the Withdrawal Agreement of January 2020.

9. EURIS, "Securing a competitive UK manufacturing industry post-Brexit", EURIS and UKTPO, 2018, http://www.euristaskforce.org/wp-content/uploads/2018/09/EURIS-A4-report-final.pdf.

10. G. Parker & D. Thomas, "Border red tape will mean 50,000 new form-fillers after Brexit", *Financial Times*, 27 February 2020.

11. M. Gasiorek, I. Serwicka & A. Smith, "Which manufacturing industries and sectors are most vulnerable to Brexit?", *The World Economy* 42:1 (2019), 21–56.

12. I. Fusacchia, L. Salvatici & L. A. Winters, "Brexit and global value chains: 'no-deal' is still costly", UKTPO Briefing Paper No. 35, July 2019, https://blogs.sussex.ac.uk/uktpo/publications/brexit-and-global-value-chains-no-deal-is-still-costly/.

13. J. Magntorn Garrett, "The UK's 'no deal' tariffs: an update", UKTPO blog, 16 October 2019, https://blogs.sussex.ac.uk/uktpo/2019/10/16/the-uks-no-deal-tariffs-an-update/#more-4074.

14. M. Gasiorek, J. Magntorn Garrett, N. Tamberi & L. Winters, "Recommendations on the UK government's global tariff proposals", UKTPO Briefing Paper No. 39, March 2020, https://blogs.sussex.ac.uk/uktpo/files/2020/03/BP39.pdf.

15. For example, M. Burrage, "The EU single market in services barely exists, and has been slowly disappearing since 2010", 3 June 2018, https://brexitcentral.com/eu-single-market-services-barely-exists-disappearing-2010/.

16. S. Benz & F. Gonzales, "Intra-EEA STRI database: methodology and results", *OECD Trade Policy Papers*, No. 223 (2019) (Paris: OECD).

17. *Ibid.*

18. *Ibid.*

19. As with border frictions, the situation will basically be the same even if the UK and EU agree a Canada-style FTA.

20. UK total service exports are approximately equal to goods exports, so this is a large amount. It is also worth noting that the EU's FTAs with third countries do little for services trade. – see J. Magntorn & L. A. Winters, "Can CETA-Plus solve the UK's services problem?", UKTPO Briefing Paper No. 18, March 2018, https://blogs.sussex.ac.uk/uktpo/publications/can-ceta-plus-solve-the-uks-services-problem/ – so these are not pertinent here.

21. HM Government, *EU Exit: Long-Term Economic Analysis*, Cm 9741, November 2018.

9

"SINGAPORE ON THE THAMES"

Alan Bollard

In the United Kingdom's early discussions about leaving the European Union, there were many proposed new models for the country's ongoing economic configurations and policies, with much argument about possible new approaches to integration. Among the most unexpected of these was the claim that the UK could follow the model of one of the smallest, most distant, and most unusual of its ex-colonies: Singapore. On the surface, the two countries would seem to have little in common: a traditional largely Anglo-Saxon country in a long historical relationship with the European continent on the one hand, and a tiny, newly founded, largely Chinese country in a poor but bustling and populous South East Asian region on the other.

However, this unlikely comparison did not go away. Indeed, it resurfaced in various forms, as politicians and commentators argued that Singapore offered a model for Britain to follow in its Brexit negotiations. This chapter considers whether these comparisons have any economic validity. Initially I recount Singapore's modern history (both the official and unofficial versions). Then I examine the Singapore development model and look for useful comparisons to make for post-Brexit Britain.

SINGAPOREAN BACKGROUND

Official histories of Singapore like to portray it as an ancient trading centre. In fact, it was little more than a swampy island at the foot of the Malay Peninsula, a tiny Malay sultanate where the harbour offered watering facilities for vessels trading between China, the East Indies Archipelago and India/the Middle East. Its key was its location: it commanded the narrow passage between the Malacca Straits and the South China Seas, the shortest route between Canton and Calcutta. Singapore was not originally a sovereign state, but rather part of a Malay sultanate, with whom Stamford Raffles contracted in 1819 to allow the East India Company to build a trading port there.

Its early role as a trading hub set the pattern of Singaporean development for the next two centuries: a small settlement that transhipped cargoes, serviced trading ships and provided fuel and provisions. It was run by a growing population of British administrators, local Malay villagers, Chinese merchants and labourers from the region.

In 1869 the Suez Canal opened, coinciding with the advent of coal-powered steam shipping. Sensing opportunity, the British imported huge coal stocks and positioned Singapore as the largest bunkering port in the world, a role it still fills today.

The British saw Singapore as a gateway to China, and a place to defend their colonial interests against the French, Dutch and Portuguese (ironically all ex-European Union colleagues today). During the Second World War, Singapore demonstrated its crucial strategic position as the key Allied garrison headquarters, but also its strategic vulnerability, with one of Britain's greatest military defeats, followed by a period of repressive Japanese occupation. Postwar, the British Administration returned, but was confronted by Chinese Communist-influenced liberation forces, a period known as "the Emergency".

Following turbulent fighting in the 1950s, the Dutch and French withdrew from their South East Asian colonies and concentrated their postwar recoveries on the European Coal and Steel Community and, later, the European Economic Community (EEC). By the time the British finally withdrew from their own colonial possessions in the East, they were already considering seeking entry to the growing EEC in the West.

The British withdrawal left an uneasy political imbalance on the Malay Peninsula. In 1963 Singapore became part of a newly independent Malaysia. It was a turbulent period, with Indonesian President Sukarno declaring "*konfontasi*": a threat to invade. By 1965 Chinese-majority Singapore split from its Malay-dominated partner, declaring independence under the leadership of Lee Kwan Yew and the People's Action Party. The party has been in power ever since.

Lee Kwan Yew famously referred to his new country as an island of Chinese in a sea of Malays. Indonesian President Bacharuddin Jusuf ("B. J.") Habibie contemptuously referred to Singapore as nothing more than "a little red dot" on a map, a belittling description that the Singaporeans took up with enthusiasm.

This was a completely new country born with a strong sense of geographical and strategic relevance, but also of its economic and political vulnerability. It was poor with no resources. Some commentators predicted it must fail, given Malaysia's control over Singapore's water, Indonesia's continuing threats to invade, worries about communism spreading out of China and serious domestic race riots in 1966. This fragile history meant that Singaporean economic policy would always follow its security concerns: maximizing self-sufficiency in a dangerous world while also allying itself with friends and rivals in the region to balance out the threats.

THE SINGAPOREAN MODEL: THE VISION

The Singapore model is unusual, being based on the clear vision of a small number of Singaporean technocrats led by the redoubtable founding prime minister, Lee Kwan Yew. The vision has been repeatedly and clearly articulated and updated in government statements and in the prime minister's bestselling books: *The Singapore Story* (1998), *From Third World to First* (2000) and *Hard Truths* (2011).

Since independence, Singapore's style of government has been authoritarian and controlling, while being embedded into a democratic system. But democracy Singapore-style has been designed to ensure the People's Action Party is guaranteed continued control of Parliament. The party has acted somewhat like a benign Communist Party, identifying talent early, investing in the education of targeted highflyers, then allocating them to positions of influence where, if they proved successful, they could expect to be cycled through key government positions, commercial roles and political offices. Expectations of their performance would be high, failure would not be tolerated and any corruption would be punished. The result has been a network of elites: for example, the current prime minister is the son of the founding prime minister, and his wife is the chief executive officer of one of the huge government investment companies.

This approach receives much local support: the People's Action Party continues to attract majority support and the political system is constructed in a way that ensures the party is very unlikely to lose power. Singapore rates only 75th on the Economist Intelligence Unit Democracy Index. The government rewards loyalty, eschews corruption and actively builds nationhood, not least through its control of the media (rated 151 on the Reporters Without Borders Press Freedom Index).

Dissidents and opposition face a tough legal system and frequent charges of legal defamation. The administration's recourse to law is famously uncompromising with a high degree of prosecution success, legal challenges to those who oppose it and legal punishments from caning (based on Victorian naval flogging procedures) to a high rate of executions.

The Lee Kwan Yew vision was about building a nation from its foundations. A key element was to be Singaporean home ownership; a huge investment programme turned substandard Asian slums into a modern high-rise apartment-dwelling nation. The government owns or controls most of the land and the official Housing Development Board, partnered with private developers, has built a huge modern housing stock, most of it sold on to Singaporeans with government financial assistance. A typical Singaporean angle is that each housing estate is required to meet Lee Kwan Yew's predetermined optimal Chinese/Malay/Indian ethnic mix. Over 90 per cent of the population now own their own apartments, and this is at the core of Singapore's nation-building.

The government's social policy is based on Confucian ideals of filial piety. Adult children are legally responsible for their ageing parents' welfare, fostered by inducements to counter the risk of diminished nuclear family responsibilities, such as encouragement to buy apartments near their parents. Singaporeans are expected to meet their retirement needs by compulsory saving through levies on their earnings to be paid into the Government Provident Fund. The household savings rate is around 55 per cent of income, one of the highest in the world. Misfortune or poverty can carry a social stigma, and poorer older people unsupported by families have little choice but to work at low-paid menial jobs. The financially successful (often through property development) are admired (the 2018 movie, *Crazy Rich Asians*, set in Singapore, was very popular).

The country has grown strongly since the 1970s (although growth has been challenged more recently by trade tensions in the region). Singapore's gross domestic product per capita at purchasing power parity is, at around $90,000–$100,000, one of the highest in the world, and about double the UK per capita income. However, the limited social safety net, low taxes and rich oligarchs have resulted in severe economic inequality: the country has a very high Gini coefficient compared to most Organisation for Economic Co-operation and Development (OECD) members.

There is a strong engineering ethos built into the Singapore vision, and this includes social engineering. In the past there have been (largely unsuccessful) attempts to encourage educated couples to have larger families and low-income families to consider voluntary sterilization. In fact, Singapore now has one of the lowest birth rates in the world, below replacement level. Today's social policies are more sophisticated but are still underpinned by the view that appropriate education helps the population become more efficient and more wedded to the national interest. Another important nationalizing device is the universal conscription of all young males into the Singaporean Armed Forces. There is a very high level of expenditure on defence, reflecting the continued political view that Singapore lives in a dangerous world.

The bulk of low-paid household and construction work is done by short-stay migrants from poor parts of the region, who live regulated lives in barracks and have no residency rights. Their numbers are manipulated in order to ensure continuing full employment for Singaporean citizens. In addition, there is an elite diaspora of international professionals in the services sector. This means there are around 5.8 million people in this small country, only 3.5 million of whom are Singaporean citizens.

The authoritarian and technically advanced nature of the Singapore government has recently been demonstrated in its response to Covid-19. Singapore was hit hard early, but quickly responded with one of the most impressive tracking, tracing and monitoring regimes. This only worked because Singaporeans accept that privacy and control should be regulated by the state, not the individual.

THE SINGAPOREAN MODEL: INDUSTRIAL POLICY

In its early years, Singapore's commerce was based on Chinese migrant merchants and small business owners. As the country developed and wages rose, it became difficult to compete with its low-labour-cost South East Asian neighbours in traditional industries. The government introduced incentives to attract higher-value Western manufacturing operations. It also invested directly in huge construction and engineering works. Remarkably, the country has expanded its land area, now estimated to be 22 per cent bigger than at independence, with further extensive land reclamation planned. Building on its historic role as an energy hub, the government constructed an artificial offshore island to house one of the largest petrochemical facilities in the world, importing crude oil and exporting a vast range of plastic, rubber and chemical value-added products manufactured by multinationals and local firms.

Singapore's modern industrial policy is based on technological advantage and value-added. It invites high-tech foreign firms to relocate to its technology parks on attractive terms. It offers zoning for innovative technological projects such as self-drive vehicles, and "sand pit" regulatory spaces for financial innovation. It rates as the world's third or fourth international financial centre, and is especially strong in bond markets, insurance, commodity markets, energy trading and wealth management. It promotes itself as a cloud computing hub in the Asia-Pacific region.

There are long-term plans for continuing economic, technical and social development. The government directs its technical training institutions and its well-funded state research institutions to meet these targets. The public is informed of the proposals, but not formally consulted about them. Development that is seen as being in the social interest will proceed rapidly and will not be slowed or obstructed by interest groups. Labour laws are tough and employer-friendly. Singaporean education rates very highly on English, mathematics and science PISA scores (the OECD's Programme for International Student Assessment), but does not rate well on creativity.

While Singapore is a state, it is also a city, with municipal operations seamlessly integrated into national policy. There are none of the complications of growth nodes and domestic regional differences. The dense population, flat land and authoritarian planning have resulted in very efficient modern infrastructure and transport, standardization and centralized control, producing economies of scale, most of it government-owned and all of it government-controlled. There are active pilot programmes to trial drones, self-drives and other innovations. A favoured regulatory technique is to establish state-controlled duopolies and seek some limited degree of managed competition between them. Most of the government's holdings are held in massive sovereign wealth funds, Temasek and GIC Private Ltd, which together hold over US$650 billion of assets, one of the largest balance sheets in the world.

With a single rate corporate income tax of 17 per cent Singapore is highly attractive for industrial relocation, although it is sometimes accused of being a tax haven. It has now established itself as the preferred South East Asian regional headquarters for most multinational firms. As the disruptions continue in Hong Kong, Singapore, always looking for competitive advantage, has quietly presented itself as a safe and efficient headquarters for the wider East Asian region, a country that can be a window into the Chinese market, but offering an independent and respected legal system.

THE SINGAPOREAN MODEL: REGIONAL POLICY

A key part of the Singapore economic vision is the idea of being a regional or world hub. It builds on Singapore's earlier history as an entrepôt. Today, Singapore produces few goods domestically, but it has the biggest transhipment port in the world, which is highly efficient, with remote-controlled cranes and advanced digital tracking, breaking down cargoes from Asian manufacturers for the long haul to European markets. A huge fleet of bunkering ships reload cargo carriers en route through the Malacca Straits. Changi Airport is the busiest air hub in the region and one of the largest in the world with (pre-Covid) one million passengers transiting through weekly; this huge airport is doubling its capacity in a ten-year expansion plan through land reclamation and centralized approval procedures (in sharp contrast to the pace of Heathrow expansion). The largest carrier is state-owned Singapore Airlines which carries Singaporean values and the brand (the "Singapore girl") to the world. The rail network is planned to join a high-speed Association of South East Asian Nations (ASEAN)-Chinese network much earlier than Britain's HS2.

Singapore has proved particularly attractive to the financial sector and it is now the largest South East Asian financial hub, and one of the world's biggest wealth management centres, assisted by low tax, strong laws, the English language, attractiveness to expatriates, a modern technology infrastructure and respected regulatory institutions. A consequence is that Singapore has also now become one of the most expensive expatriate locations.

Not only is Singapore a regional hub for transport and finance, but also for other international services, such as digital services and cloud location, health and conference tourism and bonded warehousing, playing on its strength as a technologically connected and stable epicentre in a challenging region. Singapore particularly attracts the savings and investment of the wealthy elites of South East Asia who are far more trusting of Singapore's stability than of life in Jakarta, Manila or Bangkok. Businesses show similar confidence: the majority of foreign direct investment into ASEAN comes via Singapore.

Singapore actively researches and borrows best practices from other countries. It competes relentlessly with Hong Kong as a regional headquarters. It scouts the East Asian region to induce promising firms to relocate. Its law, language and education systems derived originally from Edwardian England (although they have taken on a unique Singaporean slant). But its financial services, its bonded warehousing, its secrecy and its private wealth management model are modelled on Zürich rather than the City of London. As a trading hub, it has more in common with Dubai than with Felixstowe. As a centre for conventions, health services and education it rivals Melbourne, not Oxford.

The postwar South East Asian region was poor, populous, rivalrous and dangerous, riven by tensions centred on communist wars in Vietnam, Cambodia and Laos, and right-wing authoritarian dictators such as Filipino President Ferdinand Marcos. In 1967 the Western-leaning states, led by Singapore and others, founded the ASEAN regional arrangement. Initially it was a strategic security pact that gradually expanded into a wider economic and security arrangement among a heterogeneous group of countries. Unlike the rules-driven arrangements of the Western Europeans in the EU, ASEAN has been an agreement to talk, with aspirational visions, but with pragmatic local interests often holding sway.

The Singapore city state has grown up balancing national and regional interests and finding tactical ways to prosper in a big power world. Its regional interests are most directly reflected through the membership of ASEAN, now a ten-country grouping, focused on economic advancement, regulatory harmonization and best practice policies through the ASEAN Economic Community. This economic arrangement has high aspirations but relatively low compliance, reflecting a tolerance of different conditions: very poor member countries (particularly Myanmar, Laos and Cambodia) contrast with very high-income ones (Singapore, Brunei), and there are significant ethnic, cultural, geographical and resource differences. Like the European Steel and Coal Community, its main achievement to date has been a sense of mutual security, while it recognizes its difficult task ahead is to address assertive Chinese behaviour in the South China Sea, and erratic US policies on trade and security in the region.

Singapore is highly pragmatic, paying lip service to ASEAN economic integration, but giving priority to its own interests as an island of economic rationality in a stormy region. On big power issues, Singapore tries to maintain friendly relationships with both China and the USA, although without entering into legal commitments. But maintaining this balance is becoming increasingly difficult.

Singapore has actively pursued other regional trading arrangements, being a driver of Asia-Pacific Economic Cooperation in 1989, and more recently the Trans-Pacific Partnership and the Regional Comprehensive Economic Partnership. These large regional bodies are intended as stepping stones to a much bigger Free Trade Area of Asia and the Pacific, supported by Singapore. But regional diplomacy is hard: these prospects have now been thrown into doubt by the Trump administration.

On the international scene, Singapore is not a member of the OECD, its lack of full democracy, authoritarian legal system and tax haven behaviours being cited as reasons. On the other hand, it is a member of the World Trade Organization, but despite its huge wealth has maintained a "developing country" status entitling it to special treatment (although it has said it will not trigger these rights). The country might be described as internationalist in theory, but pragmatically nationalist when it suits.

SINGAPORE ON THE THAMES, OR LONDON ON THE MALACCA STRAITS?

What does a small tropical island on the equator have in common with a large Northern European country with ten times the population and 300 times the land area? And how well would any of its economic model be useful to a newly Brexited Britain?

The phrase "Singapore on the Thames" was first mooted by Philip Hammond, then chancellor of the exchequer during the Brexit debate, as a way to encourage the EU to agree to a softer Brexit deal for the UK. What did he mean by this? British economist Howard Davies writes: "the phrase 'Singapore on the Thames' is shorthand for Britain becoming a low tax, lightly-regulated economy, that can outcompete the sclerotic overregulated eurozone, from a strategic position only 20 miles or so offshore".[1] Asia specialist Guy de Jonqueres paraphrased the Hammond argument as Britain seeking to copy a regulatory-light, tax-light, open-for-business, modern economy attractive to foreign investors.[2]

Subsequent commentators have criticized the idea, pointing to some obvious discrepancies: Singapore is a tiny country with twice as many civil servants per capita as the UK; on top of personal income tax at 22 per cent, workers and employees are required to contribute 37 per cent of wages and salaries to the Central Provident Fund; the government is a huge shareholder in industries and owns most of the land; the country is very tightly regulated; the infrastructure is municipal rather than national.

Singapore has undoubtedly profited from its position at the centre of ASEAN, offering investors a rational investment environment. There are parallels to Britain's position vis-à-vis Western Europe. But Dublin, Paris and Frankfurt offer different opportunities and different competition than do Jakarta, Manila and Bangkok.

An additional problem for post-Brexit Britain is that the European Union has not been sympathetic to the Singapore model and is unlikely to welcome such an approach. In the past it has criticized the country as a tax haven, contributing to tax base erosion in the digital industry, with anti-labour laws and its own trade hurdles, all diverging from EU standards. The EU's "four freedoms" of goods, capital, services and labour movements are not the same as the ASEAN model. Former MEP David Martin points out that the EU–Singapore Free Trade Agreement was almost derailed in the European Parliament due to opposition to some Singaporean policies.[3]

If the low-tax, low-regulation, open-trade framework is not the true Singapore model, are there any useful features left for the UK to copy? Perhaps the most obvious feature that stands out is Singapore's tough, yet pragmatic, independent attitude to the world: Singaporeans know no one owes them a living and therefore they have to work harder. Singapore follows international rules where those are in its interests, but it can also be pragmatically nationalistic when it suits. It follows the traditional Javanese edict, "keep your friends close and your enemies even closer". It is well connected to its regional neighbours but in a way that always puts Singaporean interests first and emphasizes Singaporean independence of action.

Singapore had its own Brexit moment when it left the Malaysian Federation in 1965. It ultimately made a success of that separation, but in ways that, clearly, the UK would find it difficult to follow today.

Note for Chapter 9

1. H. Davies, "Will the UK really turn into a Singapore on the Thames after Brexit?", *The Guardian*, 17 December 2019.

2. G. de Jonqueres, "The Singapore on the Thames delusion", *Prospect*, 14 November 2019.

3. D. Martin, "Singapore on the Thames: Model for Post-Brexit UK?" RSIS Commentary, 20/19, 3.2.20.

10

THE UNITED KINGDOM AND THE COMPREHENSIVE AND PROGRESSIVE TRANS-PACIFIC PARTNERSHIP

Stephen Woolcock

This chapter provides a brief outline of what the Comprehensive and Progressive Trans-Pacific Partnership (CPTPP) is before discussing the UK government's declared objectives in potential membership of it. It then provides an assessment of what the CPTPP offers as a comprehensive free trade agreement, compared to the provisions of recent EU Preferential Trade Agreements (PTAs).[1] The EU has negotiated bilateral PTAs with CPTPP members Japan, Canada, Mexico, Chile, Peru, Vietnam and Singapore, is well advanced in negotiations with Australia and New Zealand, and negotiations with Malaysia have been initiated but not greatly advanced. Any assessment of the costs and benefits of CPTPP membership depends on the specific commitments negotiated bilaterally between the UK and each CPTPP member. This includes, in particular, detailed schedules on tariffs, tariff rate quotas, cross-border services, investment liberalization and government procurement. It may also include provisions on recognition of regulatory provisions, such as on professional qualifications, food and product standards and data protection.

A full assessment of the impact of UK membership of the CPTPP is therefore currently not possible and any comprehensive study is beyond the scope of this chapter. A general assessment of the relative gains from potential CPTPP membership is therefore provided by a comparison between the EU–Japan Economic Partnership Agreement (EPA) and Japan's commitments under the CPTPP. The chapter discusses some of the questions that will arise in any negotiation process. Finally, as the initiative to launch negotiations with the CPTPP (as well as the USA, Australia and New Zealand) is the first step towards a new independent trade policy for the UK, the chapter looks at what this tells us about how the UK might go about decision-making and negotiating future trade agreements.

THE CPTPP

The origins of the CPTPP go back to an initiative by the P4 (Brunei, Chile, Singapore and New Zealand) for the Trans-Pacific Strategic EPA that came into force in 2006. In 2008 negotiations began with eight other countries (the USA, Japan, Canada, Mexico, Vietnam, Malaysia, Peru and Australia) and in 2016 these signed the Trans-Pacific Partnership (TPP). This expansion was driven by the US decision to join in order to provide the economic underpinning of the Obama administration's "pivot to Asia". This illustrates how PTA initiatives generally have political or strategic motivations, as indeed would appear to be the case in the UK initiative on CPTPP membership. In January 2017 the Trump administration opted out of the TPP in favour of negotiating bilateral agreements.[2] The 11 other members of the TPP, however, elected to proceed without the USA and still account for 13 per cent of world gross domestic product (compared to 22 per cent for the EU) with a broadly equivalent market of 500 million people.

The CPTPP is therefore essentially the TPP less some 20 provisions that have been "suspended". Many of the 30 chapters of the CPTPP are carried over word-for-word from the TPP, with most changes to be found in the chapter on investment. In general terms, it is possible to distinguish between three broad approaches to PTAs.[3] There is an EU approach, which is derived from the way the EU has done things internally and therefore tends to be comprehensive.[4] Then there is the US or North American Free Trade Agreement (NAFTA) "gold standard" approach, which is, not surprisingly, shaped by US domestic approaches to regulation and US preferences. Lastly, there is an Asian approach, which generally entails less deep economic integration, eschews heavy institutional structures and is less binding. The CPTPP is closer to the NAFTA approach but has some of the non-binding elements of the Asian approach. Despite these typologies, modern PTAs have very similar structures and are themselves developments of General Agreement on Tariffs and Trade (GATT) or other World Trade Organization (WTO) provisions. So, the distinctions are more to do with how "WTO plus" they are on market access commitments, how they seek to reduce the costs for international business of divergent regulation and what provision they have for sustainable development (that is, provisions on labour, environmental and human rights).

THE UK AIMS: A PROVISIONAL ASSESSMENT

Any assessment of the UK's participation in CPTPP is by definition provisional. But it is perhaps possible to assess whether the UK's aims in considering membership of CPTPP are realistic. Reaching out to potential growth economies in

Asia-Pacific is clearly in line with a policy of "Global Britain". This is no doubt a reason for ministers in the current Johnson government referring to it as an objective that would be furthered by concluding agreements with the USA, Australia and New Zealand. Government statements have referred to the aims in terms of seeking to:[5]

- deepen UK trade with the future growth markets of Asia-Pacific;[6]
- create UK trade and jobs;
- contribute to shaping international trade rules, with a particular reference to rules on e-commerce; and
- support a rules-based trading system at a time when this is under threat.

Deepening UK trade relations with Asian growth markets in terms of market access all depends on how joining the existing CPTPP compares with negotiating "continuity" agreements with those economies to which UK suppliers of goods and services have preferential access under the EU's free trade agreements (FTAs). Most of these EU PTAs are recent, comprehensive and on a par with the CPTPP on most topics. Negotiating accession to the CPTPP does not offer a fast-track alternative to a series of bilateral "continuity" agreements with the EU's PTA partners in the region. The accession process to the CPTPP requires the negotiation of commitments with each member bilaterally, so there is no efficiency in opting for CPTPP membership on this score.[7] It could be argued, however, that CPTPP membership provides an alternative default option should the continuity agreements be held up. But CPTPP accession will require the agreement of all CPTPP members, so a single member could veto UK accession, something that could be avoided by negotiating the continuity agreements.

From a longer-term strategic perspective, it is worth considering the possibility of new countries acceding to the CPTPP. For the moment, Colombia, South Korea and Indonesia have expressed an interest in joining. Of these, the UK had preferential access under EU PTAs for South Korea, the most important economy of the three, and Colombia. The EU negotiations with Indonesia – the largest market in the Association of Southeast Asian Nations region – had been through ten negotiating rounds by March 2020 and considerable progress had been made. Sticking points with Indonesia appear to be palm oil, including the question of sustainable production of this in Indonesia, and non-tariff barriers to trade. There has been speculation that other countries may consider joining the CPTPP. A new US government could possibly reverse the decision of the Trump administration and rejoin, which would naturally increase the share of world trade covered by the CPTPP.[8] A more remote prospect could be China opting to seek membership.[9]

The trade and job creation objective cannot really be assessed without knowing the detailed schedules of commitments. PTAs will generally tend to have positive effects on trade, but only over time and depending on the use made of any preferences or new opportunities offered by an agreement. How effectively provisions of regulatory divergence are implemented is also more important than commitments to remove tariffs and this can only be known after years of application. The UK does have a trade surplus with the CPTPP members at the moment. Current CPTPP members account for 7 per cent of UK exports. A further factor is "gravity", in other words trade and investment are still shaped by the distance from markets. Any shift from the UK's predominant engagement with European supply chains will be at best slow and progressive. The contribution to trade and especially jobs seems likely to be very modest.

At present there is no detailed cost–benefit assessment by the government of the benefits of negotiating membership of the CPTPP. General scoping exercises have been conducted, which suggest that there would be no great difficulty for the UK membership of the CPTPP and that this could be achieved without much conflict between the demands of the CPTPP and those of the EU.[10] This is because the CPTPP does not intrude substantially on regulatory policy autonomy or does so less than some EU PTAs and especially less so than the EU itself.

In terms of the aim of contributing to shaping trade rules, this would only apply to rules developed after any eventual UK accession. The accession rules, together with the norms and expectations of the existing members, require all new members to accept all existing rules. The UK would be expected to accept the rules of the club and would not be able to negotiate the conditions of its membership, except for the bilateral commitments with each member on market access. The CPTPP rules on e-commerce are an advance on existing WTO provisions but exclude some sensitive topics. For example, the so-called "safe harbour" provisions on data protection were one of the 20 TPP topics "suspended" from the CPTPP when the USA left. For the UK, an alternative to CPTPP when it comes to shaping trade rules on e-commerce would be the plurilateral negotiations currently underway as one of the WTO's Joint Initiatives. As this initiative includes both the USA and China it is more likely to shape outcomes than the CPTPP.

With the general tendency towards more power-based trade policies on the part of the United States and – in a more discrete lower profile manner – China, anything that underpins a rules-based trading system is in the UK's interest. The CPTPP, like other regional or bilateral trade and investment agreements, contributes to such an underpinning. So, in this respect the UK joining would support a rules-based order, something that would be welcomed by the CPTPP members, caught between the USA and China. Outside the EU it would also be in the UK's interests to be seated at as many key negotiating tables as possible. The question is how important CPTPP rule making will be. A more likely scenario than the USA or even China joining CPTPP is that trade and investment rules will be shaped by plurilateral negotiations similar to those for e-commerce. The US interest in plurilateral approaches over multilateral agreements (meaning the inclusion of China, other emerging powers and potential developing country veto players) is more deep-seated than Trump's opposition to anything that is not bilateral and transactional.

On balance, the policy aim of the UK that seems to have the best prospects is therefore the symbolic one of indicating the ambition of a new global role for the country.

COMPARING CPTPP WITH EXISTING EU FTAS

In terms of tangible benefits, it is necessary to compare what the UK would achieve in trade and economic terms from CPTPP membership with what it would achieve otherwise. The alternatives to CPTPP membership should be mentioned here. These are either "WTO rules" (see Chapter 8) or (re)negotiating agreements that replicate the benefits the UK has had under the EU agreements with CPTPP members. A full assessment of these goes beyond the scope of this chapter.[11] It should be recalled that neither the CPTPP text of rules nor the CPTPP schedules are up for negotiation. But the UK will have to agree the schedules of its commitments with CPTPP members. At present, then, the best metric for a comparison is the text of the CPTPP and that of the EU FTAs with CPTPP members. Table 10.1 provides an illustration of some of the key chapters of the CPTPP with those of the EU–Japan EPA, Japan being the most important economy in the CPTPP.

Broadly speaking, Table 10.1 shows the similarity between the CPTPP and the EU–Japan EPA, and thus the EU, approach. This is not unexpected as the basic framework of rules in PTAs between developed economies tend to be similar. But there are detailed differences that will have an important impact on specific sectors or interests.

A brief commentary is needed on Table 10.1. In terms of tariffs, both the CPTPP and the EU–Japan EPA remove all tariffs on manufactures and almost all on goods. The exceptions, which are almost entirely in the food products or agricultural sector, are the same. For example, Japan's tariffs on beef are reduced to 9 per cent in both. Note that both approaches also include tariff rate quotas for some sensitive products. Japan is not an agricultural exporter and tends to be defensive on agriculture, so the UK should expect greater demands from CPTPP members (Australia, New Zealand, Chile and Canada) than the EU had in negotiating with Japan.

Both the CPTPP and the EU–Japan EPA provide for diagonal (ac)cumulation for rules of origin. This means that processing in other parties to the

Table 10.1. Comparison of key chapters of the CPTPP and the EU–Japan EPA

Chapter	CPTPP*	EU–Japan EPA**
Trade in goods	90% of tariff lines 0% on entry into force; tariffs go to 0% on manufactures after a transition period; some retained protection, for example beef 9%, milk 20%; some *Tariff Rate Quotas* for CPTPP; WTO *Tariff Rate Quotas* for some foods, for example grains and dairy products	90% of tariff lines 0% on entry into force; tariffs to 0% for manufactures after transition; 9% tariff on beef retained; tariff rate quotas for dairy and grains
Rules of origin	Diagonal accumulation across all CPTPP economies; value-added to non (CPTPP)-originating products included; self-certification with verification; a specific chapter on rules of origin for textiles and clothing	Accumulation across EU and Japan; value-added to non-(EU–Japan) products included; self-certification (exporters or importers)
Trade facilitation	Best endeavours use of international standards; electronic procedures; advanced rulings to speed customs clearance	Use of World Customs Organization standards; electronic procedures; advanced rulings to speed customs clearance
Sanitary and phytosanitary measures	Seeks to apply WTO SPS agreement more fully; stresses science-based approach	In line with WTO SPS agreement; stresses no lowering of standards; allows EU to use precautionary principle
Technical barriers to trade	Coverage of central government only for some aspects; encourages Asia-Pacific Economic Cooperation Mutual Recognition Arrangement; range of options for dealing with regulatory divergence from mutual recognition to producer declaration	Applies to regulations from all levels of government; emphasis on the adoption of international standards (for example, for cars); options for showing compliance; sector working groups to monitor non-tariff measures/ regulations
Investment protection	Up-to-date provisions on investment protection; retains the controversial ISDS	No chapter on investment protection

Chapter	CPTPP*	EU–Japan EPA**
Government procurement	Extends Government Procurement Agreement (GPA)-type rules to some CPTPP members; commitments GPA plus	Both existing members of WTO GPA; builds on coverage at sub-central government level
Services and investment liberalization	Builds on General Agreement on Trade in Services (GATS); negative listing for coverage; MFN clause; mobility for business (natural) persons; equivalence for professional qualifications; some significant exclusions in Malaysia and Vietnam; "suspensions" remove mining and raw materials; investment screening possible in countries that use it	Builds on GATS; negative listing; positive listing still; MFN clause; mobility for (natural) business persons; provision for mutual recognition of qualifications
Digital trade	Services chapter covers some less controversial e-commerce topics; prohibits data localization; "safe harbour" recognizing different national date protection regulations "suspended"	Mutual Adequacy Arrangement negotiated on data protection
Intellectual property	Builds on Agreement on Trade-Related Aspects of Intellectual Property Rights (TRIPS); reflects US preferences on pharmaceuticals	Builds on TRIPS; stronger protection for geographical indications
Sustainable development	Core International Labour Organization labour standards; compliance with existing obligations under Multilateral Environment Agreements (MEAs); dispute settlement	Core labour standards and commitments on MEAs and other environmental topics; specific reference to Paris Agreement of UNFCCC; Joint Dialogue with civil society

Notes:

* New Zealand is the depository for applications to the CPTPP. For the text of the CPTPP, see https://www.mfat.govt.nz/en/trade/free-trade-agreements/free-trade-agreements-in-force/cptpp/comprehensive-and-progressive-agreement-for-trans-pacific-partnership-text-and-resources.

** For the text of the European Union-Japan Economic Partnership Agreement, see http://trade.ec.europa.eu/doclib/press/index.cfm?id=1684.

agreement is included in any assessment of origin, thus facilitating regional supply chains. For the CPTPP this is an important feature given the number of economies included. EU PTAs envisage the extension of diagonal cumulation for other countries that conclude PTAs with the EU and use the same rules of origin. For the UK in any CPTPP negotiation, diagonal cumulation spanning the UK–EU–CPTPP would be very important as a means of ensuring that the UK manufacturing and food-processing sectors could build on their existing supply chains across the EU while trading with the CPTPP. Trade facilitation, by promoting efficient customs and border procedures, is also important for supply chains. These are common to both agreements and both essentially aim to implement the WTO Trade Facilitation Agreement. Trade facilitation is also non-preferential; in other words, improvements in customs clearance will tend to favour all traders regardless of whether their home state is a signatory to a preferential agreement.

With regards to non-tariff barriers to trade in goods and agri-food products, there are some important differences in approach that are reflected in the chapters on technical barriers to trade and the sanitary and phytosanitary (SPS) measures. The CPTPP builds on the Asia-Pacific Economic Cooperation Mutual Recognition Arrangement, which encourages mutual recognition of regulatory requirements that are equivalent. The approach is not full regulatory recognition as in the European Single Market but is not that dissimilar to the EU's approach to mutual recognition of conformity assessment in the PTAs it negotiates. The EU approach in the EU–Japan EPA places more onus on the use of agreed international standards as the basis for addressing non-tariff barriers. In terms of the SPS chapters, both refer to existing WTO provisions, which refer in turn to science-based risk assessment. The similarities in text hide some underlying differences between the CPTPP (including Japan) and the EU, over the use of the precautionary principle that the EU insists on. But just as the precautionary approach of the EU and the more purely science-based approach of Japan can coexist under the EU–Japan EPA, so could they under a UK membership of the CPTPP.

In terms of investment protection, the CPTPP incorporates the TPP approach and therefore offers a conventional form of investment protection with Investor State Dispute Settlement (ISDS) provision included.[12] The EU FTA with Japan does not include investment protection, because the EU does not have exclusive EU competence for investment protection. In the case of both the CPTPP and the EU–Japan EPA agreements, investment and services liberalization is based on so-called negative listing, meaning that only those activities explicitly listed as excluded are not liberalized. This provides for greater certainty and transparency. Mining and raw materials are excluded from the investment provisions as one of the 20 areas "suspended" when the USA withdrew in 2017. In both cases there is scope to exclude public services and for the future extension of public services. Both agreements build on GATS commitments on services. As is to be expected the CPTPP members with less developed service sectors, such as Malaysia and Vietnam, exclude some important financial services.

In the important area of the e-commerce and the digital economy, where the UK government sees potential benefits of the CPTPP in shaping emerging rules, the CPTPP "suspends" the so-called "safe harbour" provisions on data protection, whereas the EU and Japan have negotiated a Mutual Adequacy Arrangement.[13] the CPTPP prohibits data localization and therefore appears to lean more towards commercial interests than the right to regulate on this point. Otherwise, both approaches cover the less controversial elements of e-commerce.

Finally, on sustainable development the EU now insists on the inclusion of human rights, climate change (support for the Paris Agreement) and compliance with a range of international labour and environmental standards in its PTAs. These are mostly included in the CPTPP, but there is no reference to the Paris Agreement. The EU–Japan EPA also includes a direct role for civil society non-governmental organizations (NGOs) in the Civil Society Dialogue, which is seen as important by EU and UK civil society.

QUESTIONS IN NEGOTIATING MEMBERSHIP

On leaving the EU the UK is free to negotiate and conclude an agreement on membership of the CPTPP. The questions that would arise in any such negotiation process would be: what are the accession procedures for CPTPP? What would be the commitments in terms of schedules? Who might be potential veto players and how easy would it be to get domestic political support for UK membership in the CPTPP and in the UK?

As noted above, accession to the CPTPP would mean accepting the existing rules. The 11 current CPTPP members have made it clear that they will not reopen the text of the agreement or their existing schedules. Accession negotiations would take the form of a series of bilateral negotiations between the UK and every CPTPP member on the UK's commitments. Unanimity among the existing CPTPP members would then be necessary to approve UK accession. Clearly, this provides any CPTPP member with a veto if it wishes to use it. As the starting point for negotiations would be the UK's most favoured nation (MFN) commitments under the GATT/WTO, there is also scope for a CPTPP member to block approval of the UK schedules for bound MFN tariffs or for revised tariff rate quotas in order to get a UK concession. However, it is to be expected that these issues would be resolved before any serious UK–CPTPP negotiations began. Any UK accession negotiation could also be affected by other countries seeking to join the CPTPP. For example, if South Korea and or Indonesia move to accede, this would enhance the attraction of the CPTPP for the UK, but could result in the UK being moved to "the back of the queue". Any move by a new US administration to rejoin would also be a priority for the CPTPP-11.

The UK would need to negotiate tariff schedules, including the schedules on services and investment as well as those on the entities covered by rules on public procurement. The existing schedules for each of the CPTPP negotiating partners would be at least a firm starting point. From a CPTPP member country's point of view the expectation would be that the UK would offer at least the level of commitment offered by the EU in its FTA, and certainly some CPTPP members would probably seek an improvement on this, especially in sectors such as agriculture.[14]

In terms of the level of support for the UK seeking accession, there have been generally positive statements from the key countries, but this does not necessarily translate into concessions or agreement once the negotiations start. The Australian trade negotiator has, for example, expressed the view that the UK is not part of Asia-Pacific and so it is not obvious why it should be a member of the CPTPP, "obviously it's a statement of fact that the UK is not within the Pacific".[15] Commentators have expressed the view that some countries would be willing to take advantage of the UK's weak negotiating position to press for significant commitments.[16] Within the UK, there is strong opposition to the CPTPP, which is – quite accurately – seen in the same light as the TPP. International civil society advocacy groups' opposition to the Transatlantic Trade and Investment Partnership (TTIP) was extended to the TPP, which was seen as too weak on sustainable development and too strong on investment protection and liberalization of services that threaten public service provision.[17] While there is some business support for a potential British accession to the CPTPP, the service sector and, in particular, financial services do not see the prospects of major gains, with banking restrictions in Malaysia and limited scope for insurance in markets such as Vietnam. Manufacturing industry and trade unions have concerns that low-cost Chinese competition will flow via Vietnam. Trade unions oppose it on the grounds that the CPTPP is weak on labour standards and provides no role for civil society in seeking to ensure effective enforcement of provisions on labour standards. For investors, the "suspension" of mining and raw materials from the coverage of the agreement reduces the benefits. Finally, consumer organizations are concerned that existing food safety, data protection and other standards could be weakened.

AN ILLUSTRATION OF FUTURE TRADE POLICY DECISION-MAKING?

The discussion of Britain's potential membership of the CPTPP is of interest because it may give some clues as to what a Global Britain strategy would involve, but also as an illustration of what the policy-making process might look like. The debate on CPTPP, as well as PTAs with the USA, Australia and New Zealand, came just as the UK government set out its thinking on the process for negotiating FTAs.[18] The approach is an old-style trade policy approach in which the executive consults widely before deciding on the national interest/ preferences. The executive then produces a negotiating mandate and negotiates with limited parliamentary scrutiny. Finally, trade agreements are presented to the legislature as a *fait accompli*, which undermines the ratification authority of the legislature. The legislature can then only veto an agreement if it is willing to undermine the credibility of the country in trade negotiations. This sort of old-style trade policy was conducted by the EU until treaty changes and demands for greater transparency and democratic scrutiny led to changes to what might be called "new style" trade policy-making that is more transparent and provides scrutiny of preference formation, mandate and negotiations, and thus enables real powers of ratification.

The UK government consulted widely on potential membership for the UK of the CPTPP as part of a single consultation exercise on FTAs with the USA, Australia and New Zealand. There were over 600,000 responses and it has been billed as the biggest consultation exercise ever conducted by a UK government on trade. The vast majority of submissions, however, including those on the CPTPP, were common statements drafted by civil society advocacy organizations such as 38 Degrees, which campaigns against trade and globalization. (The 38 Degrees advocacy campaign material simply cut and pasted what it had used to lobby against TPP.)

On the substance of the submissions, there was not a very strong endorsement for the CPTPP. There were substantive submissions from business and trade unions but they numbered more in tens than thousands. The majority of the submissions from industry, as well as those from the Devolved Authorities, stressed the priority of retaining access to the EU market and maintaining existing supply chains across Europe.[19] The service sector, in particular financial services, was not optimistic about enhanced market access prospects. Trade unions opposed CPTPP because of the threat of Chinese imports being channelled through CPTPP members, threats to public services from the provisions on investment and the lack of any formal role for civil society. Environmental NGOs objected to the lack of any specific reference to the Paris Agreement on climate change. Apart from the broad consultation exercise, government policy and preference formation will be advised by a Strategic Trade Advisory Group made up of 14 people appointed by the government to represent a range of interests.[20]

The government's approach to making FTAs also envisages consultations with parliamentary select committees, such as the House of Commons Select Committee on International Trade. There was also a debate in the House of Commons on the proposed negotiations with the USA, CPTPP, Australia and New Zealand, which was attended by about 20 Members of Parliament. There are no formal – that is, statutory – provisions on consultation. The legal basis for negotiating and adopting trade agreements remains, at the time of writing,[21] the so-called "CRaG": the Constitutional Reform and Government Act of 2010. Under this, the government retains the (Royal) prerogative to negotiate and conclude international treaties. The Conservative government sees this as the basis for concluding trade and investment agreements. Under these arrangements there exists no right for the House of Commons to vote on a trade agreement. Its powers are limited to any implementing legislation required as a result of an agreement. As the exercise of such powers would come after an agreement had been negotiated and concluded it does not provide Parliament with the leverage needed to ensure effective scrutiny of the mandate, conduct or conclusion of any UK–CPTPP negotiation.

There is also criticism from the Devolved Authorities (Scotland and Wales in particular), which have argued that the existing, non-formal consultation procedures are inadequate. While not seeking a veto over UK trade policy they are seeking much more effective representation in trade policy and a Joint Parliamentary Committee on trade, including the House of Commons and the three Devolved Authorities.

In summary, the approach to trade policy that has been applied to possible UK membership of CPTPP is "old style" and does not provide the kind of open, transparent and accountable decision-making and negotiation that stakeholders have come to expect in EU trade policy.

CONCLUSIONS

The possible negotiation of UK membership of the CPTPP serves the government's objective of signalling its intention to play a more global role in the world economy. Membership would not create too many difficulties in terms of compatibility between the CPTPP rules and an alignment with European regulations. It is difficult to see any noticeable economic benefits from CPTPP membership in the short to medium term. Nor does negotiating membership shortcut the need to negotiate a series of agreements in order to replicate the preferences the UK has had under EU PTAs. Indeed, negotiating such bilateral "continuity" agreements avoids the risk of one or other CPTPP members blocking accession. When it comes to shaping trade rules, CPTPP is likely to be less important than seeking to shape plurilateral negotiations, such as on e-commerce, in which both the USA and China are participating. Finally, the approach to decision-making and negotiation taken for CPTPP and other PTAs is "old school" trade policy.

Notes for Chapter 10

1. PTA is used here as a more general term. Preferential agreements vary by name and in depth and scope. For example, all recent PTAs involving developed economies also cover investment and a wide range of non-tariff or regulatory questions.

2. The US proceeded to negotiate bilateral agreements with Mexico and Canada and the US Canada and Mexico Free Trade Agreement (USMCA) as well as a "deal" with Japan. It is worth noting that USMCA took over much of the new provisions that had been negotiated for the TPP.

3. See K. Heydon & S. Woolcock, *The Rise of Bilateralism: Comparing American, European and Asian Approaches to Preferential Trade Agreements* (Tokyo: UN University Press, 2009).

4. The EU EPAs have different degrees of coverage, depending on whether the partner is a developing, middle income or developed market economy.

5. See Statement by Secretary of State Liz Truss, Written Statement HCWS96, https://www.parliament.uk/business/publications/written-questions-answers-statements/written-statement/Commons/2020-02-06/HCWS96/.

6. Department of International Trade, "An information pack for the Consultation relating to the UK potentially seeking accession to the Comprehensive and Progressive Agreement for Trans-Pacific Partnership (CPTPP)", https://assets.publishing.service.gov.uk/government/uploads/system/uploads/attachment_data/file/745951/FTA_brochure_CPTPP_FINAL.pdf.

7. See D. Elms & H. Makiyama, *A Roadmap for UK Accession to the CPTPP* (Singapore: The Free Trade Initiative, 2008).

8. Although the Trump administration has adopted an extremely aggressive trade strategy based on forcing trading partners to make concessions bilaterally, there is a general, more widespread view in the USA that new approaches to trade will be needed. A Democratic administration may also face opposition in Congress to re-entering the CPTPP/TPP.

9. If China wanted to promote a regional PTA in the Asia-Pacific region it is more likely to opt for the Regional Comprehensive Economic Partnership, which it has shaped, rather than a US-influenced CPTPP.

10. Elms & Makiyama, *A Roadmap for UK Accession to the CPTPP*.

11. This would require the equivalent of the sustainable impact studies undertaken by the EU for all trade agreements for all the UK market access schedules with all CPTPP members.

12. Some CPTPP members have, however, opted out of the ISDS in side letters, illustrating the importance of detail in any assessment.

13. This actually followed the agreement on the EU–Japan EPA.

14. If the UK were to negotiate a PTA with Australia/New Zealand and Canada beforehand this would probably resolve their demands for access. But other CPTPP members have agricultural exporting interests.

15. See *Business Insider*, 17 February 2019, https://www.businessinsider.com/brexit-trade-deal-australia-says-uk-will-not-be-able-to-join-trans-pacific-partnership-2019-2?r=US&IR=T.

16. See M. Tsuruoka, "Britain in the Trans-Pacific Partnership after Brexit?", *The Diplomat*, 12 November 2019, https://thediplomat.com/2019/11/britain-in-the-trans-pacific-partnership-after-brexit/.

17. See, for example, the responses to the Department for International Trade's consultation on UK negotiations with the USA, CPTPP, Australia and New Zealand. Of the 600,000 submissions all but a few hundred were from "a few" civil society NGOs, which effectively cut and pasted their comments opposing TTIP and the TPP. See DIT Summaries of consultations on CPTPP, July 2019, https://www.gov.uk/government/news/summaries-of-consultations-on-future-ftas-published.

18. Department for International Trade, February 2019, Trade Process for Making FTA after the UK leaves the EU, https://www.gov.uk/government/publications/processes-for-making-free-trade-agreements-once-the-uk-has-left-the-eu.

19. Summary of consultations on the CPTPP, July 2019, https://www.gov.uk/government/consultations/trade-with-thecomprehensive-and-progressive-agreement-for-trans-pacific-partnershipcptpp.

20. Department for International Trade, "The process for making FTAs after the UK leaves the European Union", Policy Paper, 2019, https://www.gov.uk/government/publications/processes-for-making-free-trade-agreements-once-the-uk-has-left-the-eu.

21. The Trade Bill introduced in 2017 has been held up by, essentially, House of Lords amendments seeking stronger scrutiny powers for Parliament, https://services.parliament.uk/bills/2017-19/trade.html.

11

AUSTRALIA (AND NEW ZEALAND) AFTER THE 1973 "GREAT BETRAYAL"

Alexander Downer

AUSTRALIA AND THE "MOTHERLAND"

Great Britain has achieved much over the last 232 years, but one of its finest achievements has been the creation of modern Australia. Although initially established as a penal colony, Australia brought generations of migrants from the United Kingdom (including Ireland) and built a society which in many ways replicated the traditions and values of Britain.

Early Australian settlers did not see themselves as Australians in the way Australians do today, but as Britons living in Australia. It was not surprising, then, that when Great Britain went to war in South Africa at the end of the nineteenth century, Australian regiments rallied to the cause. New Zealanders similarly served in the Boer War. When the First World War broke out, Australia was there from the outset. Just before the war, the then Australian opposition leader and future prime minister, Andrew Fisher, said that his country would defend Britain to "the last man and the last shilling". And so it did. More than 60,000 Australians were killed in the First World War, largely on the Western Front; some 8,800 were killed at Gallipoli. A further 156,000 were wounded, gassed or taken prisoner. As a proportion of the population, Australia had the second highest casualty rate of all Allied countries, although it had not introduced conscription.

It was a similar picture for New Zealand, which was also involved from the outset of the First World War. Out of a population of just over one million, more than 100,000 New Zealanders served as troops and nurses, suffering a 58 per cent casualty rate (16,697 dead), the highest of the war, and another thousand would die of their wounds after the conflict had ended.

On the day Britain declared war on Germany in September 1939, the then Australian prime minister, Robert Menzies, said that "as a consequence

Australia is now at war". And the then New Zealand prime minister, Michael Joseph Savage, similarly declared, "It is with gratitude in the past, and with confidence in the future, that we range ourselves without fear beside Britain, where she goes, we go! Where she stands, we stand!"

In the early part of the Second World War, Australians fought in North Africa. A significant number of Australians also joined the Royal Air Force in both fighter squadrons and in Bomber Command. For the rest, Australia's war was largely with Japan. Many New Zealander soldiers similarly saw service in Greece, Crete, North Africa and in fighter squadrons and bombers.

Not only did Australians of the nineteenth and early twentieth centuries see themselves as Britons living in Australia, but Australia depended on Great Britain for its defence. This only changed in early 1942 with the fall of Singapore, when Australia realized that Great Britain no longer had the capacity to defend it. At that time, Australia turned to America for its security.

Australia's subsequent evolution from Great Britain was social and political. But it also had very substantial economic ramifications. As modern Australia began to develop, its economy needed markets. Given that its economy was primarily agricultural in the early days, those markets were not in what was then impoverished and colonized Asia but in the "motherland". Britain was the main market for the emerging Australian wool, sheep meat and beef industries. It also became the main market for Australian dairy farmers and fruit and vegetable growers. Given that agriculture was such a large percentage of Australia's gross domestic product up until the second half of the twentieth century, Australia depended very much on Great Britain for its livelihood. It was also given easy access to the British market through a system of Imperial preferences.

In the post-Second World War era the pattern of Australian trade began to change. In 1957 Australia signed the historic Commerce Agreement with Japan. That was the beginning of what became a very substantial economic engagement with North East Asia. Through the 1950s and 1960s Australia became an important national resource exporter, and although those natural resources went substantially to Great Britain the markets in Asia began to grow quite rapidly.

This was the background to Australia's reaction to plans by British governments through the 1960s to join the European Economic Community (EEC).

THE UNITED KINGDOM DECIDES TO JOIN THE EEC

Attitudes in Australia were not black and white. At one level, officials in the Australian government could understand why Britain would want to join the EEC. The British economy was struggling while continental European economies appeared to be more prosperous. Giving Britain access to European markets seemed to make good sense from Britain's point of view. Not surprisingly, Australian political leaders were more concerned with the very direct impact Britain's accession to the EEC could have on the Australian economy. There was deep and justifiable anxiety that Australia would lose access to those important British agricultural markets. Already, Australians were concerned about the EEC's infamously protectionist Common Agricultural Policy.

In 1961, the then British secretary of state for Commonwealth relations, Duncan Sandys, made a notorious trip to Australia, New Zealand and Canada. The plan was for the British government to try to reassure those countries which were at the very heart of the Commonwealth that their interests would be protected in negotiations between the UK and the EEC. Sandys was quite well received in New Zealand. Some 35 per cent of all New Zealand exports went to the UK at that time and almost all of those exports were agricultural. The New Zealand government judged that if it made special pleading it might get access even if Australia and Canada did not.

However, when Sandys came to Canberra he was received with sharp scepticism. Not only did the then government of Robert Menzies remonstrate with him about the possible loss of Australian markets in Britain, but the Australian government also worried that this would lead to an unravelling of the Commonwealth. They feared, in particular, that the British government would put its relations with its European partners ahead of its relations with its old Commonwealth family. This was of particular concern to older members of the cabinet, particularly those who had fought in the Second World War not just for Australia, but for Britain. For them, Britain's enthusiasm to join the EEC constituted something of a great betrayal of the old and historic bonds between the English-speaking peoples.

When the Conservative Party unexpectedly won the 18 June 1970 general election and the pro-European Edward Heath became UK prime minister, new negotiations began for British entry into the European Community (EC). Again, the Australian government expressed concern about the economic implications for Australia if the country were not able to negotiate continuing access to British markets for its agricultural products. The same sentiment was more strongly felt in New Zealand, which was much more dependent on British markets than Australia.

Early in the negotiations, the British government – as it had in the 1960s – gave Commonwealth countries assurances that the EEC would allow continuing access to British markets. But the Europeans fiercely resisted this, and the perception in Australia was that the British government was left with a choice: either abandon negotiations with the EEC or abandon any major concessions for Commonwealth countries.

In the event, the British government decided that membership of the EEC was substantially more important than the issue of Commonwealth access to British markets. As a result, the only country which was able to win substantial concessions was New Zealand. It did so because of the New Zealand economy's very heavy dependence on access to the British market. In Australia's case, as seen above, it had developed substantial markets in Asia, particularly for raw materials, and so the potential macroeconomic impact of losing British agricultural markets would be nothing like as severe as would be the case for New Zealand.

1973: THE PAIN BEGINS

When Britain joined the EEC at the beginning of 1973, the pain for Australia and New Zealand began. Britain signed up fully to the Common Agricultural Policy, and the doors for Commonwealth farm exports to Britain, which had substantially fed the country for over a century, were now largely closed. New Zealand did maintain substantial access to the British dairy market for some years but for Australia access to markets was close to terminated. Not surprisingly, this had a very damaging effect on the livelihoods of many Australians. The loss of British agricultural markets was not so much a macroeconomic setback but the effect on specific regions of Australia was, nevertheless, very severe. In the Adelaide Hills, the dairy industry was devastated. Dairy factories were closed and farmers gradually drifted out of the industry. The impact on beef producers was also severe as it was on exporters of fruit and vegetables.

Not surprisingly, the United Kingdom's decision to turn its back on Australian farmers generated anger. The Australian deputy prime minister at the time, Doug Anthony, who was the leader of the conservative Country Party, vowed to become a republican. That was not the reaction of most conservative politicians. They did not blame the Queen. But they did blame the British government. There was a deep underlying sense that the Heath government and the British Parliament had been disloyal to Australia. Australians had rallied to Britain in two world wars and yet Britain had been willing to sacrifice the relationship with Australia in the interests of redirecting its interests from the Commonwealth to Europe.

Worse was to come. The British government during that period decided to introduce restrictions on Australians coming to live and work in Britain. It is so often the case that the little things do the most political damage. At British airports, the Home Office decided to channel EEC citizens in one direction and non-EEC citizens in another. This enraged older Australians who perceived that the British government was giving preferential access to Europeans over their kith and kin from Australia. And, of course, they were.

By the late 1970s, matters had deteriorated further. The conservative Australian government of Malcolm Fraser launched a vigorous diplomatic attack on Brussels over the Common Agricultural Policy. Its argument was that, not only had Australian farmers been cut out of European markets as a result of Britain's accession to the EEC, but the Europeans were dumping artificially generated agricultural surpluses onto world markets, thereby depressing prices in markets that Australia had sought as a substitute for the lost British markets. As if that were not enough, the EEC then introduced a sheep meat regime, restricting Australian exports of sheep meat to Europe. The UK had been a very substantial mutton and lamb market for Australia for generations and now that market was being reduced to a small quota.

The Australian government had had enough. It threatened to ban exports to Australia of European-manufactured aircraft and military equipment. Gradually, minor concessions were made by Brussels and although the Australian government never carried out its threat to ban the import of Airbus aircraft or Mercedes Benz military vehicles, the Europeans never truly assuaged the anger of Australians towards the EEC.

Through these years of diplomatic conflict with Brussels, the Australian government could reasonably have expected the British government to provide it with support, but that support was lame. There is no doubt that the Foreign Office as well as other agencies within the British government gave a much higher priority to harmonious relations with continental Europe than they did to those with Australia and New Zealand. While British civil servants and political leaders would never admit it, Australia was downgraded very substantially in the list of British foreign policy priorities. For example, throughout the life of the Australian government of John Howard (1996–2007) and beyond, not a single British foreign secretary ever bothered to visit Australia, despite frequent visits to the UK by Australian foreign ministers. That fact alone summed up the lack of interest in the bilateral relationship with Australia in official Whitehall circles.

It would be a mistake to conclude that the elites of British politics and the civil service were hostile to Australia. They were not. They were indifferent and did not cultivate the relationship after 1973. This was in stark contrast to the sentiments of the broader British people. They retained a deep affection for Australia and New Zealand and, although these relationships were not an important component of the Brexit debate, British foreign policy, which put relations with Europe ahead of relations with traditional partners and friends in the Commonwealth, was part of the disconnect between British public opinion and the opinion of the elites.

FINDING NEW MARKETS AND MODELS

After 1973, Australia and New Zealand had to look for other markets. This did not happen overnight. It took time. But two things worked for both countries. The first was the substantial growth of the economies of East Asia and the other was the decisions taken by both Australia and New Zealand to open their economies to the outside world and to deregulate their economies internally.

The economic transformation of East Asia began with the growth of the Japanese economy and was followed by high rates of economic growth in South Korea, Taiwan, Singapore and, eventually, China. As these countries developed a new and large middle class, so they acquired a heightened appetite for the types of agricultural products that Australia and New Zealand produced. Australian and New Zealand exporters were aggressive in trying to get into those markets. Since they had lost such substantial markets in Britain, they had to be.

But it was not until the 1980s that both Australia and New Zealand realized that they not only had to change the direction of their trade, but they also had to change the fundamentals of their economic models. Up until then, Australia, in particular, took the view that its manufacturing sector should benefit from high tariffs and quotas, its currency should be regulated, financial markets should be severely constrained by government controls and its labour market centralized through an industrial court system. The agricultural sector was also tightly controlled. Although there were not significant tariffs on agricultural imports, domestic farm industries were tightly regulated and exports were managed through export marketing boards rather than individual companies.

Governments of the centre left and centre right in both Australia and New Zealand decided during the 1980s that this economic model was no longer fit for purpose. They embarked on radical deregulation programmes. In the case of Australia, this meant floating the currency, liberating financial markets, including allowing foreign financial institutions to compete in Australia, abolishing tariffs and quotas and deregulating the farm sector. The consequences of this huge liberalization programme were transformative. Many businesses became uncompetitive and closed down. That did include some aspects of agriculture. But in their places emerged new businesses and new industries which had higher levels of productivity, achieved higher rates of return and generated substantial additional prosperity. The abolition of tariffs and quotas on textiles, clothing and footwear led to the near closure of all of those industries in Australia. Instead, clothing and footwear was largely imported from Asia. But the financial and services sectors grew substantially.

The agricultural sector also went through a significant transformation. Old industries shrank as they became unprofitable without substantial protection and subsidies. New industries, such as the wine industry, emerged without government assistance and prospered in markets all over the world. A good example was the Adelaide Hills. Where once there had been dairy farms heavily supported by a highly regulated regime, those dairy farms were replaced with vineyards. The Adelaide Hills became one of Australia's leading wine-producing regions. Wine production turned out to be a good deal more profitable than dairy farming. As a result, the region was more prosperous because of the restructuring than it would have been without deregulation. Changes of this kind in agriculture occurred throughout Australia. Liberated from the constraints of government control, agricultural investors sought the most profitable enterprises, invested in them and made money.

After around 1995, the only government support available to Australian farmers was, and still is, through drought relief. This is rarely granted and does not constitute a substantial subsidy for the Australian agricultural sector.

By abolishing tariffs and quotas as a domestic economic initiative, the Australian government also made Australia a more attractive trading partner for the rest of the world. Through the 1990s and 2000s the Australian government negotiated several very substantial trade agreements. Those agreements included free trade deals with the United States, China, Japan, South Korea, Singapore and Thailand. Australia also made less liberal but still substantial trade and investment agreements with the Association of South East Asian Nations (ASEAN) in general and with Malaysia and Indonesia individually.

Economic deregulation and liberalization coinciding with trade agreements with major economies helped Australia's economy grow without a recession between 1991 and 2020. It has been an extraordinary period of prosperity unequalled in Australian history. At its heart investment has gone into the most profitable activities, be they in agriculture or other parts of the economy, rather than being directed by politicians into their preferred, but often less productive, sectors.

LESSONS FOR THE YEARS AHEAD

This recent economic history (largely) of Australia, spanning the period from Britain's accession to the European Union until Britain's departure from the European Union, does offer some lessons for the UK in the years ahead.

The UK had, until 2020, been a member of the European Union and its predecessor, the EEC, for nearly half a century. Not surprisingly, the European Union has been an important determinant of the direction of British trade and even investment. The UK has had completely unfettered trade with continental Europe and investment has been able to flow freely between the UK and continental Europe. This stands in contrast to the UK's economic relations with any other part of the world. In every case, UK exporters have to confront tariffs and sometimes quotas and investment is often restricted. Clearly, since accession to the European Union there has been substantial diversion of British trade from other markets to the EU. In 1973 some 9 per cent of British trade was with Australia. By 2020 it was less than 2 per cent. That is hardly surprising. Trade has been diverted away from countries like Australia and focused on the EU and its Single Market.

The UK now has an opportunity to restructure its trade patterns. If the British government is to develop a successful post-Brexit trade policy it will need first and foremost to try to keep trade with the 27 members of the European Union as close as possible to current conditions. That means trade free of tariffs and quotas. Naturally, UK exporters to the EU will be required to meet EU standards and likewise EU exporters to the UK will have to meet UK standards. That is not the same thing as saying EU and UK standards should be identical.

Outside of the EU, the UK will be able to build a variety of bilateral trade agreements and possibly enter into plurilateral agreements. The UK's capacity to enter into bilateral agreements and to do so quickly will depend very much on some hard decisions the UK government will have to make soon. The Australian experience is illustrative.

Australia abandoned trade protectionism primarily because restricting imports and import competition diminished prosperity, economic growth and job opportunities. Abolishing tariffs meant Australians could buy clothing, footwear and motor vehicles more cheaply than had been the case before. That left Australians with more disposable income to spend on other goods, services and activities. The net result was that abolishing tariffs and quotas enhanced economic growth and prosperity, and did not diminish it.

Incidental to this was the fact that it made trade agreements easier to enter into with other countries. The UK can surely learn from this experience.

At the moment, the UK has inherited the relatively protectionist regime of the EU. There are high tariffs on products like footwear, there are huge obstacles to agricultural trade – some of which is almost completely banned – and there are some restraints on trade in services, although services and investment policy largely fall outside the ambit of the EU.

The UK should unilaterally phase out all tariffs and quotas on agricultural products in particular. Not surprisingly, this will elicit cries of anguish from some sectors of British agriculture. The truth is, if they are producing products that the public wants of a quality the public regards as acceptable, then they will have no difficulties with competition from abroad. Furthermore, if the British government is able to strike trade agreements with other countries, British farmers will be able to develop markets elsewhere. The net effect of getting rid of tariffs and quotas on British agriculture will almost certainly be to expand British agriculture, not to reduce it.

The Australian and New Zealand experience does demonstrate that freeing up agricultural trade will lead to some restructuring of investment. Investors will move into areas of agriculture which have better market opportunities worldwide. That is what happened in Australia and New Zealand. If the UK unilaterally decides that it will dispense with tariffs and quotas, albeit over time – thereby giving industry the possibility to adjust – then the UK will find it easy to enter into trade agreements with major economies.

Take Australia and New Zealand as examples. A trade agreement with Australia could be negotiated in a matter of weeks as long as the carve-outs from free trade are limited. In all of its trade agreements, Australia does have some carve-outs from free trade as well as investment. For national security reasons, the Australian government has some limits on foreign investment in sensitive national infrastructure. There are also some constraints on foreign investment in domestic property and government approval is needed for invest-ments of greater than AUS$1 billion in commercial enterprises. Importantly, because Australia is an island with unique flora and fauna, it has strict quar-antine standards. But beyond these constraints, Australia essentially offers free trade to partners.

This free trade approach led to a free trade agreement with the United States being negotiated over a period of just 15 months. The result of that agreement is that since 2006, when it came into force, trade between Australia and the United States has grown by around 70 per cent.

In negotiating trade agreements with major economies, the UK will need to understand that agriculture is always an important issue. This is not just because agriculture is, in and of itself, an important component of most economies. It is also because agriculture has considerable political clout in countries like the United States, Canada and Australia. Politicians in those countries will simply not accept trade agreements which do not enhance agricultural trade.

This should be less of a problem for the UK than many might think. After all, the EU is a major agricultural producer and the UK currently has unfettered free trade with 27 members of the EU. Despite this, the UK has a viable agricultural sector with a surprising degree of diversity for such a relatively small landmass.

These days, trade agreements are not just a bilateral matter. The UK should look to negotiating plurilateral agreements as well. For Australia, one of the best agreements it has entered into is the Comprehensive and Progressive Trans-Pacific Partnership (see Chapter 10). This is the agreement which includes 11 countries from across the Asia-Pacific region, from Canada and Mexico to Australia, New Zealand and Singapore. Importantly, this agreement includes Japan, the third largest economy in the world.

A free-trading UK could reasonably aspire to join this agreement. In doing so it would consolidate free trade through the one agreement with 11 countries.

That would open up huge market opportunities for British exporters including agricultural exporters. In order to join existing plurilateral agreements like the Trans-Pacific Partnership, the UK would, of course, have to accept the broad terms of the existing agreement. As Stephen Woolcock points out in Chapter 10, the existing agreement could not be renegotiated between all 11 partners and the UK in order to satisfy the UK.

There is one other aspect of free trade agreements which is important to understand. That is, such agreements should not include too many other issues. If an agreement is to include complex questions of labour standards, environmental issues and human rights then it becomes much more than a trade agreement. It becomes a comprehensive international agreement. Those sorts of agreements are extremely complex and time-consuming to negotiate. One of the reasons EU agreements take so long to negotiate is that they cover a wide range of issues and do not just focus on trade and investment.

Australia's approach is that issues like the environment are better dealt with on a multilateral basis. For example, climate change is best negotiated through the United Nations.

For Australians and possibly for New Zealanders, the UK's membership of the EU over nearly 50 years has not been particularly beneficial. The UK has downgraded relations with Australia and New Zealand, trade has been diverted away from Australia and New Zealand towards the EU, and Australia and New Zealand have lost substantial markets in Europe. Brexit is an opportunity to reverse that trend, whatever other downsides there may be. Outside of the EU, the UK will almost certainly focus more of its foreign policy on its traditional friends and allies, it will have the capacity to negotiate free trade agreements with countries like the United States, Japan, Australia and New Zealand, and this greater focus by the UK on the world outside of Europe will be welcome.

12

WHAT FUTURE FOR THE CROWN DEPENDENCIES, OVERSEAS TERRITORIES AND GIBRALTAR?

Alastair Sutton

BACKGROUND

The United Kingdom is unique in the United Nations in retaining sovereignty over – and international responsibility for – more than 20 dependent territories.[1],[2] These are spread around the globe, in the Pacific, Atlantic and Indian oceans and in the Caribbean and Mediterranean seas. All, except Gibraltar, are islands. Each has its own constitution and individual relationship with the UK. All enjoy substantial internal legislative, executive and judicial autonomy, with ultimate sovereignty and responsibility for international relations[3] and defence being retained by the UK. Most of these territories have been possessions of the British Crown for hundreds of years. In some cases (Gibraltar and the Falkland Islands), UK sovereignty is contested. The relationship between the Channel Islands and England dates back to 1204, when King John withdrew English troops from Normandy. The Isle of Man came under the English Crown in 1399.

When the UK joined the European Community (EC) in 1973, all the UK territories were consulted and opted for different forms of very limited association with the Communities. Unlike the legal situation of the UK itself as an EU member state, which evolved almost beyond recognition over 46 years, the rules applying to the UK's dependencies remained unchanged in a "time warp" until Brexit in 2020. In the 2016 referendum on the UK's membership of the EU, with the exception of Gibraltar, none of the 510,000 inhabitants of the other territories were allowed to vote. Nonetheless, the legal relationship between the territories and the EU ended, as with that of the UK itself, on 31 January 2020.

Today, almost four years after the referendum and in the midst of the Covid-19 pandemic that will reshape international relations, the territories – like the UK itself – suffer from political, economic and legal uncertainty. They are all, without doubt, "fragile ships floating in a storm-tossed sea".[4]

Because of their *sui generis*, fragmentary and outdated nature, none of the treaty arrangements made for the UK dependencies in 1973 could serve as a model for the UK's future relationship with the EU after 2020. The purpose of this chapter, rather, is to examine the future prospects for these diverse jurisdictions in their relationships with the EU. This requires, however, a brief "retrospective" on their relationship with the EU, through the UK, over the 46 years ending in January 2020.[5]

In essence, all of the UK's dependent territories decided, in 1973, to remain broadly outside the (then) EC. They were then – and they are again now – "third countries" in EU parlance. Thus, although legal severance from the EU is more important for some[6] than others, the effect is far less than for the UK itself.

The Crown Dependencies[7] of Jersey, Guernsey[8] and the Isle of Man were linked to the EU through Protocol 3 to the UK's Act of Accession to the EU in 1972. This legal linkage was "minimalist" in that Article 355(5)(c) TFEU (Treaty on the Functioning of the European Union) provided that the treaties were to apply *only* to the extent necessary to ensure the implementation of the Protocol. Reflecting the view of the Islands in consultations held between 1970 and 1972, the Protocol provided for the free movement of agricultural and industrial goods between the Islands and the EU. It also contained a clause requiring non-discrimination between the Islands and all natural and legal persons of the EU.

In the 46 years since 1973, the Islands' relationship with the EU evolved from relative indifference (1973–90) to a realization that the Single Market project would affect them in fact although not in law, especially in financial services and taxation (1990–2000), and, finally, to the need to "constructively engage" with the EU, notably on tax law and policy, in order to avoid EU sanctions for failing to comply with minimum standards of transparency set by the Organisation for Economic Co-operation Development (OECD) and the EU (2000–20).

The Overseas Territories (OTs),[9] located in the Atlantic, Pacific and Indian oceans, as well as the Mediterranean and Caribbean seas, joined the French, Dutch and Danish territories as "Overseas Countries and Territories" (OCTs) under Part Four of the EC Treaty in 1973. Preferential access to EU markets and financial aid for eligible territories were the main advantage of OCT status. In 2014, a new EU Overseas Association Decision aimed at establishing a partnership for sustainable development between members of the European family. In my view this was never fully accepted by the UK's territories, not least because many of them (Bermuda, the Cayman Islands, the British Virgin Islands and the Turks and Caicos Islands) had levels of economic development higher than that of the EU average as "offshore financial centres" and in any event felt closer to the UK and their regional partners than to "Brussels".[10]

Gibraltar also had a unique status under Article 355(3) TFEU and Articles 28–30 of the UK Act of Accession outside the EU Customs Union.[11] In practice, its most important link to the EU was for trade in financial, gambling and tele-communication services. Although UK sovereignty over "the Rock" has always been contested by Spain, approximately 8,000 Spanish frontier workers cross the border every day to work in Gibraltar. The rights of these EU citizens (safe-guarded by the Protocol on Gibraltar under the Withdrawal Agreement (WA)) will continue to be important in relations between the UK, Spain and Gibraltar for many years to come.

Despite their diversity, all UK territories have a very strong sense of British identity and see themselves as members of a global British family. The churches in the Islands (and in Gibraltar) and the war graves around the world bear testimony to the sacrifices made by the territories in two world wars. Equally, each territory has understandable pride in its history, culture and tradition, perhaps none more so than the Channel Islands, with their unique, customary Anglo-Norman laws, and the Isle of Man, with Tynwald as one of the oldest parliaments in the world. It is, however, precisely the tension between UK sover-eignty and insular autonomy which presents the greatest current challenge. As a former governor of Bermuda said recently, the UK's relations with its territories are "almost fated to be difficult [and] there will always be a degree of confusion and pushing and pulling because the territories differ in what they want from the UK; some want more autonomy from the UK; some want to be closer to the UK; others are happy with the status quo".[12]

THE STATUS OF THE UK'S TERRITORIES UNDER THE WA

Like the UK, the legal relationship of all UK dependencies changed on 31 January 2020.[13] For some territories at least, the impact of Brexit has been described by British parliamentarians as "seismic". And all territories, like the UK itself, have suffered the adverse effects of political and legal uncertainty.[14] Unlike the UK, none had a "seat at the table" during the Treaty on European Union Article 50 negotiations. None (except Gibraltar) was allowed a vote on withdrawal. The territorial scope of the WA mirrors that of the EU treaties on 31 January 2020. Special provisions are however made in Protocols for Gibraltar and the Sovereign Base Areas in Cyprus.

In essence, the WA provides that, during the transition period, the totality of EU law continues to apply in and to the UK (including all its territories),[15] but the UK is excluded from the nomination, appointment or election of members of the EU's institutions, bodies, offices and agencies, as well as participation in decision-making and governance and attendance at meetings. Article 126 WA provides that the transition period is to end on 31 December 2020. Article 132 WA provides that the "Joint Committee may, before 1 July 2020, adopt a single decision extending the transition period for up to one or two years."

In terms of financial and other aid, the most tangible effect of UK withdrawal will be – for eligible OTs – the loss of funding from the European Development Fund (EDF). During 2020, UK OTs continue to be eligible under the 11th EDF which expires at the end of the year. However, Article 132(2)(a) and (b) WA provide that, if the Joint Committee decides to extend the transitional period for one or two years, the UK is to be considered a third country and thus ineligible for funding under the multiannual financial framework and own resources as from 2021. As far as projects financed under the 11th EDF are concerned, Article 152(3) WA provides that the (eligible) OTs "shall benefit from the 11th EDF until its closure and from previous EDFs until their closure".

Here also, the uncertainty caused by Brexit for many small and under-resourced jurisdictions is keenly felt. As the House of Commons Foreign Affairs Committee recommended in 2019, "the UK Government must clarify the UK's future relationship with the EU as soon as possible and analyse the impact on the OTs, what funding will be required to ensure the OTs are not losing out, and what input the OTs will have on the replacement of EU funding in future".[16]

PROTOCOL ON SOVEREIGN BASE AREAS IN CYPRUS

The maintenance of a land border between the UK and the EU after withdrawal is usually discussed in the context of the Irish border. However, the level of detail covered in the Protocol on the two sovereign base areas, as well as that on Gibraltar, shows that this is far from the case. In all three cases, UK withdrawal potentially gives rise to political and security issues, quite apart from trade in goods and services and the free movement of persons.

The Protocol builds on treaties dating back to the establishment of the Republic of Cyprus in 1960, including Protocol 3 of the Act of Accession for Cyprus to the EU, under which EU law applies in the base areas only to the extent necessary to ensure the implementation of this Protocol. After withdrawal, the base areas will remain part of the customs territory of the EU and the Cypriot authorities will continue to administer and enforce a wide range of public services, including in the fields of agriculture, customs and taxation. This is, however, without prejudice to the UK's rights to enforce UK law "in respect of its own authorities or on any immovable property owned or occupied by the Ministry of Defence, as well as any coercive enforcement power".[17] In effect therefore, jurisdiction in the sovereign base areas is henceforth to be shared between the UK and the Cypriot authorities.

Although no doubt a minor matter in substantive terms, Article 1(2) of the Protocol provides for the indefinite application of evolving EU law in the base areas, as well as the continuing jurisdiction of the ECJ.[18] The base areas remain in the EU customs territory, with EU law on customs, indirect taxation,[19] the free movement of goods[20] and the common commercial policy remaining applicable. The Cyprus authorities are responsible for customs formalities (as well as veterinary, phytosanitary and food safety checks),[21] except for military equipment and goods imported for military personnel or other persons travelling on defence or official business. Conversely, in view of the security aspects of the base areas, the UK retains responsibility for checks on persons crossing the external borders of the sovereign base areas.[22]

Finally, the Protocol provides for cooperation between the UK and Cyprus authorities in the implementation of the Protocol, including the avoidance of fraud or other illegal activities which may affect the financial interests of the Union or the UK. The implementation of the Protocol is to be managed by the Specialized Committee established under Article 165 WA, under the overall authority of the Joint Committee.

THE PROTOCOL ON GIBRALTAR

Since the initiation of the Article 50 negotiations, the only member state to have "broken ranks" with a "reservation" to the EU's united approach has been Spain. This was reflected in the Council's negotiating guidelines and in the WA itself, with the special Protocol setting rules applicable during the transition period. In its Preamble, the Protocol confirms that EU law applicable in Gibraltar during UK membership ceased to exist – for Gibraltar as for the UK itself – on 31 January 2020.

The Protocol does not prejudge the outcome, for Gibraltar, of any future agreement between the UK and the EU. It is also "without prejudice to the respective legal positions of the Kingdom of Spain and the UK with regard to sovereignty and jurisdiction". The Protocol aims to minimize any adverse economic and social effects during the transition period for the thousands of Spanish "frontier" workers coming on a daily basis from the adjacent Spanish municipalities. It builds upon the Memorandum of Understanding of 29 November 2018 between Spain and the UK on citizens' rights, tobacco and other products, cooperation on environmental, police and customs matters, as well as the agreement of the same date to conclude a treaty on taxation and the protection of financial interests.

The protection of citizens' rights – especially for frontier workers – is given priority in Article 1 of the Protocol. This Article incorporates Articles 24 and 25 WA dealing with frontier workers and is another example of the indefinite continuation of EU law (and the jurisdiction of the EU institutions) to and in the UK as a third country.[23] As provided for in Article 158 WA, the Court of Justice of the European Union is to have jurisdiction in any case commenced within eight years from the end of the transition period, on any matter covered by Part Two (citizens' rights). In addition, Article 159 WA on the monitoring of the implementation and application of Part Two is to be ensured by the establishment of an independent authority in the UK.

Four other articles in the Protocol deal with air transport law, fiscal matters, the protection of financial interests, environment protection, fishing, police and customs matters. On air transport, negotiations between Spain and the UK on the use of Gibraltar airport are to continue, with both sides notifying the Joint Committee when an agreement is reached.

Similarly, and most importantly from the EU's perspective, both sides are to establish frameworks for full transparency in tax matters, as well as "an enhanced system of administrative cooperation to fight against fraud, smuggling and money laundering and to resolve tax residence conflicts". In essence, this aims at ensuring the continued respect – by the UK and Gibraltar – for the standards established under the G20 and the OECD on good fiscal governance, transparency, exchanges of information and harmful tax practices, as well as the economic substance criteria established by the OECD Forum on Harmful Tax Practices, "which *shall* be complied with in Gibraltar, with a view to Gibraltar's participation in the OECD's Inclusive Framework on base erosion and profit-shifting (BEPS)".[24]

The mandatory nature of these provisions,[25] as well as those on the prevention of illicit trade in tobacco products (a particularly acute problem across the Straits of Gibraltar) and the EU system for tracking and tracing tobacco products,[26] (1) indicates the EU's concern regarding the possible harm to the EU as a result of Gibraltar's law and practice in the field of tax, financial services and economic crime, and (2) provides an indication of the approach to be adopted by the EU in negotiations (if any) on the future relations of other UK territories with the EU.

A specialized committee, in which the EU is to participate, is to be established as a forum for regular discussion, *inter alia*, on waste management, air quality, scientific research and fishing. A similar committee is to be set up for monitoring and coordination on police and customs matters.

The emphasis in the Protocol on issues such as tax and customs fraud, evasion and smuggling reflects the strong concern by EU member states and institutions on the vulnerability of the Union due to Gibraltar's strategic location and the capacity of the UK authorities in Gibraltar to take the action necessary to deal with these issues.

WHAT FUTURE FOR THE UK'S DEPENDENT TERRITORIES WITH THE EU?

At the time of writing (May 2020), three preliminary points need to be made:

1. The Covid-19 pandemic will have a fundamental effect at every level across the globe: for states and other jurisdictions, international organizations as well as the private sector;
2. The intransigent approach of the Johnson government in the negotiations for a future bilateral agreement with the EU, excluding by legislation any extension of the transition period under Article 132 WA, increases the likelihood of a "no deal" outcome at the end of December 2020; and
3. The territorial scope of any future EU–UK agreement is open for negotiation, although the EU's opening position is to *exclude* all the UK's territories.

Against this background, there are three possibilities[27] for the territories:

1. Those territories which consider it in their interest to do so could remain without any formal legal link to the EU;
2. Those territories that wish to maintain a legal relationship with the EU (through the UK) could request the UK to seek an agreement with the EU, on an individual basis,[28] for groups of territories (such as the Crown Dependencies) as was the case between 1973 and 2020 or on a "mixed" basis; or
3. At least some territories could seek to be covered by any UK agreement with the EU, assuming both parties accept such an extended territorial scope of the agreement.

Arguably the most acute difficulty facing the UK and its territories flows from the latter's constitutional autonomy.[29] In law, the UK is responsible for the external relations of all its territories. However, the increasing overlap between internal and external policies – and the fact that, in virtually all policy areas, the territories follow different approaches from the UK – is a serious obstacle to the inclusion of the territories in the UK's agreements or in the negotiation by the UK of legally separate agreements for the territories.

In 2019, the House of Commons reported that "for the OTs, Global Britain is a living reality and they have a valuable part to play in it".[30] The main theme of this chapter is that, particularly as a result of Brexit and the probable effects of the Covid-19 pandemic, both of these propositions are questionable. The UK's capacity and even its political will to promote, defend, represent and negotiate for more than 20 disparate and autonomous islands is already seriously weakened, even before the economic recession that will inevitably follow the Covid-19 crisis.

In 1982, 255 British soldiers died fighting to preserve British sovereignty over the Falkland Islands, 13,000 km from the UK. Today, 1,300 British troops are stationed in these remote islands. And today, nearly 40 years later, the UK–Argentina dispute over sovereignty remains as unresolved as that between the UK and Spain over Gibraltar. UK withdrawal from the EU removes the support of 26 member states for the maintenance of the status quo as regards Gibraltar as well as EU support for the UK in the United Nations as regards the dispute with Argentina.

In 2012, the Cameron administration[31] identified five specific benefits brought to the UK through the OTs:

1. A global presence;
2. A set of strategic assets of current operational and long-term strategic value;
3. Economic and financial opportunities, notably through the international financial centres in the territories;
4. Natural and environmental resources (fisheries, minerals, hydrocarbons and biodiversity);
5. Talent and diversity (students, workers and members of the armed forces).

The 2012 White Paper also identified the benefits brought by the UK to the OTs as being: defence and security, economic and technical assistance, international support and "reputation". For their part, OTs were expected to maintain the rule of law, respect for human rights and integrity in public life, delivering efficient public services and building strong, successful communities.

In 2012 the then UK minister for international security strategy in the Ministry of Defence, Gerald Howarth, said (presciently) that: "We will have to work harder, and in different ways, to advance and protect British interests as the world around us evolves. British OTs play an essential role in furthering those interests."[32]

In 2019, a Parliamentary Committee[33] underlined the need for the territories to be treated more as "partners" of the UK in a rapidly changing world, notably (at that time) as a result of Brexit. Although the committee focused on the OTs, its conclusions could apply equally to the UK's relations with the Crown Dependencies.

A number of OTs,[34] in their evidence to the House of Commons Committee, underlined the adverse impact which the loss of EU funding would have for them. The report concluded that "the UK Government must clarify the UK's future relationship with the EU as soon as possible and analyse the impact on the OTs, what funding will be required to ensure that the OTs are not losing out, and what input the OTs will have on the replacement of EU funding in the future".[35]

In my view, the relationship between the UK and its territories between 2020 and 2050 is not merely a matter of money. Many UK territories (those which are "finance centres") are financially self-sufficient. Rather, the future relationship of the UK and all its territories is intrinsically linked to the UK's political, economic and security role in the world outside the EU. For the UK, the priority now is clearly to finalize its new relationship with the EU. But it is also to replace its role in the EU's partnership agreements with new agreements with the UK's strategic partners around the globe. This will not simply be a "copy and paste" task, but rather lengthy negotiations with seasoned negotiating partners who will all seek a better "deal" (for example in terms of market access for goods, services and investments) with the UK as an independent state, rather than as a member state of the EU.

It is difficult to imagine (practically and legally[36]) that the UK will wish to expend valuable political capital in seeking – at least at the same time – new international relationships for its territories, which have different interests from the UK. It is also doubtful (to say the least) whether the UK's main international partners – any more than the EU itself – have any serious interest in concluding agreements covering the UK's territories.

It may be added that, in May 2020, the economic impact of the Covid-19 pandemic, both on the UK internally and in its international capacity, can only make the effective discharge of the UK's responsibilities for 20[37] or more OTs (all without a vote or representation in the UK Parliament) more challenging, including in representing their interests in relations with the EU. The fact that the OTs are "managed" by the Foreign and Commonwealth Office (FCO) (and by governors nominated by the FCO), while the Crown Dependencies are the responsibility of the Ministry of Justice, appears dysfunctional.[38]

THE FUTURE RELATIONS OF THE UK'S TERRITORIES WITH THE EU: THE END OF AN ERA?

In the absence of any draft texts published by the UK (in contrast to the EU's policy of transparency with a draft text published on 12 March 2020),[39] it is impossible to know precisely what approach the UK will take to the territorial coverage of the future bilateral agreement with the EU. However, in the White Paper published in February 2020[40] the government stated that it would negotiate not only on behalf of the devolved administrations (Scotland, Wales and Northern Ireland) but also: "on behalf of all the territories for whose international relations the UK is responsible. In negotiating the future relationship between these territories and the EU, the UK Government will seek outcomes which support the territories' security and economic interests and which reflect their unique characteristics."[41]

The minister responsible for the OTs (Lord Ahmad of Wimbledon) has stated that, "as we head into the next phase of the negotiations and take up the opportunities afforded by our departure from the EU, including the ability to negotiate our own trade agreements around the world, the continuing priority for the British Government is to ensure that the voices of our OTs are heard – and that your priorities inform our approach to the negotiations every step of the way".[42] The minister did not mention the Crown Dependencies, although their economic importance (and population of around 250,000) matches, if not outweighs, that of the OTs combined. It is crucial that the UK adopts a more coherent and "holistic" approach to its territories, whatever their "internal" constitutional status, in defining its global strategy after Brexit and the Covid-19 pandemic.

Although it is clear that all the UK's territories are reflecting on their future after 2020, none appear to have taken a final decision on the extent to which they wish any future EU–UK agreement to be extended to them. The Channel Islands, for example, have stated that the Islands will be following closely the negotiations in 2020 between the EU and the UK on the future relationship and "will make informed judgments about whether it would be in their interests to request the eventual UK–EU agreement on the future relationship to be extended in whole or in part to the Islands. Any such agreement would of course be subject to the agreement of the UK and the EU27."[43]

In addition, at least as far as the Channel Islands are concerned, agreement has been reached between them and the UK on "customs arrangements which will take effect after the end of the transition period,[44] when the UK and the Islands leave the EU Customs Union" and, crucially, "agreement was also reached with the UK in October 2019 over the extension to Guernsey and Jersey of the UK's membership of the WTO [World Trade Organization] which will also take effect at the end of the TP [Transitional Period]".[45]

As far as the OTs are concerned, which are all monitoring the situation, many have expressed concerns, notably on the continuing legal, political and economic uncertainty, and none have opted clearly for one or other solution on their future relationship with the EU.

In its draft text,[46] the European Commission (following informal consultations with all member states, the European External Action Service and the European Parliament) proposed to *exclude* all UK territories from the territorial scope of the future agreement.[47] The following comments are relevant in this context:

- The Commission's draft was finalized and published in March (2020) after the publication of the UK's White Paper in February. It may therefore be assumed that the EU were aware of the UK's intention to negotiate "on behalf of all territories for whose international relations the UK is responsible" and rejected this approach, at least as a matter of principle on the opening of negotiations.
- The initial attitude of the EU[48] is not surprising given that: the EU has no (obvious) strategic, political or economic interest in entering into bilateral treaty relations with *any* of the UK's territories, either "independently"[49] or through the UK; that many of the more important UK territories have been "problematic" for the EU in the past as "offshore financial centres" or "tax havens"; and that issues arising in or with these non-sovereign jurisdictions of a third country can be dealt with by the EU unilaterally as necessary.
- The year 2020 is not 1973 and there is no incentive now, as there was when the UK acceded to the EC, for member states to accommodate UK requests that are not clearly in the EU's interests.
- Despite the intention of the UK to negotiate "on behalf" of its territories, there would be serious difficulties in reaching agreement with them (jointly or severally) due to the, at one and the same time, narrowness and wide variety of their economic interests, the significant differences between their laws, policies and interests and those of the UK, and the resulting legal difficulties in negotiating, implementing and enforcing agreements with the EU on their behalf.

It is clear that for some territories (the Falkland Islands, Pitcairn, Gibraltar and Anguilla) the loss of preferential access to EU markets has serious implications. For others (Bermuda and the Crown Dependencies), however, there is no legal reason why, in the short term at least, recognition granted by the EU in the form of equivalence decisions should be rescinded.[50]

Similarly, the fact that all UK territories were, in fact if not in law, "third countries" before UK withdrawal, should mean that there is no change in their new status, other than the loss of UK support and influence in the EU institutions.[51] Thus, for example, bilateral tax information exchange agreements between UK territories and individual EU member states are unaffected by UK withdrawal.

THE STATUS OF UK TERRITORIES IN THE UK'S
AGREEMENTS WITH OTHER THIRD COUNTRIES

In parallel to negotiations with the EU, the UK has initiated discussions with most third countries previously linked to the UK through trade or partnership agreements concluded by the EU. The United States is an exception, in the sense that there is no comprehensive trade agreement between the USA and the EU. For all the reasons set out above (especially the constitutional autonomy of the UK's territories), it is unlikely that either the UK or its partners would wish to delay or complicate negotiations for their new partnerships over the extension of the territorial scope of these agreements. At best – and assuming the political will exists in the UK, in third countries and in the territories themselves – negotiations on behalf of the territories with, for example, the United States, will only be considered once the UK's relationship with the EU and its most important third countries is settled.

CHALLENGING TIMES AHEAD FOR THE UK AND ITS TERRITORIES

The combined effect of Brexit, the Covid-19 pandemic and a probable global recession will seriously handicap the UK's ambitions to re-establish itself as a global power outside the EU. There is a real risk that *all* the UK's territories, whatever their constitutional status, will suffer "collateral damage" in this situation.

As indicated at the outset, the UK is unique in the world in having responsibility for more than 20 OTs. These are geographically, strategically, constitutionally and economically diverse. Gibraltar and the Falkland Islands present unresolved issues of sovereignty. Each territory is, to a greater or lesser extent, constitutionally autonomous, linked to the UK only through the Crown, and not Parliament. None, however, apparently seeks to exercise its right to self-determination and seek independence. No single territory or group (not even the Channel Islands) offers the potential for reciprocal interest for most major international partners. Many, labelled as "offshore financial centres", have a track-record of conflict with the EU (and, in certain cases, with the UK itself) in tax, financial services, corporate transparency and the fight against international economic crime.

A recent illustration of the constitutional conflict and uncertainty between the UK and its dependencies is the imposition of mandatory transparency requirements for public registers of beneficial ownership of companies in all UK OTs, against the will of some.[52]

The UK itself has left the EU "under a cloud". It is sometimes forgotten that the UK's decision to withdraw from the EU in the 2016 referendum followed

156

more than 40 years of equivocation (at best) on the European project, illustrated by the 1975 referendum and a series of "opt-outs" from core EU policy areas. The absence of preparation for withdrawal, as well as of alternatives to EU membership, and the repeated delays and uncertainties in the Article 50 process, have left their mark among the 27 member states and the institutions. In addition, the lack of preparation and intransigence of the UK in the ongoing negotiations for a new partnership have added to an atmosphere of frustration and mistrust in the EU. The refusal of the EU to contemplate (at this stage at least) the negotiation of new relationships with the UK's territories must be seen against this background.

Finally, the establishment of a comprehensive new framework relationship with the EU for the UK itself (not to mention its territories) now seems unlikely for some time (possibly years) to come. Recovery from the Covid-19 pandemic will in any event take priority, for the UK, for the EU and for their partners around the world. Against this background, the political and legal uncertainty that has characterized the UK's relations with Europe for more than 70 years is unlikely to be removed soon.

Given this backdrop, the UK's political and legal responsibility (or "duty of care") for its worldwide "family" of dependent territories will be greater than ever in the 30 years till 2050. A more proactive approach to "constructive global engagement" on both sides (but especially in London) is needed now that the links with the EU have been removed. Although the diverse (and sometimes vague) constitutional relationship between the UK and its territories is rooted in history (including the process of decolonization since 1947), it may be questioned whether, in 2020, this contributes to the political and legal certainty that trade and investment need. This issue, in my view, is not unrelated to the unresolved issue of the status of Northern Ireland (and the possible reunification of Ireland) which, like Gibraltar and the Falkland Islands, has been highlighted by Brexit, as David Phinnemore discusses in Chapter 13.[53]

Consideration should be given to a more coherent approach, whereby all UK territories – whatever their different historical, political and constitutional backgrounds – are treated "under one roof" in London.[54] Whatever the differences between their constitutional links with the UK (especially important in the case of the Crown Dependencies), for the outside world (including the EU) they are all objects and not subjects of international law, under UK sovereignty. Thus, the "modalities" for international engagement by, or on behalf of, the territories – notably the issue of "entrustments" – needs urgent consideration. This requires deliberation about the principle and scope of possible entrustments for individual jurisdictions, and then securing the recognition of these by potential international partners, including the EU.

In light of the limited resources of many dependencies, greater consideration could be given to how they might cooperate more effectively in the defence and promotion of their common interests. In this context, the role of the UK Overseas Territories Association and the possible extension of its membership to include the Crown Dependencies might be considered. The success of the Channel Islands Brussels Office as the "eyes and ears"[55] of Jersey and Guernsey with the EU's institutions might be seen as a model for the UK's 20 or more territories, not only in Brussels but also in London and other key capitals around the world. Likewise the representative office of Gibraltar in Brussels.

The effective representation of the diverse interests of more than 20 autonomous jurisdictions in international governmental or non-governmental organizations is also crucial. Many territories already have "independent" status in organizations such as the Global Forum in the OECD, the International Association of Insurance Supervisors, the International Organisation of Securities Commissions, the Financial Action Task Force and the Basel Group of Off-Shore Banking Supervisors. However, especially in the wake of the Covid-19 pandemic, the work of UN Specialized Agencies such as the World Health Organization, the WTO and the World Customs Organization (WCO) will have a new priority, including for the UK's territories.

For the hard-pressed UK government, understanding the diverse needs of its territories for international engagement and then representing, promoting and defending their interests will pose a significant challenge in the years ahead. This is the case not only for UK ministries in London, but also for UK embassies and missions abroad, which – for the most part – had not, until 2016, seen it as part of their function to represent the UK territories in the states or international organizations to which they are accredited.[56]

AN UNCERTAIN CONCLUSION

Against this background, there is no clear answer to the question posed in the title of this chapter on what the future holds for the UK's unique global patrimony that its 20-odd[57] territories represent. It is not clear, either, that the UK government, or even the territories themselves, have a clearly defined and agreed strategy for their cooperation over the next 30 years or more. Such a strategy is vital if the territories are not to be mere "relics of Empire",[58] but genuine partners of the UK in areas such as climate change, maritime safety and conservation and biodiversity, not to mention the UK's aspirations in global security.[59]

It would be unfortunate if the UK's withdrawal from the European project were to prove the latest step in a process involving, *inter alia*, global disengagement through decolonization, a weakening of the relationship with the United States,[60] "unfinished business" in Ireland[61] and the fragmentation of the "United" Kingdom. The way in which the UK discharges its "duty of care" in resetting its relationship with its wider "family" will be one test of its ambition to become "Global Britain".[62]

Notes for Chapter 12

1. My previous papers on the relationship of the UK's dependent territories with the EU include "Jersey's changing constitutional relationship with the EU", *Jersey Law Review* 9:1 (2015), https://www.jerseylaw.je/publications/jglr/PDF%20Documents/JLR0502_Sutton.pdf; and "Relics of empire or full partners of a new global United Kingdom? The impact of Brexit on the UK Crown Dependencies and Overseas Territories", *Constitution Society* (2018), https://consoc.org.uk/wp-content/uploads/2018/06/Alastair-Sutton-Relics-of-Empire-or-Full-Partners-of-a-New-Global-United-Kingdom.pdf.

2. I use the term "dependent territories" here generically, although in law, with the exception of the Crown Dependencies, the term "Overseas Territories" replaced the term "dependent territories" as a result of the British Overseas Territories Act 2002. The term "colony" in relation to the OTs has never been abolished but is not used nowadays.

3. See later in the chapter for the extent to which a degree of responsibility for external relations has been delegated to certain dependencies, especially – in recent years – in areas such as taxation.

4. An expression used by the Japanese government in the 1970s, during its trade conflicts with the EC and the United States, to describe Japan's external dependence on imports, notably of energy products. The EU's 2013 Overseas Association Decision also notes (preamble paragraph 23) that "the OCTs are fragile island environments requiring adequate protection".

5. An exhaustive analysis of these unique treaty arrangements is set out in my paper, "Relics of empire or full partners of a new global United Kingdom?"

6. Notably the poorer OTs in receipt of EU financial assistance and preferential access for their exports of, for example, fish products.

7. Total population is around 250,000.

8. Including Alderney and Sark.

9. Anguilla (population 15,000), Bermuda (64,000), British Antarctic Territory, British Indian Ocean Territory (4,000 military personnel), Cayman Islands (65,000), Falkland Islands (3,000), Gibraltar (32,000), Montserrat (5,900), Pitcairn (70), St Helena (Ascension and Tristan da Cunha) (6,600), South Georgia and the South Sandwich Islands (30), Sovereign Base Areas of Akrotiri and Dhekelia (15,700 mainly military personnel and families), Turks and Caicos Islands (56,000) and the British Virgin Islands (28,000). Total population around 290,000.

10. It is also likely that the Euroscepticism which characterized the UK's EU membership "rubbed off" on many of its territories, perhaps especially in the Crown Dependencies, although not Gibraltar.

11. Similarly, EU indirect tax and other areas of EU law, such as the free movement of goods and the common agricultural policy, did not apply in or to Gibraltar.

12. House of Commons, Foreign Affairs Committee, "Global Britain and the British Overseas Territories: resetting the relationship", HC 1464 (2019), 6.

13. OJ C 66/1/1 of 19.2.2019.

14. House of Commons, Foreign Affairs Committee, "Global Britain and the British Overseas Territories: resetting the relationship", HC 1464 (2019), 5.

15. Article 3 WA.

16. House of Commons, Foreign Affairs Committee, "Global Britain and the British Overseas Territories: resetting the relationship", HC 1464 (2019), 23.

17. Protocol Article 13.

18. See also Article 12 on supervision and enforcement.

19. Protocol Article 3. Tax exemptions apply to goods imported for use by the UK armed forces or civilian staff accompanying them, or for supplying messes or canteens.

20. As set out in Articles 34–6 TFEU.

21. Protocol Article 6.

22. Protocol Article 7.

23. As indicated above, the other "indefinite" provisions are those dealing with the Irish border, the Sovereign Base Areas in Cyprus, and the provisions in Part Three of the Withdrawal Agreement on Separation Provisions.

24. Article 3 (2) of the Protocol, my emphasis.

25. As well as those aimed at preventing and deterring the smuggling of alcohol and petrol.

26. Article 3 (3) provides that the "UK shall ensure that its ratification of the Framework Convention on Tobacco Control (2003) and the Protocol to eliminate Illicit Trade in Tobacco Products (2012) is extended to Gibraltar by 30 June 2020".

27. These are developed in more detail in my paper, "Relics of empire or full partners of a new global United Kingdom?"

28. For purely practical (as well as political) reasons, this seems unlikely.

29. Under UK constitutional law, this is more developed for the Crown Dependencies than for the OTs. However, the internal autonomy combined with the non-sovereign status of *all* the UK's territories raises serious difficulties for them and the UK itself in representing their international interests.

30. House of Commons, Foreign Affairs Committee, "Global Britain and the British Overseas Territories: resetting the relationship", HC 1464 of 21 February 2019.

31. The Overseas Territories, Security, Success and Sustainability (White Paper), June 2012, Cm 8374.

32. *Ibid.*, 23.

33. House of Commons, Foreign Affairs Committee, "Global Britain and the British Overseas Territories: resetting the relationship", HC 1464.

34. St Helena, Gibraltar, British Virgin Islands, Falkland Islands, Cayman Islands and the Turks and Caicos Islands.

35. House of Commons, Foreign Affairs Committee, "Global Britain and the British Overseas Territories: resetting the relationship", HC 1464, 21 February 2019, 31.

36. Given the legislative, executive and judicial autonomy of all the UK's territories (including, especially in this respect, the Crown Dependencies), requiring separate consideration for these territories in negotiations with partners such as the United States, Australia, New Zealand, Canada, Brazil, India and other major partners.

37. I include, for these purposes, the five Crown Dependencies in this number.

38. In addition, unlike their French and Danish counterparts, none of the UK's territories are represented in the UK Parliament. See further, House of Commons, Foreign Affairs Committee, "Global Britain and the British Overseas Territories: resetting the relationship", HC1464, (2019), 7–17, The OTs and the FCO and the OTs and Parliament.

39. Task Force for Relations with the United Kingdom (UKTF) (2020) 14.

40. The Future Relationship with the EU – The UK's Approach to Negotiations, CP211, February 2020, paras 10–11.

41. *Ibid.*, 11.

42. Lord Ahmad & C. Pincher, "A post-Brexit comment", *The Bermuda Gazette*, 30 January 2020.

43. "The future relationship with the EU: the UK's approach to negotiations", CP211, February 2020, 11.

44. Note, however, that even during the transition period, as has been the case throughout the UK's membership of the EU, the Crown Dependencies have been a part of the EU's customs union by virtue of the terms of Protocol 3 to the UK's Act of Accession.

45. Press notice issued by the Channel Islands Brussels Office on the Channel Islands and the EU following the UK's withdrawal (Brexit) on 1 February 2020.

46. Draft text of the Agreement on the New Partnership between the EU and the UK, 12 March 2020, UKTF (2020) 14.

47. Draft Article FINPROV. 1 – territorial scope. The territories specifically referred to are Gibraltar, the Crown Dependencies, the Sovereign Base Areas of Akrotiri and Dhekelia in Cyprus and Anguilla, Bermuda, the British Antarctic Territory, the British Indian Ocean Territory, the British Virgin Islands, the Cayman Islands, the Falkland Islands, Montserrat, Pitcairn, Saint Helena, Ascension and Tristan da Cunha, South Georgia and the South Sandwich Islands and the Turks and Caicos Islands.

48. I use the term "EU" on the basis that the draft agreement published by the European Commission in March 2020 had been the subject of consultation with all member states, as well as with the European External Action Service and the European Parliament.

49. For example, as in the past the EU entered into bilateral textiles agreements with Hong Kong and Macau.

50. These include decisions on insurance and audit for Bermuda; audit for the Cayman Islands; and audit, credit institutions and investment firms for Jersey, Guernsey and the Isle of Man.

51. This was, in any event, not always forthcoming, especially in areas such as tax, financial services and the fight against international crime; the territories laws and policies conflicted with those in the UK.

52. In 2018, the UK Sanctions and Anti-Money Laundering Act was extended – without the consent of some – to all of the UK, but, due to their greater constitutional autonomy, not to the Crown Dependencies.

53. The same may be said as regards the future "devolved" status of Scotland and Wales, highlighted both by Brexit and the Covid-19 pandemic.

54. As indicated above, currently the Crown Dependencies are the responsibility of the Ministry of Justice (although not in any way related to the justice system) and the other territories are dealt with by the FCO.

55. It would be unrealistic to expect a private sector body such as the United Kingdom Overseas Territories Association to represent or speak on behalf of individual territories.

56. Such as the OECD, WTO, WCO, World Health Organization and other organizations in the UN "family" of specialized agencies.

57. Depending on how they are counted.

58. Recognizing that this term is not an accurate description of the Channel Islands and the Isle of Man.

59. For example, in the Asia-Pacific region to address the expansionist policies of China in the region.

60. Notably as a result of participation in conflicts in Iraq and Afghanistan.

61. With Brexit having highlighted the potential difficulties on the border with Ireland, in addition to the disputes with Spain and Argentina on sovereignty over Gibraltar and the Falkland Islands.

62. House of Commons, Foreign Affairs Committee, "Global Britain and the British Overseas Territories: resetting the relationship", 2019.

13

THE PROTOCOL ON IRELAND/NORTHERN IRELAND: A FLEXIBLE AND IMAGINATIVE SOLUTION FOR THE UNIQUE CIRCUMSTANCES ON THE ISLAND OF IRELAND?

David Phinnemore

Negotiating its withdrawal from the European Union was a painful, protracted process for the United Kingdom. It was also a process that saw it concede ground to the EU on most withdrawal issues. Unsurprisingly, the EU was often presented in much of the UK media and particularly by supporters of Brexit as inflexible and short-sighted. There were accusations that it was not only refusing to show any appreciation of the UK position, but also intent on "punishing" the UK into leaving. Such accusations overlook the fact that, on the question of Northern Ireland, at least, the EU adopted a position of relative flexibility. Conscious of the challenges that Brexit posed for the island of Ireland, the EU and the UK agreed a dedicated Protocol providing for a set of arrangements unique in the EU's external relations. While the EU is quick to point to the flexibility it has shown in agreeing special terms for Northern Ireland, these are not without their problems for the UK and the EU.

That the Withdrawal Agreement contains a dedicated Protocol on Ireland/ Northern Ireland is due to a range of challenges that UK withdrawal from the EU poses for Northern Ireland and the island of Ireland more generally and, importantly, the EU's and the UK's willingness to respond to these challenges. The willingness was evident as soon as then Prime Minister Theresa May, on 29 March 2017, submitted her letter to Donald Tusk, president of the European Council, notifying the EU of the UK's intention to withdraw, and in so doing setting in motion the Article 50 withdrawal process. That notification recognized the need to pay attention to the UK's "unique relationship" with Ireland and "the importance of the peace process in Northern Ireland". Hence, a "return to a hard border" on the island of Ireland should be avoided and the Common

Travel Area (CTA) between the UK and Ireland maintained. Moreover, the UK had "an important responsibility to make sure nothing is done to jeopardize the peace process in Northern Ireland, and to continue to uphold the [1998] Belfast ['Good Friday'] Agreement".[1]

The EU was of a similar mind. The European Parliament insisted that "the unique position of and the special circumstances confronting the island of Ireland must be addressed in the withdrawal agreement", and urged that "all means and measures" consistent with EU law and the Good Friday Agreement be used "to mitigate the effects" of UK withdrawal on the land border between Ireland and Northern Ireland. It also insisted on "the absolute need to ensure continuity and stability of the Northern Ireland peace process and to do everything possible to avoid a hardening of the border".[2] The European Commission was also concerned about the land border, noting "the particularly sensitive situation that might arise in Northern Ireland" if customs checks were reintroduced.[3] All this was reflected in the European Council's response to the UK's Article 50 notification. In their guidelines for the withdrawal negotiations, EU leaders were clear:

> The Union has consistently supported the goal of peace and reconciliation enshrined in the Good Friday Agreement in all its parts, and continuing to support and protect the achievements, benefits and commitments of the Peace Process will remain of paramount importance. In view of the unique circumstances on the island of Ireland, *flexible and imaginative solutions will be required*, including with the aim of avoiding a hard border, while respecting the integrity of the Union legal order.[4]

What form these "flexible and imaginative solutions" might take was not, however, clear. First, the challenges to which solutions were needed had to be agreed. With the May government's "red lines" including commitments to leaving the Customs Union and the Single Market, a priority question was how could a hardening of the border on the island of Ireland be avoided? The UK being outside the EU Customs Union and the Single Market would respectively require customs as well as regulatory checks and controls, and so physical infrastructure on a border whose invisibility had become a key symbol of the peace process and made a major contribution to reducing the salience of the border question in politics on the island. There was then the question as to how flexible the UK and the EU could be in devising and agreeing a solution. How far was the UK government willing to contemplate some form of differentiated treatment for Northern Ireland and so, according to unionist concerns, potentially weaken its position in the "union"? If the UK government did agree special arrangements for Northern Ireland, how could it resist Scottish government[5] calls for a "differentiated solution" for Scotland, where a larger majority than in Northern Ireland had voted for the UK to remain in the EU? On the EU side, how much flexibility was possible if the integrity of its Single Market and legal order more generally were to be upheld?

No immediate answers were available; these were unprecedented circumstances. But ideas were circulating.[6] Could Northern Ireland be granted some form of "special status" within the EU as some political parties in Northern Ireland were arguing? Could Northern Ireland remain in the European Economic Area? Could it remain in the EU Customs Union? For the moment, the questions remained unanswered. What was clear from the EU's position at least was that the Irish dimension to Brexit was a priority. So, reflecting Donald Tusk's insistence when inviting the EU-27 leaders to their first "Art. 50" European Council that Ireland, alongside people and money, "must come first",[7] it was quickly accepted that addressing the "unique circumstances on the island of Ireland" would be a first-phase issue in the withdrawal negotiations. The UK agreed. Following the formal opening of the withdrawal negotiations, Michel Barnier, the EU's chief negotiator, consequently reported that not only had the EU and the UK established a dedicated "dialogue on Ireland/Northern Ireland", but that their objective for the first phase was to agree "the main principles of the key challenges for the UK's withdrawal as soon as possible", and that this would include "the question of the borders, in particular in Ireland". Barnier also noted that the EU and the UK recognized that the "protection of the Good Friday agreement and the maintenance of the Common Travel Area (CTA) are the most urgent issues to discuss".[8]

THE WITHDRAWAL NEGOTIATIONS

Despite the priority being given to the Irish dimension, progress on agreeing which issues had to be addressed and what potential solutions might be adopted was slow. The UK in August 2017 did publish a "Position Paper" on Northern Ireland and Ireland, but it was generally vague on how to address the four issues it highlighted: upholding the Belfast ("Good Friday") Agreement in all its parts; maintaining the CTA and associated rights; avoiding a hard border for the movement of goods; and aiming to preserve north–south and east–west cooperation, including on energy.[9] This, and UK attempts to leverage the EU's willingness to show flexibility on Northern Ireland to secure concessions on the wider future UK–EU relationship, led to frustration on the EU side. Barnier made this clear when presenting the EU's "Guiding principles for the Dialogue on Ireland/Northern Ireland".[10] Any arrangement for the Irish border would be "unique" and "cannot preconfigure the future [EU–UK] relationship ... What I see in the UK's paper on Ireland and Northern Ireland worries me." Barnier also reminded his audience that there were limits to the EU's flexibility: "Creativity and flexibility cannot be at the expense of the integrity of the Single Market and the Customs Union."[11] The *acquis* had to be upheld.

The lack of progress meant that the European Council in October 2017 was unable to agree on the move to the second phase of the withdrawal negotiations. Instead, the decision was postponed until its next meeting in December of the same year. In the meantime, it was becoming clearer that the only way in which a hardening of the border on the island of Ireland could be avoided, given the UK's red lines of leaving the Customs Union and the Single Market, was for Northern Ireland to remain, in effect, in the EU Customs Union and to maintain regulatory alignment with the EU's Single Market, at least as far as the free movement of goods was concerned. As much was duly recognized by the UK government in December 2017 when EU and UK negotiators eventually produced a "Joint Report" on the state of the negotiations, a process temporarily halted in its tracks by opposition from Northern Ireland's Democratic Unionist Party (DUP) on whose support May's government depended for a parliamentary majority.

The Joint Report acknowledged the need to protect the Good Friday Agreement, with the UK also reaffirming its commitment to protecting north–south cooperation on the island of Ireland and "to its guarantee of avoiding a hard border", and accepting that "[a]ny future arrangements must be compatible with these overarching requirements".[12] As the Joint Report also noted, the UK intention was to achieve these objectives through its future relationship with the EU. It continued: "[s]hould this not be possible, the United Kingdom will propose specific solutions to address the unique circumstances of the island of Ireland". And, if there were no "agreed solutions", the UK would "maintain full alignment with those rules of the Internal Market and the Customs Union which, now or in the future, support North–South cooperation, the all-island economy and the protection of the 1998 [Good Friday] Agreement".[13]

Debate would rage for much of the remainder of the withdrawal negotiations over what paragraph 49 of the Joint Report meant, with the UK government seeking on several occasions, primarily for domestic political reasons, to push back on its commitments. The political difficulties the UK government had on delivering on its commitments tended to overshadow any discussion of what the Joint Report meant in terms of finding "flexible and imaginative" solutions to address the "unique circumstances" on the island of Ireland. In agreeing paragraph 49, the EU was effectively signalling that it was willing, for the sake of avoiding a hard border on the island of Ireland, to allow part of a non-member state to participate in its Customs Union and its Single Market. This would confer on Northern Ireland a unique and – at least in respect of Single Market participation – unprecedented status. The inclusion of part of a non-member state in the EU customs territory had a precedent: Jungholz and Mittelberg in Austria from 1968 until Austria's accession to the EU in 1995. Further evidence of "imagination" and "flexibility" on the part of the EU came in its willingness to forego the asserted indivisibility of the four freedoms of the internal market and grant Northern Ireland continued access for goods alone.

Whether such an unprecedented arrangement would have to be put in place would depend on whether the UK could come up with the "specific solutions" envisaged in the Joint Report. It did not. The Commission Task Force for the withdrawal negotiations therefore sought to convert what had been agreed in the Joint Report into a draft withdrawal agreement. A first draft was published on 28 February 2018 and included a draft Protocol on Ireland/Northern Ireland with what became known as a set of "backstop" arrangements to address the "unique circumstances" on the island of Ireland and in particular avoid a hard border. They would only enter into force if the still-to-be-negotiated future UK–EU relationship failed to deliver the same outcomes.

So, under this proposed "backstop", Northern Ireland – but not the rest of the UK – would remain part of the EU's custom territory and retain access through "a common regulatory area" and continued alignment with the relevant – but as yet unspecified – *acquis* to the EU Single Market for goods, including agricultural products (but excluding fish).[14] EU legislation on value-added tax and excise as well as state aid would continue to apply in Northern Ireland, as would EU rules allowing for the continued functioning of the single electricity market on the island of Ireland. Certain environmental legislation would also continue to apply.

And it was envisaged that, in addition to having a UK–EU Specialized Committee for the Protocol and a Joint Consultative Working Group, the UK in respect of Northern Ireland would be granted an EU decision-shaping role of sorts through invitations to attend "exceptionally" and on a "case-by-case basis" comitology committees as well as meetings of Commission expert groups and "other similar entities, or of bodies, offices or agencies". Overall responsibility for the implementation of the Protocol would be in the hands of a UK–EU Joint Committee. Any disputes relating to EU law would be referred to the European Court of Justice (ECJ).

Although the UK government accepted the principle of the backstop, as well as certain drafted provisions on maintaining the single electricity market on the island of Ireland, state aid, continued north–south cooperation and the Specialized Committee, the proposed common regulatory area was rejected.[15] There was also opposition to the idea of Northern Ireland remaining part of the EU customs territory since this would require checks and controls on the movement of goods between Great Britain and Northern Ireland: a "border in the Irish Sea". Opposition was most vocal among those unionist political forces in the UK who believed that such a border threatened the integrity of the UK internal market and indeed Northern Ireland's position within the UK. The fact that the May government's survival since the 2017 election depended on the support of a DUP implacably opposed to any differentiated treatment of Northern Ireland, at least as regards the terms of withdrawal from the EU, meant that an alternative form of backstop had to be found. The only way to minimize the checks and controls in the Irish Sea while avoiding a hard border on the island of Ireland was for the backstop to include the UK in a customs union with the EU. Such an arrangement was eventually conceded by the EU, and the withdrawal negotiations concluded.[16]

But the May government was unable to secure domestic parliamentary approval for the Withdrawal Agreement. And the main reason was the back-stop. However, as became increasingly clear during the course of 2019, the key objection was less the differentiated treatment that the backstop arrangements would mean for Northern Ireland, but more the fact that if the backstop entered into force it would tie the UK as a whole into a customs union with the EU. Consequently, the UK would not have the freedom to pursue an independent trade policy, a key demand of many pro-Brexit MPs. Pro-Brexit insistence on an independent UK trade policy trumped the unionist cause. There were also concerns – voiced in particularly by the DUP – that the backstop arrangements contravened the principle of "consent" in the Good Friday Agreement. With May eventually resigning following repeated failures to secure a parliamentary majority for the Withdrawal Agreement, it was left to the new prime minister, Boris Johnson, to see if he could deliver on his call to "ditch" the "undemocratic" backstop through a renegotiation of the Withdrawal Agreement.

With both the UK and the EU keen to avoid a "no deal" Brexit, agreement was reached in October 2019 on a revised Protocol on Ireland/Northern Ireland. Johnson was certainly able to claim that the backstop had gone; with the revised Protocol,[17] the UK was no longer committed to a customs union with the EU if the future UK–EU relationship did not deliver on avoiding a hard border on the island of Ireland. The reason was simple: in exchange for dropping the UK-wide Customs Union with the EU, Johnson had agreed that the Protocol's differentiated arrangements for Northern Ireland would be the default position at the end of transition. The backstop had become a "frontstop", and irrespective of the outcome of the negotiations on the future UK–EU relationship, Northern Ireland would in effect remain part of the EU's customs territory and Single Market for goods. Despite Johnson's insistence to the contrary, there would therefore be customs checks and regulatory controls on goods moving across the Irish Sea from Great Britain to Northern Ireland.[18] Moreover, in the absence of a comprehensive UK–EU free trade agreement, there would also be tariffs.

As with each of the previous versions, the revised Protocol on Ireland/ Northern Ireland eventually agreed by the EU and the UK in October 2019 attracted vocal opposition from the DUP. Other political parties in Northern Ireland and business groups, previously content with May's "backstop" version of the Protocol, albeit welcoming the fact that the UK would not be leaving the EU without a deal, also voiced their concerns. With Johnson securing a majority in the December 2019 general election, however, his government was no longer dependent on the DUP for a parliamentary majority and was able largely to ignore the concerns being voiced, particularly in Northern Ireland. The Withdrawal Agreement was duly approved by a majority of MPs in votes in December 2019 and January 2020, and the UK left the EU on 31 January 2020.

THE RESULTING PROTOCOL

Viewed from the perspective of European integration, the Protocol on Ireland/ Northern Ireland agreed as part of the Withdrawal Agreement can be regarded as a flexible and imaginative solution to address the challenges posed by the UK's withdrawal from the EU to the "unique circumstances" on the island of Ireland. The Protocol – assuming its effective implementation – will avoid a hard border on the island of Ireland and the physical border will remain as is, that is, invisible and only marked by changes in road markings and the occasional, often vandalized, "Welcome to Northern Ireland" sign.

Goods, at least, will continue to move freely on the island. And, as such, producers in Northern Ireland have been granted privileged access to the EU internal market for almost all goods, including agricultural goods. The one exception is fish. This has generally been welcomed. However, to avoid any physical hardening of the border on the island of Ireland, the external border of the EU Customs Union and internal market has simply been placed, somewhat controversially, in the Irish Sea, and so within the UK, thus threatening to disrupt the UK internal market. For many, particularly unionists, this further weakens Northern Ireland's position in the UK. For many businesses it will mean additional costs, the consequences of which – both for economic activity generally and more specifically in terms of increased prices for consumers – remain to be seen.

These are two sources of criticism of the Protocol. Another is concerned far less with the constitutional implications of the Protocol for the future of the UK and Northern Ireland's economic and social well-being. Instead, the criticism is focused on the lack of imagination and flexibility shown in the Protocol. In various respects, the Protocol is a minimalist and suboptimal response to the challenges that UK withdrawal from the EU poses for the unique circumstances on the island of Ireland. It focuses on the absolute minimum of what is required to avoid a hard – primarily physical – land border. The free movement of services, however, goes. This clearly calls into question the extent to which the Protocol delivers on the Joint Report's commitment to find solutions that support the "all-island economy". Indeed, the reference to such a commitment in the "back-stop" version of the Protocol agreed with the May government was subsequently dropped for the revised version agreed with the Johnson government.

The free movement of people will also no longer apply. UK and Irish citizens will be able to move freely across the border due to the CTA. Indeed, the Protocol expressly provides for the UK and Ireland to "continue to make arrangements between themselves relating to the movement of persons between their territories". However, free movement does not apply to non-Irish EU citizens. Their access to the Northern Ireland labour market will be determined by UK policy. This brings uncertainty for cross-border workers. It has also raised serious concerns for employers of seasonal workers in Northern Ireland. Also, although those resident in Northern Ireland who hold Irish citizenship – a birth right under the Good Friday Agreement – will continue to be able to exercise certain EU citizenship rights elsewhere in the EU beyond Ireland, those residents who have not, prefer not or cannot avail of such a right to Irish citizenship will not have those rights.

Other features of the Protocol also suggest a lack of either imagination or flexibility or both on the part of the UK and the EU in agreeing its content. Whereas Northern Ireland will remain subject to a significant amount of the internal market *acquis*, with future amendments and replacements automatically applying, it has no formal involvement in their adoption at EU level or in UK–EU decisions in the Joint Committee on the inclusion of new EU legislation in the Protocol. Any formal influence for Northern Ireland will be through the UK government and the UK–EU bodies responsible for the implementation of the Protocol; and for these a Northern Ireland presence relies on an invitation to participate from the UK government. Even the dedicated Specialized Committee does not automatically provide for the involvement of Northern Ireland officials. The same applies to the Joint Consultative Working Group, the forum for information exchange on forthcoming legislation relevant to the Protocol that was agreed instead of the decision-shaping role of sorts provided for in the initial draft of the Protocol. Invitations to comitology and other committee meetings as well as those of EU agencies never made it to the final text. The EU was concerned that UK officials attending in respect of Protocol-related issues would exploit their presence to pursue wider UK interests.

A further criticism of the Protocol is that it is essentially a static arrangement with limited scope for revision or expansion except through the wider

UK–EU relationship. This reflects the fact that, as originally conceived, the Protocol contained "backstop" provisions that would only come into force if the still-to-be-negotiated post-transition UK–EU relationship did not deliver on the commitments contained in the Joint Report. And, even then, the arrangements were intended to be temporary. That all changed with the 2019 revision of the Protocol and its shift to being a "frontstop" and potentially the basis for permanently differentiated treatment of Northern Ireland within the UK–EU relationship.

However, no provision was made for an amendment mechanism or an "evolution" clause, as often found in agreements that create such a close relationship as part of the EU's external relations. The Withdrawal Agreement does allow the Joint Committee to adopt, during the four years after transition, "such amendments … necessary to correct errors, to address omissions or other deficiencies, or to address situations unforeseen when [the] Agreement was signed". However, early EU assessments regard this as a mechanism for addressing technical issues and not a general enabling provision. The only enabling clause in the Protocol concerns, as noted, further UK–Irish measures on the CTA. However, Article 4 of the Council Decision on concluding the Withdrawal Agreement does allow the Council, on "a duly justified request" from the Irish government, to authorize Ireland "to negotiate bilateral agreements with the United Kingdom in areas of exclusive competence of the Union" where an agreement "is necessary for the proper functioning of the arrangements set out … in the Protocol on Ireland/Northern Ireland".[19] The anticipated scope of such agreements is not indicated, and again the focus may be on addressing technical issues. However, the provision is striking in that it demonstrates a willingness on the part of the EU potentially to consider additional flexibility around the *acquis* to ensure the Protocol can deliver on its objectives on the island of Ireland.

HOW FLEXIBLE? HOW IMAGINATIVE?

A fundamental reason for the Protocol not delivering more in terms of flexibility and imagination was the absence of UK "asks". Indeed, UK opposition to the differentiated treatment of Northern Ireland, an opposition that only hardened following the 2017 general election and the May government's reliance for a parliamentary majority on the support of the DUP, meant that it barely engaged with the idea of pursuing "flexible and imaginative solutions" unless they applied to the UK as a whole. Even when it eventually accepted that there would have to be some differentiated treatment, the UK government was desperate to keep that to an absolute minimum and to avoid any opportunities for the Protocol and the arrangements it established to be used to further any differentiated treatment, even where that might be in the interests of Northern Ireland and in the spirit of commitments made in the Joint Report.

One example relates to whether Northern Ireland – in effect, part of the EU's Customs Union – should be able to benefit from access to the markets of those third countries with which the EU has trade agreements. The question has yet to be resolved, but the strengthening – at the UK's insistence – of the language in the Protocol around Northern Ireland being part of the UK customs territory has reduced the scope for such access being secured. Northern Ireland producers may have to rely just on access to the UK's trade agreements with non-EU countries, although that could be complicated by its position vis-à-vis the EU.

A second example concerns north–south cooperation on the island of Ireland. Here the role of the Protocol is to "maintain the necessary conditions for continued … cooperation" (Article 11). Yet, despite an extensive mapping exercise to consider the implications of Brexit,[20] the Protocol provides no detail beyond listing areas of cooperation (that is, environment, health, agriculture, transport, education and tourism, as well as in the areas of energy, telecommunications, broadcasting, inland fisheries, justice and security, higher education and sport). There is reference neither to the content or findings of the mapping exercise nor to the substance of the cooperation and how it shall be maintained. Moreover, the UK government's reluctance to see implementation of the Protocol as potentially facilitating further north–south cooperation was evident during ratification of the Withdrawal Agreement. Under the European Union (Withdrawal Agreement) Act 2020, UK ministers are precluded by law from agreeing in the Joint Committee to any recommendation altering arrangements for north–south cooperation even where the recommendations come from the North South Ministerial Council established to promote north–south cooperation under the Good Friday Agreement.[21]

This is not to say that the EU would necessarily have agreed to additional arrangements that would have accorded even greater access to the Single Market had the UK made an "ask". During the negotiations, voices could be heard on the EU side expressing reservations over the privileged access being granted to producers in Northern Ireland. There were also concerns about whether the Protocol's arrangements for the UK to implement checks and controls on the movement of goods into and through Northern Ireland were sufficiently robust to secure the integrity of the EU's Customs Union and Single Market. Such concerns were only heightened by UK foot-dragging on preparations for the implementation of the Protocol during transition and UK government attempts to deny the need for checks and controls on the movement of goods from the rest of the UK across the Irish Sea into Northern Ireland.

This raises questions regarding how willing the UK and the EU will be to show any further flexibility and imagination on the development of Northern

Ireland's position within the UK–EU relationship, particularly under the Protocol. Will further differentiated treatment of Northern Ireland be sought and if so will it be facilitated? This will depend on many factors, not least what is deemed acceptable politically in Northern Ireland.

And here we come to a final example of flexibility and imagination in the Protocol: the provisions on democratic consent that allow members of the Northern Ireland Assembly to determine on a regularized basis, potentially every four years, whether essential provisions concerning the movement of goods in particular – and so the nature of the land border and east–west checks and controls – remain in place. The future of unprecedented arrangements agreed by the EU has been placed in the hands of regional politicians from a non-member state. A first vote, assuming transition ends on 31 December 2020, is expected towards the end of 2024. That will be a key moment in determining whether the "flexible and imaginative" arrangements contained in the Protocol on Ireland/Northern Ireland will remain the agreed solutions to the challenges Brexit poses for the "unique circumstances" both the UK and the EU agree exist on the island of Ireland.

Notes for Chapter 13

1. UK Government, Prime Minister's letter to Donald Tusk triggering Article 50, London, 29 March 2017, https://assets.publishing.service.gov.uk/government/uploads/system/uploads/attachment_data/file/604079/Prime_Ministers_letter_to_European_Council_President_Donald_Tusk.pdf.

2. European Parliament, Resolution of 5 April 2017 on negotiations with the United Kingdom following its notification that it intends to withdraw from the European Union (2017/2593(RSP)), Strasbourg, 5 April 2017, https://www.europarl.europa.eu/doceo/document/TA-8-2017-0102_EN.html, 20.

3. European Commission, minutes of the 2205th meeting of the Commission held in Brussels (Berlaymont) on Wednesday 22 March 2017 (morning), PV(2017) 2205 final, Strasbourg, 4 April, https://ec.europa.eu/transparency/regdoc/rep/10061/2017/EN/PV-2017-2205-F1-EN-MAIN-PART-1.PDF, 22.

4. European Council, Special meeting of the European Council (Article 50) (29 April 2017) – Guidelines, EUCO XT 20004/17, Brussels, 29 April 2017, https://www.consilium.europa.eu/media/21763/29-euco-art50-guidelinesen.pdf, 1, emphasis added.

5. Scottish Government, *Scotland's Place in Europe*, Edinburgh, 20 December 2016, https://www.gov.scot/publications/scotlands-place-europe/.

6. See B. Doherty *et al.*, "Northern Ireland and Brexit: the European Economic Area option", EPC Discussion Paper, European Policy Centre Brussels, April 2017, http://www.epc.eu/en/publications/Northern-Ireland-and-Brexit-the-European-Economic-Area-option~20b124; and D. Phinnemore, "The language of 'flexible and imaginative' solutions is unique to the Irish dimension of Brexit", LSE Brexit Blog, 6 November 2017, https://blogs.lse.ac.uk/brexit/2017/11/06/the-language-of-flexible-and-imaginative-solutions-is-unique-to-the-irish-dimension-of-brexit/.

7. European Council, letter from Donald Tusk to EU(27) leaders, Brussels, 28 April 2017, https://www.consilium.europa.eu/media/24061/invitation-letter-ec-art-50-29-april-2017.pdf.

8. European Commission, speech by Michel Barnier, the European Commission's chief negotiator, following the first round of Article 50 negotiations with the UK, SPEECH/17/1704, Brussels, 19 June 2017, https://ec.europa.eu/commission/presscorner/api/files/document/print/en/speech_17_1704/SPEECH_17_1704_EN.pdf.

9. UK Government, "Position Paper: Northern Ireland and Ireland", August 2017, https://www.gov.uk/government/publications/northern-ireland-and-ireland-a-position-paper.

10. European Commission, Guiding Principles for the Dialogue on Ireland/Northern Ireland, TF50 (2017) 15 – Commission to UK, Brussels, 20 September 2017, https://ec.europa.eu/commission/sites/beta-political/files/dialogue_ie-ni.pdf.

11. European Commission, Statement by Michel Barnier on the publication of the Guiding Principles for the Dialogue on Ireland and Northern Ireland, SPEECH/17/3145, Brussels, 7 September 2017, https://ec.europa.eu/commission/presscorner/api/files/document/print/en/speech_17_3145/SPEECH_17_3145_EN.pdf.

12. European Commission, Joint Report from the negotiators of the European Union and the United Kingdom Government on progress during phase 1 of negotiations under Treaty on European Union Article 50 on the United Kingdom's orderly withdrawal from the European Union, TF50 (2017) 19 – Commission to EU 27, Brussels, 8 December 2017, https://ec.europa.eu/commission/sites/beta-political/files/joint_report.pdf, 49.

13. *Ibid.*

14. European Commission, Draft Withdrawal Agreement on the withdrawal of the United Kingdom of Great Britain and Northern Ireland from the European Union and the European Atomic Energy Community, TF50 (2018) 33 – Commission to EU 27, Brussels, 28 February 2018, https://ec.europa.eu/commission/sites/beta-political/files/draft_withdrawal_agreement.pdf.

15. European Commission, Draft Agreement on the withdrawal of the United Kingdom of Great Britain and Northern Ireland from the European Union and the European Atomic Energy Community highlighting the progress made (coloured version) in the negotiation round with the UK of 16-19 March 2018, TF50 (2018) 35 – Commission to EU27, Brussels, 19 March 2018, https://ec.europa.eu/commission/sites/beta-political/files/draft_agreement_coloured.pdf.

16. Official Journal, Agreement on the withdrawal of the United Kingdom of Great Britain and Northern Ireland from the European Union and the European Atomic Energy Community, C 66 I, 19 February 2019, https://eurlex.europa.eu/legalcontent/EN/TXT/PDF/?uri=CELEX:12019W/TXT&from=EN.

17. Official Journal, Agreement on the withdrawal of the United Kingdom of Great Britain and Northern Ireland from the European Union and the European Atomic Energy Community, L 29, 31 January 2020, https://eur-lex.europa.eu/legal-content/EN/TXT/PDF/?uri=CELEX:12020W/TXT&from=EN.

18. S. Weatherill, "The Protocol on Ireland/Northern Ireland: protecting the EU's internal market at the expense of the UK's", *European Law Journal* 45:2 (2020), 222–36.

19. Official Journal, Council Decision (EU) 2020/135 of 30 January 2020 on the conclusion of the Agreement on the withdrawal of the United Kingdom of Great Britain and Northern Ireland from the European Union and the European Atomic Energy Community, L 29, 31 January 2020, https://eur-lex.europa.eu/legal-content/EN/TXT/PDF/?uri=CELEX:32020D0135&from=EN, Article 4.

20. European Commission, Negotiations on Ireland/Northern Ireland, Mapping of North–South cooperation, TF50 (2019) 63 – Commission to EU 27, Brussels, 21 June 2019, https://ec.europa.eu/commission/sites/beta-political/files/mapping_of_north-south_cooperation_0.pdf.

21. UK Government, European Union (Withdrawal Agreement) Act 2020, January, http://www.legislation.gov.uk/ukpga/2020/1/contents/enacted, 24, no. 3 (2020).

14

EU–UK SECURITY RELATIONS
AFTER BREXIT

Gijs de Vries

No member state has been as influential as the United Kingdom in shaping EU policies to fight serious crime, including terrorism. Paradoxically, no country has been more effective in blocking initiatives to have the EU play a role in defence. In both domains, the effects will be felt long after the UK has left the EU. This chapter discusses the UK's chequered legacy in European security policy, and how this may affect future cooperation. Will police forces and intelligence agencies continue to act in concert to mutual advantage, or – as will be argued below – are data exchanges and mutual assistance more likely to suffer? Will European military and security cooperation benefit from the UK's departure, or will the EU's credibility and effectiveness diminish? What measures could prevent unnecessary damage to European and British security?

This chapter proceeds in three stages. First the effects of Brexit on criminal justice cooperation will be assessed. The discussion then turns to the external dimension of foreign policy, security and defence. The final section reflects on repercussions for the future.

INTERNAL SECURITY

The United Kingdom played a leading role in shaping the EU's internal and external security policies. It was the 2005 British presidency that proposed, jointly with the EU Counterterrorism Coordinator, the EU's counterterrorism strategy, which still directs EU policy. The European Commission's first two directors for criminal law and justice were British (Adrian Fortescue, 1999–2003, and Jonathan Faull, 2003–10), as was the first president of Eurojust (Michael Kennedy, 2002–7). Rob Wainwright, a former Security Service (MI5) agent, directed Europol for nearly a decade (2009–18). Claude Moraes chaired the European Parliament's Committee on Civil Liberties, Justice, and Home

Affairs (2014–19). Britain's last commissioner, Julian King (2016–20), was in charge of security. It is a record unmatched by any other member state.

Following Brexit, the UK will lose its voice in the institutions, preparatory committees and agencies that decide and implement EU security policy. It will be out of the room when the European Council, the Council, the Commission or the European Parliament set policy. The Home Office will lose its seat in the Standing Committee on Operational Cooperation on Internal Security, the EU's prime preparatory body for internal security; the Foreign Office will lose its ambassador in the Council's Political and Security Committee, which is charged with external security; the Secret Intelligence Service (MI6) and MI5 will lose their roles in EU INTCEN (EU Intelligence and Situation Centre), the EU's centre for strategic intelligence; the Metropolitan Police and the National Crime Agency will no longer shape Europol's priorities, and the UK will no longer be able to initiate or lead Joint Investigation Teams via Eurojust. Personal contacts and professional friendships, constructed over decades, will atrophy; networks will unravel; trust will dissipate. European security, this much is certain, will diminish. Britain, too, will be less secure.

Serious and organized crime affects more UK citizens, more frequently than any other security threat. Serious and organized crime, National Crime Agency (NCA) Director, Lynne Owens, noted, kills more British citizens every year than terrorism, war and natural disasters combined.[1] The majority of serious and organized crime in the UK, the NCA points out, retains a clear international dimension, and the threat is growing both in volume and complexity. The UK's longstanding investment in European security thus reflected an obvious national interest.

In a "no deal" scenario, bilateral intelligence cooperation and exchanges through the Counter-Terrorist Group (a non-EU body) would be least affected; intelligence is not an EU competence. Intelligence, however, is only part of the picture. The British approach to domestic security and terrorism is one of integration between intelligence agencies and law enforcement agencies. The latter will bear the brunt of Brexit. Three areas will be particularly affected: information exchange, criminal justice and influence on EU policies and instruments.

Should the EU and the UK fail to agree on their future relationship after 31 December 2020, or on an extension of the transitional period, the UK will be disconnected from all EU networks, information systems and databases, such as the Schengen Information System (SIS II), the Europol Information System, Eurodac (fingerprints) and the European Criminal Records Information System. These systems are in high demand; in 2017, for example, British security forces accessed the SIS 539 *million* times. No good alternative to the SIS exists. Interpol's database is not as useful. Reports of Interpol alerts being abused by certain governments to target political opponents and other critics have made some EU member states reluctant to upload notices on wanted suspects.

Judicial cooperation would also suffer. Without an agreement, the UK and the EU could no longer use the European Arrest Warrant (EAW; 1,277 cases in 2019). The EU-27 jointly issue more EAW requests to the UK than vice versa, as their relative population size would suggest, but the damage would affect both sides. EAWs played (and play) a crucial role in police cooperation between Northern Ireland and Ireland. The Council of Europe's 1957 Convention on Extradition would be a poor alternative; none of the four protocols has been ratified by all EU member states. Some countries, such as Germany, would no longer be able to extradite national citizens. Besides, extradition outside the EAW can cost four times as much and take three times as long.[2]

Third, the UK would no longer have a say in steering the activities of agencies such as Europol, Eurojust or the European Agency for Cybersecurity. Even an operational agreement between the UK and Europol, based on existing third-country models, would represent "a clear diminution in the UK's security capacity".[3]

Data Protection

To the EU, personal data protection is a fundamental right. It is governed by the European Charter of Human Rights (Article 8), which is legally binding on the EU and on member states as they implement EU measures. It is an essential prerequisite for the free flow of personal data across borders: under EU law, the EU is prohibited from exchanging data with non-EU countries unless these are deemed to have "adequate" privacy protection. Such adequacy decisions are taken by the European Commission and are subject to the jurisdiction of the European Court of Justice (ECJ).

As a member state, the UK has been co-responsible for all EU privacy legislation and its implementation record is second to none. At first sight it should thus be easy for the European Commission to grant the UK a green light. In reality, things are more complicated. Prime Minister Johnson warned that the UK, "will in future develop separate and independent policies in areas such as … data protection, maintaining high standards as we do so".[4] This caught the EU off guard. Why would the UK want to deviate from EU data protection standards it had helped to design, and which are widely considered as leading in the world? Was London planning to lower its standards? Or was it perhaps intent on complicating the negotiations about post-Brexit relations even further?

Whatever the case may be, data protection was always going to be one of the most difficult issues to solve. In 2015, the ECJ struck down an agreement between the EU and the USA to share passenger name records. It argued that the mass surveillance by US intelligence agencies violated the privacy rights of EU citizens. A somewhat revised agreement was approved by the European Commission, but this too is being challenged before the ECJ. As British intelligence agencies also practice mass surveillance the Commission must weigh the risks to privacy before granting an adequacy decision. Crucially, it must also take account of the privacy risks caused by the UK's sharing of sensitive data with US intelligence services and other partners (Five Eyes). In the past, Britain did not face this type of Commission scrutiny; member states are fully sovereign as regards security policy. Ironically, Brexit will subject the UK to greater EU data protection oversight.

Human Rights

Human rights are fundamental to the European Union's legal order (Treaty on European Union Article 2). In 2009, the EU gave legal force to its Charter on Fundamental Rights by including it in the Lisbon Treaty. All EU member states are parties to the European Convention on Human Rights. EU trade agreements with third countries are conditional on each partner's respect for human rights.

Naturally, a human rights clause could be expected to figure in any legal framework governing EU–UK relations after Brexit. In practice, however, the subject has proven remarkably contentious. The European Court of Human Rights (ECHR) is a *bête noire* in British domestic politics (see Chapter 15), particularly on the right. British tabloids have long railed against the Strasbourg Court, occasionally mistaking it for the EU Court in Luxembourg.[5] In 2015 the Conservative Party included a promise to break with the ECHR in its election manifesto. In 2016 Theresa May bolstered her campaign for her party's leadership through an attack on the ECHR: "The ECHR can bind the hands of parliament, adds nothing to our prosperity, makes us less secure by preventing the deportation of dangerous foreign nationals – and does nothing to change the attitudes of governments like Russia's when it comes to human rights." In fact, Mrs May argued, "it isn't the EU we should leave but the ECHR and the jurisdiction of its court".[6] In its 2017 election manifesto, the Conservative Party said it would consider the UK's human rights legal framework, "when the process of leaving the EU concludes"; in 2019 it promised to "end the supremacy of European law".

One particular irritant for its detractors is the ECHR's application of human rights law to British military operations. Since the ECHR ruled in 1978 that the British army's use of five interrogation techniques on detainees amounted to cruel and inhuman treatment, judges and human rights campaigners have been accused of vexatious accusations against British troops. These concerns have found an echo on the other side of the Atlantic. US General David Petraeus warned that "[t]he extension of the European Convention on Human Rights to the battlefield has made extensive litigation against British soldiers inevitable [...] In Afghanistan, it undermined the British military's authority to detain enemy combatants and also to work with [...] NATO allies".[7] Against this it has been pointed out that the Iraq war alone resulted in 326 settled cases that prompted £20 million in UK payouts. "If the government paid out", the former legal adviser to the British army argued, "these (cases) are not vexatious and not spurious. They are proven and the MoD [Ministry of Defence] have admitted liability."[8] This is not to everybody's liking. In 2020 the UK minister for defence introduced legislation that would compel the government to derogate from the ECHR in any overseas military operation.

To the EU, however, continued British adherence to, and application of, the ECHR is an "essential element" of future relations. In fact, the Political Declaration commits the EU and the UK to "continued adherence and giving effect to the ECHR, and adequate protection of personal data, which are both essential prerequisites for enabling the cooperation envisaged by the Parties". The UK appears to have changed its mind. In March 2020 it informed the EU that it did not want to commit to applying the Convention. A major test of wills is on the cards.

Altogether, then, the prospects for cooperation in the fight against crime after Brexit are not very good. Data sharing between police forces and other security actors will become more cumbersome, expensive and slow, as will extradition of suspected criminals. Joint analysis will become more difficult. Personal relationships and mutual trust are likely to erode. Two politically sensitive and emotive subjects – privacy protection and the role of the ECHR – could well deepen divisions.

EXTERNAL SECURITY

Cooperation on defence and external security may be affected to a lesser degree, although the relative weakness of a negative does not equate to a positive. On the positive side, the UK and its partners broadly share the same perspective on the main security challenges of our time. The five strategic objectives of the EU's Global Strategy (security, resilience of states and societies to the EU's east and south, an integrated approach to external conflicts and crisis, cooperative regional orders and global governance) largely reflect British thinking, as do the priorities of the European Agenda on Security (terrorism, organized crime and cybercrime). The UK's 2015 national security strategy is structured around similar priorities.

The UK is the only European country that meets both the North Atlantic Treaty Organization (NATO) target of spending 2 per cent of gross domestic product on defence and the UN target of spending 0.7 per cent of gross national income (GNI) on international development. With its seat on the UN Security Council, nuclear deterrent and capable military, its contribution to European security is valued highly. At the same time, however, the UK has often thwarted initiatives to strengthen the EU's role in security. It blocked an increase in the budget of the European Defence Agency (EDA) for many years, refused to participate in the EDA's largest projects, and vetoed the proposal of the EU's then High Representative for Foreign Affairs and Security Policy, Baroness Ashton, to create a European military headquarters, to mention only some examples. On foreign and security policy, from 2009 to 2015, the UK voted against the majority 35 per cent of the time, the highest figure of any member state.[9]

To maximize British influence post-Brexit, Prime Minister May originally proposed a security partnership that included regular structured UK–EU-27 consultation, up to leader level; reciprocal secondment of staff, including in the EU Military Staff and the European External Action Service; and collaboration in EU INTCEN and European Union Military Staff Intelligence. UK–EU external cooperation was to go beyond foreign, security and defence policy and include development, defence research, sanctions policy and space security.[10] It would have been a security partnership of unprecedented scope, far more ambitious than the EU's usual arrangements with third countries. Under Boris Johnson, the UK changed direction. Foreign Minister Dominic Raab is said to be more interested in bilateral cooperation and ad hoc arrangements such as the E3 on Iran (UK, France, Germany). This leaves several issues to be resolved. These include crisis management, defence collaboration, access to Galileo, cooperation on foreign aid and sanctions policy.

Crisis Management

Between 2003 and 2019, the EU ran 34 crisis management operations in 25 countries on three continents, of which 22 were civilian, 11 military, and one mixed (Darfur). Currently, 16 operations are ongoing (ten civilian, six military). On average, the EU deploys 3,000 troops and 1,500–2,000 civilian personnel each day.[11] While there have been some notable successes,[12] most missions have been modest in size, limited in means and relatively unambitious. Increasingly, military operations tend to focus on armed forces training, with no executive dimension. The battalion-size EU Battlegroups (2,500 troops), created to perform tasks at the higher end of the military spectrum, reached operational capacity in 2007 but have never been deployed.

The United Kingdom's record in EU crisis management operations is mixed. While it often sought (and obtained) a role in designing and occasionally leading EU operations, it has been reluctant to put boots on the ground. In terms of personnel, between 2003 and 2018 the UK has accounted for just 2.3 per cent of member state contributions. This puts it on a par with Greece.[13]

The UK's aloofness reflected a trend. As Heisbourg notes, Britain ceased to invest politically or militarily in the European Security and Defence Policy from the Iraq crisis of 2002–3 onwards.[14] Whitman observes that the 2015 National Security Strategy and Strategic Defence and Security Review placed the EU in "a minor supporting role" in the UK's defence and security.[15] Following the 2016 referendum, the number of UK staff represented in the European External Action Service has been constantly decreasing in all categories.[16] Britain was due to lead an EU Battlegroup in 2019, during the Brexit transition period, but it pulled out.

The effects of Brexit on EU civilian and military missions and operations are therefore likely to be limited. The UK's analytical skills and military nous will be missed, but the EU's operational capacity will not be significantly affected. The UK, for its part, will lose influence. The headquarters of the European Union Naval Force anti-piracy mission has already been relocated from its base in north London to Rota in Spain. As a non-EU member state, the UK could still participate in an EU operation using NATO assets under Berlin Plus, but it would need an invitation to take part in an autonomous EU operation. In that scenario, the UK could not be a lead nation or provide headquarters or operation commanders.

To avoid having to play second fiddle to the EU, the UK will seek to work through NATO, to the extent that its interests coincide with those of the US administration. It will probably also try to expand its bilateral and multilateral ties with European states. It already provides airlift capability (helicopters) to support France's Operation Barkhane against Islamist militants in the Sahel. With France, the UK is building a Combined Joint Expeditionary Force which could provide up to 10,000 personnel for crisis response in Europe and beyond. The UK forms part of the European Intervention Initiative, a French-led forum to reinforce defence ties (currently 13 European members). London has signed a bilateral defence treaty with Poland and is working to set up a 10,000-strong Joint Expeditionary Force with eight northern European countries (Denmark, Estonia, Finland, Latvia, Lithuania, the Netherlands, Norway, Sweden). Still, there will be limits to the UK's willingness to work with European partners. When France in 2019 proposed a European maritime surveillance mission in the Persian Gulf, the UK announced its intention to join. It subsequently changed its mind and joined the US-led initiative, Sentinel, instead.

Brexit, regardless of its shape and cost, will compound the pressure on Britain's defence budget. The 2010 Strategic and Defence Review reduced the UK armed forces' conventional capacity by about a third.[17] Since then levels have been cut further: in 2019 the size of Britain's armed forces fell for a ninth consecutive year.[18] American generals have expressed concerns that Britain would find it difficult to deploy a division (about 20,000 troops) alongside US troops in a European conflict.[19] Equipment, too, has suffered. Research by the Royal United Services Institute found that the army would be "comprehensively outgunned" in a conflict with Russia.[20] The remedy – the Ministry of Defence's equipment plan which accounts for over 40 per cent of spending – is deemed unafforda-ble.[21] Parliamentarians consider that the funding model for defence is broken, as the Treasury does not fund the government's defence ambitions properly.[22] Further reductions to the conventional capabilities of the UK's armed forces, the International Institute for Strategic Studies (IISS) has warned, may be likely.[23] Although the UK still has the largest defence budget in Europe, the gap between its foreign policy ambition and its military capacity is widening. In a rational world this would strengthen rather than weaken the case for UK–European defence collaboration.

Defence Industry Cooperation

The European Union's Global Strategy posits strategic autonomy as an objective for the Union. Strategic autonomy is defined as the "ability to act and co-operate with international and regional partners wherever possible while being able to operate autonomously where and when necessary". At present, this ability is still limited to the lower end of the operational spectrum. Current procurement plans of the EU-27 up to 2030 are not expected to close the capability short-falls.[24] For years, initiatives to have the EU help to close the gap foundered on the rock of British resistance.

Once the UK had voted to leave, however, an opportunity arose for the EU to expand its role. The 2014–19 Juncker Commission leapt at the chance and launched proposals for a European Defence Union. These include the setting up of a European Defence Fund, initiatives for Permanent Structured Cooperation on defence (PESCO), a type of joint military headquarters (Military Planning and Conduct Capability) and annual reviews of national defence planning. Crucially, the Commission also proposed to use the EU budget. Its draft multiannual spending plan 2021–7 included €13 billion to create a European Defence Fund and €6.5 billion to facilitate military mobility, as well as €10.5 billion for an off-budget European Peace Facility. This would significantly boost defence-related spending from current levels (€2.8 billion in the period 2013–20).[25] Separately, the European Investment Bank Group scaled up its financing for dual-use technology, cybersecurity and civilian security to €6 billion (2018–20).

As on previous occasions, the EU's new multiannual budget has proved contentious and the Commission's proposals were unlikely to survive the negotiations unscathed. In July 2020 the European Council adopted an unprecedented economic recovery package of up to €750 billion. At the same time, it scaled down the EU's multiannual budget to €1.074 billion, allocating €7 billion to the European Defence Fund and €1.5 billion to military mobility, as well as €5 billion to the European Peace Facility. The European Parliament is unlikely to significantly increase these amounts.

Regardless of the ultimate size of the sums involved, third countries such as Norway, Turkey, the USA and the UK are naturally keen to obtain a share. In 2018 the UK requested a bespoke arrangement with the EDA, arrangements for participation in the European Defence Fund and the option to participate in PESCO. Industrially, these suggestions made sense. Britain's defence industries are among the strongest in Europe and the UK takes part in numerous bilateral and multilateral defence industrial projects with European partners. Industries on both sides would benefit from maintaining and even strengthening these ties post-Brexit. Politically, however, it was a different story. France, Spain and Italy worried about Anglo-Saxon dominance while Cyprus was keen to prevent Turkey from getting its foot in the door. In the end, it was agreed that third countries may participate in PESCO on a case-by-case basis, provided they bring substantial added value to the project. Decisions will require unanimity, which will make Turkish participation unlikely. Companies based outside the EU will also be allowed – subject to conditions – to take part in European Defence Fund-supported projects but will not receive funding. Britain will therefore find its way in, if it so wishes. But the suggestion that the UK should be free to exclude EU companies from defence contracts after Brexit to ensure maximum benefits for the British economy, raised in a report commissioned by the Ministry of Defence, had best not be taken up.[26]

Galileo

In 2018 a bitter row erupted over British access to Galileo, the EU's answer to the US global positioning system and Russia's global satellite and navigation system Glonass. Galileo's 26 satellites provide access to civilian service providers across the world. To its EU-based partners Galileo also provides a secure, encrypted Public Regulated Service (PRS) for use by police forces and the military. Although initially hostile to the Galileo project – known in London as "the Common Agricultural Policy in space"[27] – the UK gradually warmed to its potential. In 2018 the British government proposed that, post-Brexit,

British security providers should retain access to the encrypted service and that British companies, which had played a leading part in designing the security provisions, should be allowed to continue bidding for contracts. Both requests were rejected by the EU, which recalled the commonly agreed restrictions on third-country involvement in the Galileo PRS. These restrictions had been hailed by the British government at the time as a negotiating success.[28] London sensed foul play: a blatant effort on the part of France, Germany and Spain to take advantage of Brexit.

In an effort to force the European Commission's hand, the British government next threatened to veto the procurement of satellites by the European Space Agency (ESA), which acts as the EU's procurement body. To avoid being outmanoeuvred, the EU agreed to assume all liabilities that the ESA would normally incur by taking on the contract. This allowed the decision to be taken by majority vote. In response, the UK ended the talks about Galileo and announced it would develop its own, sovereign satellite system. However, as estimated costs rose to £5 billion, in 2020 the British satellite project was put on hold.

A compromise can perhaps still be found. The EU has offered the UK access to the Galileo PRS "in the context of Union operations or *ad hoc* operations involving its Member States". The UK would be required to take part in the non-security related activities of the Union's space programme, or grant the Union access to the envisaged United Kingdom Global Navigation Satellite System.[29] At the time of writing, negotiations were ongoing.

Foreign Aid

As one of only a handful of countries that spend at least 0.7 per cent of GNI on official development assistance (ODA), the UK has put its stamp on European development policy. In 2018 it channelled 10 per cent of its ODA expenditure (£1.4 billion) through the EU budget and the European Development Fund. The ensuing policy synergy benefitted both sides. For the UK, channelling aid through the European Commission also helped to keep administrative costs low.

In a "no deal" scenario it would serve both parties to continue to work closely together, notably in areas such as peace and security, migration and humanitarian aid. However, prospects for continued alignment would depend on wider policy developments, such as a possible realignment of British aid policy. Boris Johnson has called for the 0.7 per cent to be spent more in line with Britain's political, commercial and diplomatic interests.[30] As announced by the UK prime minister in June 2020, the merger of the Department for International Development with the Foreign Office, apparently in an effort to give substance to the notion of "Global Britain", may well cast a pall over development cooperation with the EU. Acrimonious relations post-Brexit would have a similar effect.

Sanctions

Sanctions are an oft-used instrument of European foreign policy. Only the USA uses sanctions more frequently. The EU's most widely used measures are asset freezes, visa bans, arms embargoes, financial measures such as bans on bank transfers, flight and shipping bans and trade measures such as limits on oil exports to North Korea.[31] In 2018 the EU had 42 sanctions programmes in place. Ten of these served to implement UN measures. In another eight cases, the EU applied its own sanctions in parallel to those of the UN (e.g. Iran and North Korea). In 24 cases the EU operated sanctions autonomously, without a UN framework. These include sanctions against Russia's energy, financial and arms sectors in response to Russia's annexation of Crimea and its destabilization of Ukraine. In recent years the EU has also responded to gross violations of human and civil rights by suspending aid (Burundi, Fiji, Togo, Zimbabwe) or by suspending preferential trade access (Myanmar, Belarus, Sri Lanka, and Cambodia). Among other instruments, Brussels has adopted a blocking regulation to protect EU entities and individuals against US extraterritorial sanctions, including against Iran.

The UK has often been influential in shaping EU sanctions. Prospects for continued alignment after Brexit are unclear; according to British MPs "[l]ittle high-level thought appears to have been given to UK priorities for post-Brexit sanctions".[32] Although London has said it will continue to apply the European measures against Russia and Iran, in other cases political or commercial interests may lead it to deviate from the EU. Thorny questions abound. Will the UK, for example, include EU-compatible human rights clauses in its future trade agreements with non-EU countries? If so, will it operate these clauses in concert with the EU? The EU has recently imposed trade sanctions on Cambodia. Will the UK, Cambodia's principal European trading partner, continue to apply these sanctions, or will it attenuate them, as Hun Sen claimed London has promised?[33]

CONCLUSION: REPERCUSSIONS FOR THE FUTURE

Can the UK retain global influence after Brexit? Whether in respect of counter-terrorism, cybercrime, international sanctions or foreign aid, as an EU member state Britain has often been in the driving seat. Its loss of influence post-Brexit will be commensurate, not only in Brussels but also in Washington, where the UK has become less relevant as an interlocutor in Europe. Outside the EU, its military operations have been unsuccessful. Sir Simon Fraser notes: "We have reserved the right to act independently or in military coalitions drawn from the EU, NATO or beyond, as we did in Iraq, Afghanistan, and Libya. This reminds us that the EU does not have a monopoly on foreign policy failure."[34]

Brexit is unlikely to have a major effect on European military security. Its effects will be more keenly felt in the fight against serious crime, which will become more difficult. The principal repercussions of Brexit will be geopolitical. At a time when China is flexing its muscles and the USA has become less reliable as an ally, the EU has been weakened by the loss of a key member state.

Meanwhile, the risk of further damage to both sides is high. Whereas Theresa May aimed for a security partnership with the EU, Boris Johnson has shown no such interest. On the contrary: now that the UK has regained its notional sovereignty it may wish to demonstrate its independence. Compared to Washington and Beijing, Brussels looks the softest target. Economically, the UK will become a competitor to the EU. The prospect of Britain and the EU feuding publicly is growing rather than diminishing.

Can the tide still be turned? Jolyon Howorth wrote that, in recent times, "no leading UK politician, from either party [Conservative or Labour], had a clear view of what sort of future defence relationship Britain might entertain with the EU".[35] He might have added that a similar void existed on the EU side – as indeed it still does. Much the same could be said about foreign policy in general. The lack of strategic thinking is palpable: neither side has a clear idea about how to deal with the US, Russia, or China. Britain, where Leave voters are three times as likely to see the UK's relationship with the Commonwealth as equally important as that with the EU, is mired in "postcolonial melancholy".[36] EU foreign policy, for its part, lacks leadership, instruments and ideas. President Macron's trial balloon, a European Security Council to accommodate the UK, failed to take off, weighed down by concerns over powers, composition, relations with EU institutions and London's allergy to things European. With Global Britain and Sovereign Europe shrouded in mist, helmsmanship is lacking on both sides and the relationship is adrift. The passengers seem resigned to wait for better times. It could be a while.

Notes for Chapter 14

1. Speech by director general, Lynne Owens, National Crime Agency, London, 14 May 2019.

2. Theresa May (2018), speech at the Munich Security Conference, 17 February 2018.

3. House of Commons, Home Affairs Committee (2018), UK–EU security cooperation after Brexit, Fourth Report of Session 2017–19, 3.

4. Written statement, "The government's proposed approach to the negotiations with the EU about our future relationship", HCWS86, 3 February 2020.

5. Even The Times confuses the two. Bruno Waterfield and Oliver Wright, "EU demands its judges keep control after Brexit: Strasbourg would rule on future UK trade rights", front page, The Times, 28 January 2020.

6. Home secretary's speech on the UK, the EU and our place in the world, London, 25 April 2016.

7. General David Petraeus, "Foreword" in R. Ekins & J. Marionneau (eds), *Resisting the Judicialisation of War* (London: Policy Exchange, 2019), 4.

8. J. Elgot, "Theresa May will oppose 'vexatious' allegations against Iraq UK troops", *The Guardian*, 21 September 2016.

9. S. Hix & S. Hagemann, "Does the UK win or lose in the Council of Ministers?", UK in a Changing Europe, 2 November 2015.

10. HM Government, Framework for the UK–EU Security Partnership, London, 7 May 2018.

11. U. Krotz & K. Wright, "CDSP military operations" in H. Meijer & M. Wyss (eds), *The Handbook of European Defence Policies and Armed Forces* (Oxford: Oxford University Press, 2018), 870.

12. Examples include the missions to Indonesia (Aceh), the Democratic Republic of Congo, the Horn of Africa (Atalanta) and Somalia.

13. House of Lords, European Union Committee (2018), Brexit: Common Security and Defence Policy missions and operations, 16th Report of Session 2017–19, 36.

14. F. Heisbourg, "Brexit and European security", *Survival* 58:3 (2016), 13.

15. R. Whitman, "The UK and EU foreign and defence policy after Brexit: integrated, associated or detached?", *National Institute Economic Review* 238 (2016), R2.

16. European External Action Service, Human Resources Report 2018, 49.

17. International Institute for Strategic Studies (IISS), *The Military Balance* (2019), 82.

18. BBC News, "Strength of British military falls for ninth year", 16 August 2019.

19. *The Economist*, "Shoulder pips squeaking", 9 December 2017, 35.

20. J. Watling, *The Future of Fires: Maximising the UK's Tactical and Operational Firepower* (London: RUSI, 2019), 2.

21. National Audit Office, *The Equipment Plan 2019 to 2029* (2020).

22. House of Commons & House of Lords, Joint Committee on the National Security Strategy (2019), Revisiting the UK's national security strategy, Fourth Report of Session 2017–19, 3.

23. IISS, *The Military Balance*, 86; see also J. Lindley-French, "UK military operations" in Meijer & Wyss, *Handbook of European Defence Policies and Armed Forces*, 828.

24. D. Barrie *et al.*, Protecting Europe: Meeting the EU's Military Level of Ambition in the Context of Brexit (IISS/DGAP, 2018), 3.

25. For an excellent analysis, see P. Haroche, "Supranationalism strikes back: a neofunctionalist account of the European Defence Fund", *Journal of European Public Policy* (2019), DOI: 10.1080/13501763.2019.1609570.

26. D. Bond, "Report urges government 'to safeguard freedom of manoeuvre' in procurement post-Brexit", *Financial Times*, 9 July 2018.

27. J. Rankin, "EU may give UK unique deal after Brexit", *The Guardian*, 27 July 2016.

28. House of Commons, European Scrutiny Committee, 49th Report of Sessions 2017–19, 14.

29. Council decision authorizing the opening of negotiations with the United Kingdom, COM(2020) 35 final, 3 February 2020.

30. P. Wintour, "Boris Johnson backs call for multibillion cut to UK aid budget", *The Guardian*, 11 February 2019.

31. M. Russell, "EU sanctions: a key foreign and security policy instrument", European Parliamentary Research Service, May 2018.

32. House of Commons Foreign Affairs Committee, "Fragmented and incoherent: The UK's sanctions policy", 23rd Special Report of Session 2017–19 (2019), 3.

33. C. Dunst, "How Brexit could undermine human rights in Cambodia", Politico.EU, 23 February 2020.

34. S. Fraser, "Can the UK retain global influence after Brexit? Policies and structures for a new era", The Policy Institute, King's College London, 2017.

35. J. Howorth, "EU defence cooperation after Brexit: what role for the UK in future EU defence arrangements?", *European View* 16 (2017), 194.

36. A. Menon & A. Wager, "Taking back control: sovereignty as strategy in Brexit politics", *Territory, Politics, Governance* 8:2 (2020), 282.

15

THE UK STILL IN EUROPE? IS THE UK'S MEMBERSHIP OF THE COUNCIL OF EUROPE IN DOUBT?

Martyn Bond

The UK is a founding member of the Council of Europe and has played a leading part in its activities. But recent evidence suggests that the UK government may be under pressure to reconsider its traditional position, in particular in the wake of the Brexit decision.

TODAY

A recent disquieting sign was noted by the House of Lords EU justice subcommittee in January 2019. It pointed to a change in the UK government's wording of the post-Brexit Political Declaration agreed with the European Union. The draft declaration suggested the future relationship should incorporate the UK's *commitment* to the European Convention on Human Rights and Fundamental Freedoms. However, the final version released in November 2018 had changed the wording to a commitment to *respect the framework* of the Convention. Clarification supplied by the parliamentary under-secretary of state for justice simply stated that the government would not repeal or replace the act while Brexit was ongoing, but added, "It is right that we wait until the process of leaving the EU concludes before considering the matter further."[1]

"Considering the matter further" perhaps implies that it has had some consideration already. It certainly does not inspire confidence that the decision is already secure and that the UK will remain committed both to the Convention and – *a fortiori* – to the Council of Europe.

There are other straws in the wind that might give credence to some doubts on this front. The latest revision to the Protocols of the European Convention on Human Rights (Protocol 16) has neither been signed nor ratified by the

UK. The UK is not alone in this, but it has a particular sensitivity about taking advice from what it might see as a "foreign" court, and this opens that possibility. Protocol 16 creates an optional system by which the highest national courts can seek advisory opinions from the European Court on the interpretation of the Convention. The UK government justified its hesitant position by stating it would observe "how the system operates in practice, having regard particularly to the effect on the workload of the Court, and to how the Court approaches the giving of opinions". That was six years ago, under the 2010–15 Conservative–Liberal Democrat coalition, and the view of government has not changed since.

Might that suggest that opposition to the European Convention on Human Rights is more embedded and has been so for longer than more recent indicators suggest? It would be ironic, given the major role that British lawyers played in the original concept and drafting of the Convention. At their insistence, it became a regional adaptation of the Universal Declaration of Human Rights, but with a mechanism – the European Court of Rights (ECHR) – for adjudicating cases of abuse, something which made it exemplary in its day and still an object of admiration around the world.

Opposition to the ECHR and its jurisdiction has gained traction, particularly within the Conservative Party, and also among some lawyers of a more conservative persuasion. This development is subsequent to the introduction of the Human Rights Act (1998), which incorporated the Convention into UK law and was passed while a Labour government was in power. This was seen at the time as a practical and useful measure which allowed many human rights cases to be settled within the UK rather than being referred to Strasbourg, hence avoiding both extra cost and delay.

A Bill of Rights Commission composed of senior lawyers was set up in its wake (in March 2011) and considered some of the questions it raised, including whether a UK Bill of Rights should be created. Indirectly, it also discussed potential withdrawal from the European Convention on Human Rights, and its report in 2012 revealed widely divided opinions in the Commission on the main question of whether a UK Bill should replace the Human Rights Act. Some members thought the UK would become a "pariah state" if it voluntarily withdrew from the Convention, suggesting that any member state, "deciding to withdraw from the Convention and therefore no longer bound to comply with it or to respect its enforcement procedures could, in certain circumstances, raise concern as regards the effective protection of fundamental rights by its authorities".[2] Others asserted the opposite: it was "axiomatic to record that the UK would continue to adhere to an ethical foreign policy and promote adherence to the safeguarding of fundamental freedoms and civil liberties at all times".[3] The matter was adjourned undecided, waiting for clarity in relation to Brexit.

Another straw in the wind, blowing in the same direction, was a private member's bill proposed by a Conservative MP, Charlie Elphicke, who suggested that the Human Rights Act of 1998 should be repealed and substituted with a UK Bill of Rights and Responsibilities. This bill received some publicity and support and reached its second reading in March 2013 before it was withdrawn. Leaving the European Convention on Human Rights, however, became one of the promises in the Conservative Party manifesto for the 2015 election, with a view to replacing the Human Rights Act with a British Bill of Rights, allegedly giving the UK more control over the laws it implements: "We will scrap Labour's Human Rights Act and introduce a British Bill of Rights which will restore common sense to the application of human rights in the UK. The Bill will remain faithful to the basic principles of human rights, which we signed up to in the original European Convention on Human Rights."[4]

Some judicial decisions from Strasbourg have touched a sensitive nerve recently in UK political or public opinion and contributed to souring relations with Strasbourg. For example, in 2011 the then UK prime minister, David Cameron, remarked that an ECHR judgement which required the UK to give prisoners the vote – a basic human right – made him "physically ill".[5] But the issue was never as simplistic as that. It has since been quietly resolved with a minor administrative adjustment to the terms of sentencing of prisoners, not offering a blanket right but a selective one. It was enough to satisfy the Court judgement, but not so much that it proved impossible to pass into law and practice in the UK. Yet it became for a while a cause célèbre in the struggle between Europhiles and Europhobes at Westminster and unnecessarily politicized the ECHR in the eyes of the UK media and public opinion.

It may be that there was some confusion in public opinion between the European Union and the Council of Europe. Some of the animus of the debate around Brexit may well have spilled over onto other institutions, notably the Council of Europe and the ECHR. But not only is the Council of Europe clearly not the same organization as the European Union, but also the ECHR, in Strasbourg, is quite distinct from the European Court of Justice, in Luxembourg. Opposition to the EU on occasion merges into opposition to the Council of Europe simply because they are both European. Eurosceptics prefer something more British and less European, even when it comes to human rights.

The UK media has also played a particularly damaging role in the ongoing debate about the ECHR and interpretation of the Convention. The most flagrant example of this was on the occasion of the 2012 High-Level Conference on the Future of the ECHR, held under the auspices of the Council of Europe, but under the chairmanship of the United Kingdom (which at that moment held the rotating presidency), in Brighton. It was a significant moment for the ECHR to progress its reform agenda, putting in place new procedures to clear the backlog of human rights cases that had accumulated over the years.

Such was the animosity towards the ECHR in some political quarters, however, that in the run-up to the conference a popular UK tabloid newspaper featured on its front-page pictures of the judges in their robes under the headline: "Named and Shamed: The European Human Rights Judges Wrecking British Law".[6] Even by the rough-and-tumble standards of the British press, this was a frontal assault on a judicial institution that the United Kingdom had done much to create, to which the British government subscribed and of which a distinguished British judge, Sir Nicholas Bratza, was president. Needless to say, the accompanying article was uninformative and biased. A notional apology presented to the Press Commission some months later went unpublicized and unnoticed.

Given its good intentions, it is all the more surprising that the UK 1998 Human Rights Act, which incorporated the rights and freedoms set out in the European Convention on Human Rights into domestic British law, is now in the sights of those who declare that they want "more control". The Human Rights Act offered domestic redress without recourse to Strasbourg, lessening the caseload of UK applications to the ECHR, speeding up the delivery of justice and lowering its cost. Many more decisions that might have required consideration in Strasbourg have since then been dealt with in the UK. For its critics, however, the Human Rights Act incorporates the wrong rights, and gives them to everybody, even foreigners who may be in Britain, not just to British subjects.

YESTERDAY

The contemporary situation inevitably has roots in the past and reviewing the origins of the Council of Europe and the establishment of the ECHR may uncover how far the underlying issues of the past still influence the present.

In May 1949 the United Kingdom, along with nine European countries, established the Council of Europe. At that stage neither the European Coal and Steel Community nor – *a fortiori* – the European Economic Community had been thought of. But the Treaty of London that created the Council of Europe was a compromise between two competing visions of Europe that also struggled for control of the process that led to the European Union.

In the aftermath of the Second World War, some countries were still self-confident and unquestioning of their national identity, while others had a less secure grasp of nationhood. They had seen at first hand the political divisions that defeat, occupation, collaboration and resistance had inflicted on their peoples. These different experiences influenced the views their governments took about the nature of European unification. Were they to rebuild on old foundations or were they to seek greater assurance in something new that did not carry with it the risk of repeating their previous painful experiences? Were they traditionally intergovernmental in their outlook, or were they prepared to share some of their sovereignty in a joint venture that might be greater than the sum of its parts?

Among the ten founding states, the UK had a strongly confident self-image, personified in the bulldog defiance of Winston Churchill. Ireland and Sweden had been neutral and had some sense of guilt as sometimes involuntary accomplices with the wrong side in the war. The remaining seven states – Belgium, Denmark, France, Italy, Luxembourg, the Netherlands and Norway – had all been occupied by Nazi Germany. Only recently had they re-established democratic governments and they were, in a political sense, new and possibly fragile states, however far back into the mists of history and legend they might trace their cultural roots.

Of all these states, only the United Kingdom was clearly in a position to take the lead and set the tone, but the new Council of Europe reflected a compromise between these various positions. The statutes of the Council of Europe would foresee a Committee of Ministers on the one hand and a Parliamentary Assembly on the other. The Parliamentary Assembly would debate and put forward resolutions agreed on, as any parliament might, by majority vote. The Committee of Ministers, on the other hand, which retained the responsibility to decide, would represent the member states, and each would retain its autonomy with a power of veto: its decisions would be made on a unanimity basis. The Assembly would be made up of MPs delegated to it by their national parliaments and would be at liberty to help in *making* decisions, but the Committee of Ministers would work on an intergovernmental basis and would be responsible for actually *taking* decisions.

Other factors beyond the governments and their perceived interests also contributed in a major way towards forming the climate of opinion from which the Council of Europe emerged. Churchill, out of power in the UK since the landslide Labour victory in the July 1945 election, was searching for a role that would match his experience and his stature as a victorious wartime leader, and he found it in the cause for European unity. He made sure that his views on Europe mattered. Britain's diplomatic task was to balance and secure all her varied interests but, with his personal experience, Churchill could see a particular role for himself, while he was leader of His Majesty's Opposition, as cheerleader for a united Europe.

In a speech at Zürich University in September 1946, Churchill took as his theme the future of Europe. The continent was in a state of flux and, barely

18 months since the end of hostilities, he surprised his audience by calling for a "partnership" between the arch-enemies France and Germany: a "spiritually great France and a spiritually great Germany". He also echoed a 1943 broadcast he had made, calling for a Council of Europe to be established after the war, "a real effective League, with all the strongest forces concerned woven into its texture, with a High Court to adjust disputes, and with forces, armed forces, national or international, or both, held ready to impose these decisions".[7]

Churchill's efforts culminated in the Congress of Europe, held in The Hague in early May 1948. The conclusions of this Congress were noted by governments, but they took different views on the demand that it made for a constituent assembly for Europe. A French government initiative to call a conference to promote the resolutions of The Hague was immediately backed by the Benelux states. But the Labour government in London did not want such an initiative to spiral out of control and endorse what it saw as unrealistic federalist proposals. So, London took the reins into its own hands and called a conference itself, opening the invitation to a wider circle of interested states. That allowed it better to dictate the agenda and steer the conclusions.

As a result, the Council of Europe of 1949 was an organization where the voice of governments far outweighed the voice of parliamentarians. The Parliamentary Assembly was far from being a *constituent* assembly and initially even its agenda had to be approved by the Committee of Ministers in advance. It was forbidden by statute from discussing matters concerning defence, which were reserved for governmental discussion. Referring to the Parliamentary Assembly, Ernest Bevin, the then British foreign minister noted, when making his final concession in the negotiations, "We can give them this talking shop".[8]

Despite this inherent tension, however, the Treaty of London, which established the Council of Europe, was presented publicly as a milestone on the road to a united Europe, the first comprehensive institutional result for the widespread postwar concern for peace that swept political circles after 1945. There would now be a Council of Europe which might, some speculated, one day develop into a government for the whole continent. For the first time in history there would also be a Parliament for Europe (even if it began only as a "talking shop").

As it turned out in practice, the early Council of Europe was something of a curate's egg, good in parts and bad in others. Paul-Henri Spaak, former Socialist prime minister of Belgium and first chairman of the UN General Assembly, chaired this European Assembly in its struggle with the Committee of Ministers, seeking by as many procedural ruses as possible to increase its powers to the point where it might legitimately take on the role of a constituent assembly. But after two years of unremitting stonewalling by the Committee of Ministers, in particular the British delegation, he finally resigned in disgust at the end of 1951.

The Council of Europe remained essentially a creature of the governments, with some parliamentary gloss, following the British desiderata. It was not the creature of parliaments, controlling a government at European level, as some of the more federalist continentals would have preferred.

However difficult relations were between the Parliamentary Assembly and the Committee of Ministers, in those two years the Council of Europe achieved a major step forwards in terms of guaranteeing respect for human rights in Europe. Within less than a year the first Convention was agreed by all member states and signed in Rome in November 1950: the European Convention on Human Rights and Fundamental Freedoms. It was a moral milestone, marking the moment when all states agreed together in a legal text that Europeans would never again suffer the abuse of human rights that so many had witnessed under war and fascist domination.

THE ISLAND PERSPECTIVE

From a British point of view, the working relationship with the Council of Europe had begun well. The UK was holding the line in the struggle with Spaak and the Parliamentary Assembly, and British lawyers played a major role in drafting the European Convention on Human Rights, drawing on the Universal Declaration of the United Nations and adapting it to the contemporary European situation. At the insistence of the Committee of Ministers, submitting to the jurisdiction of the Court would remain optional for member states, not mandatory, and cases could only be brought with the agreement of the states concerned. It was a good piece of work, and the UK was the first state to ratify the Convention when it passed through the British Parliament in 1951.

As external circumstances changed, the European Convention on Human Rights also slowly developed. The civil and political rights covered by the Convention were expanded through additional protocols agreed by all member states to include a dozen or more additional rights, and the governmental filter on individual applications to the ECHR was removed.

In 1965 the UK government took a major step, exercising an option under Article 25 of the European Convention on Human Rights. It accepted the jurisdiction of the ECHR in relation to individual complaints, although only on a provisional basis that had to be renewed every five years. In 1980 the optional clause was debated in Westminster again, this time amid charges that the ECHR was "interfering with the exercise of parliamentary sovereignty" and "limiting (the UK's) freedom of action", the first signs of greater opposition to come. However, in 1981 and subsequently Westminster accepted the optional clause again, each time for five more years.

In 1994, during the negotiation of Protocol 11, one of the periodical progressive amendments to the European Convention on Human Rights, the then UK home secretary, Michael Howard, an unabashed Eurosceptic, tried in vain to ensure that the right of individual petition would remain optional. The possibility of non-renewal of individual petition to the ECHR, he suggested, might act as a check on it overreaching its authority. However, there was little support for this view in other countries and Protocol 11, making the right of individual petition compulsory, entered into force on 1 November 1998.

In 2012, under the UK chairmanship, the Council of Europe adopted the Brighton Declaration, a package of reforms to tackle the excessive backlog of cases pending before the ECHR and simplify some of its procedures. At the same time it also emphasized that the main responsibility for guaranteeing human rights rested with national governments, parliaments and courts, stressing in a new Protocol 15 the principle of subsidiarity and the doctrine of the margin of appreciation for national courts when interpreting Strasbourg judgments.

The ECHR stands as a beacon of judicial authority at an international level, and it is hardly surprising that on occasion governments should chafe at the potential guardianship it may exercise over their actions. That is, after all, what it was created for. It operates a form of judicial review of government action; peer review, in the sense that many other governments are in the same situation. And the UK government – through its participation in the Council of Europe and respect for the European Convention on Human Rights – is part of that system. It is normal that the governments concerned should be in a position to adjust the rules of the game, but only when they all agree to do so.

It is also easy to exaggerate the practical impact of the judgements of the ECHR in the more developed and stable democracies, the UK among them.

The ECHR delivers several hundred judgments every year, relating to between 2,000 and 3,000 cases (often cases are joined if they raise the same point of law). On average, nearly half of these concern five member states: Turkey, Italy, the Russian Federation, Poland and Romania. The rest relate to the other 43 members of the organization. The UK is on average responsible for less than 3 per cent of the violations found by the ECHR.

In 2019, for instance, there were just six judgments issued involving the UK government and half of these related to what are described as "repetitive" issues. Clearly, the number of cases in which the ECHR finds *against* the UK government is very small indeed. As an ad hoc measure, the "just satisfaction" awards made by the UK authorities to successful plaintiffs that year amounted to a paltry €71,385, hardly a serious burden on the national budget.

Having the ECHR ensures that human rights are applied with some measure of consistency in 47 countries, now the whole of Europe after the fall of the Berlin Wall and the collapse of communism. But ensuring a measure of consistency does not mean that the ECHR writes the law in any of these countries. It makes a judgement when something is considered "incompatible" with protected human rights and requires the government in question to decide how to fix the incompatibility. The Convention and the resulting case law of the ECHR has been vitally important in raising standards and increasing awareness of human rights across all member states, but it is not a legislature.

Indeed, the most important impact of the Convention and the ECHR is really to be found not in the violations which come before the ECHR, but in the respect of its standards within European societies. It is not an effect to be measured, but to be experienced, seen and appreciated in the degree of tolerance shown in different societies, in the way in which public authorities behave in respect of minorities and issues of equality, in the rights enjoyed by individuals and by groups, in the quality of justice and the responsibility of government in countries where the people own the government, not where the government owns the people. The quality of life is what is maintained by respect for the Convention and the ECHR, and that is what is damaged when they are undermined.

Critics ask whether these rights would not be better protected with a specifically British Bill of Rights, rather than by the European Convention on Human Rights, which "requires" the country's "subjection" to an international jurisdiction. It is precisely the question that is asked in a country which has not been occupied by a foreign power for a thousand years. Many other countries in the Council of Europe know better than to trust to one's own government so blindly.

The underlying issue thrown up by this debate indeed touches on the issue of parliamentary sovereignty. Who does have the final say? Is it the elected parliament, which maintains the government in each member state, or is there a higher order, a constitutional order? In the case of the United Kingdom, the constitution is not codified, but it is to be found in both statute and precedent, and partly in precisely such treaties as the Treaty of London, which gives the judiciary a role within an international framework.

Apologists for parliamentary sovereignty in its purest form will argue that Parliament is sovereign in the sense that it can rescind or alter its decisions at any time by a simple majority vote, and one Parliament does not bind its successors. At any time, Westminster can make or unmake the law, just as it can make or unmake governments.

This gives rise to tension with the conduct of foreign relations, which usually works to a much longer time frame than the life of one parliament, and engages the state in a network of benefits and obligations that are not so easily undone. And it is precisely with those neighbouring countries that the government may wish to go further in sharing this authority. This was the case with the European Union, and it remains – now under scrutiny – the case with the Council of

Europe. Criticism of the Human Rights Act has been the trigger for this debate, and the process has been accelerated by Brexit.

Seen from Elsewhere

Brexit is, in essence, a voluntary secession by the UK from the European Union. It is the first time that the European Union has faced such an issue, being much more accustomed to voluntary accessions than secessions. The Council of Europe is in a similar situation. It has grown from the original ten founding members to 47 and has only come close on three occasions to excluding a member state precisely for contravening the European Convention on Human Rights. Close, but never quite.

In the case of the 1967 Colonels' Coup in Greece, four member states brought a case against Greece in the ECHR, which ruled against Greece in November 1969. A resolution to suspend Greece's membership of the Council was prepared for discussion and decision, but the Greek government withdrew from the Council and denounced the Convention just before the Committee of Ministers was called upon to take the decision. Greece was readmitted to the Council of Europe in October 1974 after free elections, following the collapse of the Colonels' regime the same year.

In the case of Turkey, the military coup of September 1980 ushered in a period of human rights abuse in that country. The initial response of the Parliamentary Assembly of the Council of Europe was to threaten to recommend to the Committee of Ministers to expel Turkey unless it respected the Convention, released political prisoners and returned quickly to a democratic system of government. In 1982, several member states brought cases against Turkey to the ECHR, but slow procedures in Strasbourg and partial relaxations of military rule in Turkey meant that the issue was never brought to a head. Turkey remained a member, although a much-criticized member, until the return of democratic elections in 1983.

The third case was more recent. In March 2014 Russia invaded Ukraine and annexed Crimea. In response, the Council of Europe stripped Russia of its voting rights. Russia then boycotted the Parliamentary Assembly from 2016 and refused to pay its dues, leaving a budget deficit of over €30 million annually, since it is one of the four largest contributors to the budget. In the subsequent to and fro between Moscow and Strasbourg, Russia went onto the offensive, threatening to leave the Council of Europe and cease to be party to the European Convention on Human Rights unless all sanctions on its delegation in Strasbourg were lifted. A compromise was eventually reached in 2019 at a meeting of the foreign ministers, allowing Russia to participate again with full rights and paying the sums owed. This decision, however, badly damaged relations with Ukraine and some other adjoining states, as it appeared to them that Russia had in no way faced consequences for its armed aggression and breaches of the Convention. For them, this undermined the very values on which the Council of Europe was based.

Continuing membership of the Council of Europe while simultaneously denouncing the European Convention on Human Rights would certainly be without precedent, even though de facto some members – as above – have not been excluded even though they have offended against the Convention. In principle, the Council of Europe requires its member states to respect certain standards of human rights. It has long been the Parliamentary Assembly's practice, when formulating its opinions on membership applications, to make accession to the Convention a condition of Council of Europe membership.

But it has never faced a situation where a member state wishes to remain a member of the Council of Europe while at the same time declaring its intention to renounce its accession to the European Convention on Human Rights. From past experience, it seems unlikely that the Parliamentary Assembly and the Committee of Ministers would tolerate such an anomaly. Thus, in denouncing the Convention the United Kingdom would, in all probability, also be voluntarily leaving the Council of Europe, a violent aftershock following the political earthquake of Brexit.

THE PRICE OF INDEPENDENCE

In leaving the Council of Europe, the UK would be leaving much more than just the European Convention on Human Rights and the ECHR. Over the years, the Council of Europe has grown into a multifaceted network of activities involving member states in various combinations, always in pursuit of its central goal: achieving a greater unity between its members for the purpose of safeguarding and realizing the ideals and principles which are their common heritage and facilitating their economic and social progress. In that process it has set up a large number of other procedures for monitoring or promoting good behaviour by its member states.

One such mechanism is the Social Charter. This reviews the effective respect for social and economic rights in the member states, but through procedures which do not involve the ECHR. It works instead through a committee reporting to the Committee of Ministers, keeping monitoring of sensitive rights concerning housing, education and social support subject to review by member states rather than the Court.

Other mechanisms bolster the Council of Europe's approach to defending rights, frequently linked to conventions that member states initially agree together, but then may sign and subsequently ratify, each in their own good time. The prevention of torture and the struggle against racism and intolerance, for instance, are the tasks of commissions set up by the Council as a result of conventions. These commissions attempt to improve the behaviour of member states in practice by setting common standards, supported by a process of mutual monitoring, inspection, comparison and advice. For some activities, the work of the convention is supplemented by a commissioner or ombudsman who may conduct her or his own investigations or receive complaints as a means of ensuring that the mechanism of peer review by member states fulfils the objectives set in the relevant conventions.

The Council of Europe applies a similar set of principles to what are known as Partial Agreements among member states. These are arrangements aimed at improving the practical application of common standards in a wide variety of areas, from the preparation and licensing of safe medicines to ensuring standards of care for handicapped persons, from gathering audio-visual statistics to promoting modern languages, from drugs policy to advising on new constitutional laws. Member states decide whether they wish to sign up for these particular agency activities, and in exchange for having a say in how they operate; they also accept that they will improve their own practice in the light of better experience which may come to light elsewhere. With goodwill, and a minimum of publicity, these agencies represent a remarkably useful and practical mechanism that operates in a positive way to improve standards internationally.

The extent of this mutually helpful cooperation is reflected in the fact that the Council of Europe has until now agreed close to 200 conventions, at least a score of them encouraging a process of mutual monitoring and comparison among member states with a view to improving standards of official authorities' behaviour. They range across a varied field including issues as diverse as prison conditions and social security, the recognition of university diplomas and adoption, the preservation of archaeological heritage and the status of au pairs. All this activity has helped to create a climate of increasing civility between European nations, what the participants at the European Congress of The Hague at the start of this lengthy process would have recognized under the heading of "Culture", what they had lost in the war and wished to enjoy again in peace.

The route from the 1940s to where the Council of Europe is today has not always been smooth. Member states were, for example, seriously divided when deciding how to enlarge the membership to include the new states of Eastern Europe after 1989, and even more so when considering the candidacy of Russia. There were many issues to consider, but one principle to decide: whether to admit these states before they had implemented reforms, or to condition their entry on actually meeting the criteria established for a modern democracy.

The decision taken to admit them was on condition that they would accept a monitoring procedure by which existing member states would inspect and verify if they met the necessary criteria. A generation later, that monitoring procedure has matured and is applied across the board, all member states now being fully recognized within the organization and themselves forming part of the monitoring teams operating in every state to raise standards. It is a largely unpublicized way for all member states to operate "soft power" through coordinating their efforts with like-minded democracies in a common effort. It ensures that Europe as a whole lives up to better standards than might be expected if states were impervious to inspection and opposed to internal reform.

But the process relies on mutual goodwill. Hence the strains and, indeed, breakdown of such processes when there is blatant abuse of the basic principles of the European Convention on Human Rights. States that are not easily embarrassed may even exploit such situations, for instance Russia's behaviour in the recent quarrel following the annexation of Crimea. But most states are concerned about their standing in the court of public opinion internationally and, although soft power has its limits, it can achieve a great deal.

Membership of the Council of Europe allows all member states, the UK included, to take a stand for human rights globally. The UK is rightly proud of its tough stance around the world on human rights. Opting out and reducing our engagement on this front – trimming human rights to match "British values" – would undercut the British position when questioning practices elsewhere, such as in Iran, China or even the United States.

Membership of the Council of Europe is seen as a kite mark for good behaviour. Losing it really should damage a country's standing. For a founding member state to throw it away must surely be unimaginable.

Notes for Chapter 15

1. For a full analysis of the exchanges around this incident, see Baroness Kennedy & A. Horne, "Rights after Brexit: some challenges ahead?", *European Human Rights Law Review* 5, October 2019.

2. "Is adherence to the European Convention on Human Rights a condition of European Union membership?" House of Commons Library, Standard Note SN/IA/6577, 25 March 2014.

3. *Ibid.*

4. See, The Conservative Party Manifesto 2015, http://ucrel.lancs.ac.uk/wmatrix/uk manifestos2015/localpdf/Conservatives.pdf.

5. See, "UK may be forced to give prisoners the vote in time for May elections", *The Guardian*, 1 February 2011, https://www.theguardian.com/society/2011/feb/01/ prisoners-vote-may-elections-compensation-claims.

6. See, "Named and shamed: the European human rights judges wrecking British law", *Daily Mail*, 5 February 2011, https://www.dailymail.co.uk/news/article-1353860/Named-shamed-The-European-human-rights-judges-wrecking-British-law.html.

7. See, Winston Churchill, speech delivered at the University of Zurich, 19 September 1946, https://rm.coe.int/16806981f3.

8. Cited in A. N. Wilson, *After the Victorians: The Decline of Britain in the World* (New York: Farrar, Straus & Giroux, 2015), 514.

AFTERWORD

Michael Leigh

The options presented in this book may appear, at first sight, mainly of academic interest because the United Kingdom has already left the European Union and the British government appears bent on a minimal agreement providing for free trade in goods, accompanied by limited provisions on services and a number of sectoral agreements. It is even ready to envisage a "no deal" Brexit, falling back on World Trade Organization (WTO) non-preferential terms, if no agreement is reached in the limited time available. However, as this volume goes to press, it would be a mistake to conclude that a thin deal or "no deal" Brexit is the last word on the future relationship.

The negotiations are taking place in an unusually fluid environment, in which Brexit is a lesser priority for both sides than coping with the overwhelming public health and economic crises. The two chief negotiators and the British prime minister succumbed to the Covid-19 virus for several weeks in spring 2020 and the negotiations have been conducted fitfully at a distance. Any agreement reached in the crisis atmosphere of 2020 is by nature provisional.

This Afterword draws attention to a number of considerations that might lead British and EU leaders to reconsider the nature of the future relationship in the months and years ahead: (1) the extraordinary circumstances in which the negotiations are being held; (2) geopolitical turbulence; (3) changes in the British political scene; and (4) different scenarios for the EU's own future. The Afterword concludes with tentative reflections on other models presented in earlier chapters that may prove instructive in the further evolution of UK–EU relations.

NEGOTIATIONS LIKE NO OTHERS

The negotiations between the EU and the UK to define their future relationship began in March 2020 and were always going to be difficult. The two sides' objectives diverged widely on key provisions and the time available to overcome these differences was very short.[1] Unless the UK requested and was granted by the end of June 2020 an extension to the transition period that was due to expire on 31 December 2020, the negotiations needed to be concluded, signed and ratified in less than ten months. Both parties agreed to make best endeavours to reach an even earlier agreement on the sensitive questions of fisheries and financial services by 1 July 2020.[2] Failing an overall agreement, another cliff edge, with reversion to trade on non-preferential WTO terms, loomed at the end of 2020.

The most fundamental differences between the two sides were the UK's vision of a series of separate sectoral agreements versus the EU's preference for a single overarching agreement with one governance structure; the UK's request for far-reaching equivalence agreements and the mutual recognition of regulations governing trade in goods; the UK's more ambitious objectives for the removal of barriers to the cross-border provision of services; the more restrictive UK approach to the recognition of EU geographic indicators; the role of the European Court of Justice in dispute settlement pursuant to the future relationship agreement; and, above all, EU insistence on enforceable "level playing field" commitments covering workers' rights, competition and state aids, as well as social and environmental protection.[3]

In light of this forbidding agenda, the scant progress made, the overwhelming Covid-19 and economic crises and the need to avoid another major economic shock, spokespeople for the European Peoples Party (EPP), the largest group in the European Parliament, called on the UK at the end of March to request a prolongation of the transition period. According to the EPP, "The coronavirus pandemic complicates the already very ambitious schedule."[4] Representatives of the Scottish government suggested a two-year extension, with Scotland facing the additional blow of collapsing oil and gas prices.[5] The managing director of the International Monetary Fund (IMF), Kristalina Georgieva, gave this plea a global dimension: "It is tough as it is", she told the BBC, "Let's not make it any tougher ... My advice would be to seek ways in which this element of uncertainty is reduced in the interests of everybody, of the UK, of the EU, the whole world."[6]

However, the British government indicated that it would not request an extension and would reject any such request from the EU side, claiming that this would prolong the negotiations and add to business uncertainty.[7] A last-minute change of heart in November or December could not be ruled out. But this would require a full treaty procedure, possibly involving ratification by 27 parliaments in the EU.[8] British legislation rules out a decision to extend the transition period by the Joint Committee established under the Withdrawal Agreement.[9] But the EU is adept at finding eleventh-hour solutions, if there is good will on all sides.[10]

In the course of the negotiations, Michel Barnier, the EU's chief negotiator, has repeatedly warned of the lack of significant progress in the talks and the need to make haste to meet the Withdrawal Agreement's deadlines.[11] Any agreement concluded in the depths of the Covid-19-induced recession, or an abrupt exit with no agreement in place, can only be regarded as provisional. When the UK–EU relationship comes to be revisited, the two sides will seek inspiration from the models discussed in this book, even though the eventual result will be a *sui generis* arrangement adapted to the perceived interests of the two sides.

GEOPOLITICAL TURBULENCE

Brexit occurred at a time of immense geopolitical turbulence, accentuated by the Covid-19 pandemic and recession. Flushed with fervour for recovering sovereignty and taking back control, British government representatives brushed aside questions as to whether a middle-sized country of some 67 million people could cope alone with global challenges in a world approaching 8 billion inhabitants. But British exceptionalism did not necessarily provide an adequate response to the dire geopolitical, public health and economic risks facing the country.[12]

The Brexit negotiations took place against a background of strategic competition between China, the United States, Russia and Europe, economic strains within and between states, increased inequality, disruptive technology and efforts to reconcile climate concerns with the need to kick-start stricken economies. This could well be a "Suez moment", with power shifting from the United States to China, Moscow – implausibly – claiming partner status with Beijing, in the name of Eurasia, and an increasingly detached United States, intent on reshoring and reducing dependence on the outside world. The collapse of energy prices led to increased tensions between the United States and Russia, over the latter's efforts to strike a blow at the American oil and gas industry by forcing prices down further.[13] The pre-electoral climate in the United States encouraged heightened polemics, while China, Russia and Iran stepped up disinformation campaigns in order to spread discord and fear in the United States and Europe.[14]

The asymmetric impact of the pandemic accentuated north–south disparities, with a collapse in commodity prices, trade, investment and income from remittances.[15] Poorer countries lacked resources for costly recovery plans as in Europe and the United States. By mid-April 2020, 102 countries had requested emergency assistance from the IMF.[16] A debt crisis threatened many developing countries.[17] Renewed population pressures seemed likely, with migration already a touchstone for polarized politics on both sides of the Atlantic.

Many of the vulnerabilities revealed by the pandemic have been attributed to globalization, which has characterized the last half century. The realization that 97 per cent of the antibiotics used in the United States, as well as many other pharmaceuticals, come from China jolted American opinion into calls for greater self-sufficiency.[18] Awareness in Europe of dependence on China and India for medical supplies, although somewhat less acute, also spread rapidly, bringing globalization under intense critical scrutiny and prompting the EU to develop a strategy to address supply chain problems revealed by the crisis.[19]

Calls grew for better regulation of markets and a greater role for the state in the economy, especially in public health and safety.[20] Measures to tighten anti-takeover rule were adopted in France.[21] Commission Executive Vice-President Margrethe Vestager said in April that European companies should take stakes in exposed businesses to stave off Chinese takeovers.[22] Nationalization has been accepted even by a British Conservative government as a counterpart for state bail outs.[23] But there have also been warnings about the risks of deglobalization and of beggar-thy-neighbour economic policies, which bedevilled world politics and economics during the great depression of the 1930s.[24] The Trump administration had already weaponized trade tariffs before the onset of the pandemic.

Some of these inchoate geopolitical shifts could well influence Britain's relations with the EU, the United States, China and other actors after Brexit. The ambition of British governments since the April 2016 referendum has been for the country to become a kind of "multipolar middle power",[25] initially referred to as "global Britain".[26] A multipolar Britain would aim to develop close links with both China and the United States.

Before the pandemic, China was widely seen as a source of political and economic strength for Britain, epitomized by the UK's rush to become a founder member of the Beijing-sponsored Asian Infrastructure Investment Bank and to benefit from Belt and Road contracts.[27] There were expectations at first that Britain's close relationship with the United States would lead to an early and far-reaching free trade agreement. In this vision, advantageous political and economic connections with the world's top two would be accompanied by privileged trade and investment links with Commonwealth countries. The North Atlantic Treaty Organization would assume increased importance as Britain's principal international strategic anchor after Brexit.

Yet the geopolitical turbulence, exacerbated by the Covid-19 epidemic and recession, have thrown this vision into disarray. Britain's enthusiastic opening to China has been replaced by a far more critical stance, with calls to hold China accountable for the spread of the epidemic. At the same time, prospects for an early UK–US free trade agreement have been clouded by differences over such issues as Huawei's involvement in building Britain's 5G network infrastructure, the price of drugs used by Britain's National Health Service and food safety standards.[28] Trade talks between the UK and the United States got underway in

May.[29] But there are many obstacles to overcome and any resulting agreement will await a new administration in Washington.

The pandemic has accentuated a number of international trends which heighten the vulnerability of a middle-sized country like the UK, adrift from its former EU partners. The weakening of multilateralism, the further withdrawal of the United States from world affairs and the growing self-confidence of Chinese leaders, as well as heightened tensions between Washington and Beijing, create an unstable and unpredictable environment for post-Brexit Britain. An international investigation into the origins of the pandemic is essential but finger wagging by a medium power like Britain does not move leaders in Beijing.[30]

In 2019 the EU labelled China a systemic rival and strategic competitor, an assessment not dissimilar from the prevailing view in Britain.[31] Like Britain, EU representatives also stressed that China was an indispensable partner in addressing global challenges.[32] The UK will be drawn to coordinate more closely with the European Union in navigating a path between Washington and Beijing. For example, it would make sense to be associated with the EU's system of information sharing on investment screening and coordinated efforts to reduce dependence on China for vital medical supplies.[33] In spring 2020 the director of Chatham House, Britain's leading foreign policy think tank, wrote that "If Covid 19 creates a long-term schism between China and the US, with Europeans caught on its edge, this could do deep damage to world order."[34] He did not suggest that Britain's interests differed in any respect from those of other Europeans in this rapidly deteriorating situation. But, for now, the assertion of British exceptionalism seems to take priority over concerted action.[35]

Geopolitical turbulence will continue throughout the UK–EU future relationship negotiations and beyond. Nonetheless, the ministerial statement that summarized Britain's negotiating objectives in this process played down cooperation on foreign and security policy, by comparison with the ambitious vision in the Political Declaration that accompanied the Withdrawal Agreement.[36] The final form of these documents, while changing few formal provisions from the previous version, placed greater emphasis on the need to respect the autonomy of the decision-making structures of both parties.[37] When the dust settles from Brexit and the British side is more influenced by the need to address common challenges than to assert Britain's "sovereign equality", arrangements for cooperating with the EU on foreign policy and security may well be revisited.

CHANGES IN THE BRITISH POLITICAL SCENE

The outcome of the 2020 future relationship negotiations can also be regarded as provisional because of the domestic political circumstances under which they were negotiated. The December 2019 general election gave a landslide victory with an 80-seat majority to the Conservative Party. This reflected the compelling simplicity of the party's promise to "get Brexit done" and the weakness of the Labour Party, which suffered from poor leadership, a confused message about Brexit and internal problems, especially a failure to deal with antisemitism in the party.[38]

On the basis of this victory, the new prime minister, Boris Johnson, cemented his government's uncompromising approach to Brexit and relied on his parliamentary majority to approve a reworked Withdrawal Agreement and a more qualified Political Declaration. However, the negotiations began in March without a broad consensus on the government's extensive redlines among different currents of opinion in the Conservative Party and in the country. There was considerable unease about the dominant role of the prime minister's chief adviser, an uncompromising advocate of Leave and an outlier on the government's Covid-19 strategy.[39]

Sir Keir Starmer was elected, on 4 April 2020, as leader of the Labour Party and, hence, became leader of the official Opposition.[40] The studied ambiguity of his predecessor, Jeremy Corbyn, on EU issues had contributed to a climate favourable to Brexit and to a minimalistic view of the future relationship. At the same time as he became Labour Party leader, Starmer gained control of the party's National Executive Committee, where a majority had previously echoed Mr Corbyn's views.[41] This put him in a strong position to advance his own more pragmatic agenda.

Frances O'Grady, the general secretary of the Trades Union Congress, has called for an agreement with the EU that "protects people's jobs, rights and public services".[42] The EU's insistence on a "level playing field" in future relations with the UK implies that the country should remain committed to a high level of social and economic rights. The prime minister, however, insists on Britain's right to diverge from EU principles, while claiming that workers' rights will be adequately protected through domestic legislation. This difference of view is unlikely to be resolved in the short period available for the negotiations.

Nonetheless, the government can rely on its solid parliamentary majority, public relief that the divisive Brexit debate is over, three years after the referendum, and the overwhelming priority of combatting the Covid-19 epidemic, to create a permissive political space for the negotiations. The negative economic impact of a thin deal or "no deal" Brexit at the end of 2020 is likely to be masked to a considerable extent by the profound recession induced by the epidemic. The government benefitted from "rally round the flag" sentiment at the peak of the crisis but delays and contradictions in its Covid-19 suppression strategy, and in its approach to the EU future relationship negotiations, are likely to come under closer scrutiny when the crisis is passed.[43]

The Labour Party, whether in opposition or in government, in the years ahead will examine the deal emerging from the 2020 future relationship negotiations critically. Various sectors of opinion in Britain will be pressing for high standards of environmental, labour and data protection, in line with evolving EU norms. The science, innovation and research community will be seeking association rather than limited third-country status under the EU's framework research programme, Horizon Europe, so that cooperation with colleagues in the EU in cutting edge fields, including medical research, can continue.[44]

One of the most controversial features of the Withdrawal Agreement is its Protocol on Ireland and Northern Ireland.[45] In the rush to "get Brexit done" after the December 2019 general election, the administrative barriers created by the agreement were largely overlooked. But, as Chapter 13 documents, new obstacles to trade and transport between Great Britain and Northern Ireland and between the UK and the EU will become realities at the end of the transitional period, in the midst of the deepest recession since the 1930s.[46]

A modest UK–EU trade agreement, or reversion to WTO rules, will not foreclose demands for smoother economic relations in the years ahead. The experience of other countries in their relations with the EU, reviewed in this volume, can provide useful hints on ways to adjust UK–EU relations, when and if the two parties decide to revisit the conditions under which the UK left the EU.

SCENARIOS FOR THE FUTURE OF THE EU

Much of the Brexit debate in Britain was premised on the assumption that the EU had outgrown the economic entity that the UK joined in 1973 to become a European superstate in the making. But the assumption that the EU is headed in a federal direction was doubtful long before the British 2016 referendum and is even more questionable today. If, in the course of time, a British government seeks to revisit the country's relations with the EU, it might well find that the EU is on a different path from any envisaged until now.

As the future relationship negotiations go forwards, the EU is once again at an inflection point, at which its future development may take different directions. The negotiations were necessarily based on the *acquis* of the European Union – that is, its existing laws, rules and procedures as well as the relevant UK legislation. Nonetheless, the political, economic, legal and regulatory environment will continue to evolve, on both sides of the Channel, and the two unions, the EU and the UK, may themselves face existential challenges.[47] The unprecedented public health emergency and recession that formed a backdrop to the negotiations in 2020 make it particularly hard to discern the EU's future course. Mutual perceptions and reciprocal interests will depend to a considerable degree on the direction taken by both parties in the years ahead.

In conditions of uncertainty, "scenarios" can help to sketch possible alternative futures. A European Commission White Paper set out five scenarios for the future of Europe in 2017.[48] At that time, pandemics figured inconspicuously among global risks that were routinely cited without any sense of clear and present danger. In light of subsequent experience and with considerable simplification, three broad scenarios can be outlined, as possible backdrops to future UK–EU relations.

The first can be called the *"relaunch" scenario*; its main current proponent is the French president, Emmanuel Macron.[49] He advocates a future path for the EU based on greater integration, solidarity and burden sharing and sees the eurozone as the core of the EU in the years ahead. His vision is of a union that reinforces democracy, the rule of law and multilateralism and which opposes illiberalism and nationalist excesses. He wants "a Europe that protects", both in the sense of ensuring the security of its citizens and of preventing job losses through unfair competition and offshoring. He sees Europe becoming more "sovereign" by conditioning access to its markets on respect for the EU's labour and environmental standards.[50]

This scenario attributes to the EU a key role in regulating global trade, reviving the multilateral system, reconciling climate goals with the needs of economic recovery, creating a digital single market, protecting data privacy and coordinating preventive and responsive measures in the field of public health. It also sees a greater role for the state and for the EU in industrial policy, especially in supporting national and European "champions", and in controlling foreign investment. Foreign policy, security and defence are areas expected to be pursued by the European Union more vigorously after Brexit, under this scenario, without having to overcome British reticence.

The "relaunch" of the EU was to be piloted by a Conference on the Future of Europe, promoted by the European Commission president, Ursula von der Leyen, and the former Belgian prime minister and member of the European Parliament, Guy Verhofstadt.[51] The conference was to gather the views of citizens on the major challenges facing Europe and generate proposals for EU reform. Its "bottom up" approach would contrast sharply with previous elite-driven reform efforts. Recommendations generated by the Conference might eventually lead to treaty changes, although national governments remain wary of possible referenda. However, the conference was postponed because of the epidemic, with tentative efforts by supporters to keep popular consultation features alive online.[52]

In any event, President Macron found that his original scenario, in which Germany would back his EU relaunch programme in recognition of the profound reforms that he had brought about inside France, had failed to materialize. It fell victim both to German reluctance to accept his proposals for strengthening the eurozone, particularly debt mutualization, and his own difficulties in mobilizing support for domestic reforms.

Still, the relaunch scenario takes comfort from Jean Monnet's much-quoted dictum: "Europe will be forged in crises and will be the sum of the solutions adopted in those crises."[53] But some observers have concluded, on the contrary, that crises reveal fragility, following a series of setbacks going back to the global financial crisis of 2008.[54] And fragility may lead to disintegration, unless solutions are found to underlying problems.

There have been frequent alerts of the risk of disintegration and even collapse throughout the first decades of the twenty-first century. As early as 2010, German chancellor Angela Merkel warned that "if the euro fails so will the idea of European Union".[55] In April 2020, the French finance minister, Bruno le Maire, said that unless the 27 managed to reach agreement on debt mutualization the European Union and the eurozone were destined to disappear.[56] The Italian prime minister, Giuseppe Conte, and other ministers have regularly warned of the risk of EU collapse unless it responded with greater solidarity to various crises that have beset the Union in recent years.[57] Differences over the EU's response to the pandemic produced further warnings of impending disintegration interspersed with reaffirmations of confidence in the EU's future.[58]

Such declarations can be considered hyperbole, negotiating tactics or efforts to pre-empt nationalist voices at home. However, by dint of repetition they lend credibility to a *disintegration scenario* that otherwise might be dismissed as scaremongering or intellectual conceit. There are many versions of such a scenario. A common underlying feature, though, is the notion that the single currency, the Schengen open borders system and the EU's enlargement to include 11 former communist countries may have amounted to overreach. The geopolitical benefits of these processes are compromised, in this reading, by fundamental flaws. The single currency is impaired by the prohibition of fiscal transfers, the Schengen system by the weakness of burden sharing on external border controls and the processing of requests for asylum, and enlargement by backsliding on democracy and the rule of law.[59]

Brexit itself is the first case of the departure of a member state and amounts to disintegration in the most literal sense. Initial fears that this might lead to "contagion" have receded as the difficulties of Brexit discouraged other would-be secessionists. But Eurosceptic nationalists could still wield the threat of secession whenever they deem it a vote winner.

The disintegration scenario depicts the euro as promoting divergence rather than convergence and sees the EU gradually disbanding into groups of states with disparate interests. In its most benign form, this is referred to as multi-speed

Europe. The euro and migration crises of the past decade have, according to this hypothesis, produced less rather than more integration, with member states showing little solidarity and defending often misconceived national interests.

This has provided political capital to Eurosceptic nationalist political movements that are on the rise in the member states and that captured close to a third of the seats in the European Parliament in the 2019 election. While nationalists tend, by definition, to be disunited, they embody intolerant values that are opposed to the principles on which the EU is founded. The EU's largely ineffective rule-of-law actions against Hungary and Poland confirm its inability to enforce respect for "EU values".

The disintegration scenario sees the epidemic and recession as giving a boost to Eurosceptic nationalists, once the acute phase of the crisis has faded. The epidemic reinforces national authorities rather than the EU, inequalities, within and between countries and distrust (both north–south and east–west). Divergent borrowing costs – expressed in the notorious "spread" – hollow out the notion of a single monetary policy. Potentially distorting state bailouts for ailing companies threaten the Single Market and increase inequalities, as poorer countries have fewer means to support their industries and unemployed.

The suspension of deficit, state aid and free movement rules comfort this scenario. Fully 84 per cent of French respondents favoured closing the country's borders to foreigners, according to a poll published in April 2020.[60] While the temporary suspension of such EU rules is permissible in exceptional circumstances, proponents of the disintegration scenario raise the question of whether they will remain temporary, citing the French adage: *seul le provisoire perdure* (only the provisional endures). This fits with a more general sentiment that life will never be the same again after the pandemic.[61]

The disintegration scenario also points to the risk of "beggar-thy-neighbour" policies and subsidy wars of the kind that proved so damaging during the great depression of the 1930s. Overall, this scenario sees the EU sleepwalking towards further euro crises fuelled by excessive debt, and questions whether northern countries will again summon the political will to come to the support of their weaker southern brethren. If not, a break-up of the eurozone, and with it the EU, cannot be excluded according to the disintegration scenario.

A third scenario sees the EU mainly as *a resurgent regulator* whose key characteristic is its ability to regulate markets and to deliver public goods both within the Union and across the globe. Proponents of this view consider the two previous scenarios as based on a false dichotomy because elements of integration and disintegration coexist in the EU as it goes forwards.[62]

Indeed, the juxtaposition of a "relaunch" and a "disintegration" scenario seems to reflect a rise and fall view of history, which ignores the complexities of today's interdependent world. It also reflects Walter Hallstein's much-quoted bicycle analogy whereby the EU will only continue to exist if it moves forwards.[63] A variant of this notion is the image of "the European project" as an automobile that will break down unless it manages to overcome obstacles and move forwards. Proponents of this view sometimes depict Europe as on the "edge of the abyss" unless it has a grand project on the horizon.[64]

A far more pragmatic view of the EU's future focuses primarily on the results it is able to deliver. The European Commission itself has recognized that the EU's effectiveness will be judged less on the principles it proclaims or its "narrative" than on the tangible results obtained. "Only a collective resolve to jointly deliver on the things that matter will help close the gap between promises on paper and people's expectations", it wrote in 2017.[65]

In the EU's response to the Covid-19 crisis needs were so acute that only results mattered. According to one observer this presaged a major change in approach, with delivery of public goods becoming primordial: "Emergency action to enhance healthcare and unemployment insurance might signal a paradigm shift for the union from market integration to providing public goods."[66]

That said, the response of the EU to the epidemic and accompanying economic downturn is a mixed picture. After a shaky start, the European Central Bank assumed its full responsibilities, while the Commission launched several public health and economic initiatives, including an innovative recovery fund on which the member states reached a consensus in July 2020 following difficult negotiations.

The Covid-19 pandemic may lead the EU to play a greater role in the field of public health in the future, despite the absence of a strong treaty base. But this does not necessarily imply a "spill-over" process leading to a higher state of integration but, rather, a pragmatic response to the basic needs of the population. Intervention by the EU authorities often aims to protect the EU's existing achievements, especially the Single Market, the euro or the Schengen open borders system. Thus, contrary to the bicycle analogy, this scenario sees the consolidation of past accomplishments as legitimate and necessary.

This type of analysis differs markedly from earlier theorizing about European integration in that the EU's ability to deliver public goods does not depend on progress towards a more federal Europe. Anu Bradford in a noteworthy study denies that "further integration is needed for the EU's revival and relevance".[67] Instead, she claims, "Even in the absence of a European federation, the EU is already able to advance its interests both within and beyond its borders", through a process that she calls "the Brussels Effect".[68] This is defined as "the EU's capacity to regulate the global marketplace".[69] This power owes much to the EU's size and legal authority as well as the absence of any other regulator with global reach. She pays particular attention to the EU's ability to ensure market competition, regulate the digital economy and protect the environment.

Clearly, this rather down-to-earth scenario requires further elaboration and will contend with other more dramatic views of the EU's future. For present purposes, it is sufficient to conclude that a future British government may be more inclined to draw closer to a European Union whose appeal depends primarily on the delivery of public goods and better regulation than on one perceived as intent on building a European federation.

OPTIONS FOR BRITAIN

This Afterword has drawn attention to a number of factors that in the future might lead the British government of the day to revisit the UK's relations with the EU. The future relationship negotiations in 2020 took place in a highly charged atmosphere, due to their compression into a few months, looming cliff edges, the somewhat rigid positions defended by both sides and the simultaneous public health and economic crises. This relegated the UK–EU negotiations to a second-order priority, which did not favour compromise solutions, even though the outcome would determine the framework for the British economy for years to come and would affect the prospects for economic operators and citizens on both sides of the Channel.

This was a period of intense geopolitical turbulence that made it difficult for British ministers, officials and diplomats to chart a clear path for the country's future outside the EU. As tensions between Beijing and Washington increase, the British government may well seek to coordinate its own position more closely with the EU and its member states.

In 2020 the government was still intent on demonstrating the viability of British exceptionalism. But as economic difficulties build up through the combined effect of the epidemic-induced recession and Brexit, British leaders may come around to the view that a closer relationship with the EU should be explored. This could become more likely if the EU's own future development is in a pragmatic rather than a federalist direction, in which the delivery of public goods and better regulation are priorities.

The British government that took the country out of the EU in January 2020 may not be the one to undertake a review of relations with the Union. But politics is a dynamic process and leaders of whatever party is in office in the years ahead may wish to reconsider the arms-length relationship decreed by their predecessors. In any event, most international agreements include review clauses.

Under these circumstances, British and European policy-makers may seek inspiration from the options presented in this book. No single model will suit the United Kingdom, which will continue to shun the role of "decision-taker" implied by full participation in the Single Market, along the lines of the European

Free Trade Area countries. This book shows that Australia, Canada, Singapore, Turkey, Ukraine and New Zealand have diverse interests to defend that distinguish them from the United Kingdom. Geographic location matters more than is often assumed. Nonetheless, the varied experience of the EU's different partners provides useful hints as to possible arrangements that may be of interest to the United Kingdom in the future.

Notes for Afterword

1. Institute for Government, "UK–EU future relationship: UK and EU mandates", https://www.instituteforgovernment.org.uk/explainers/future-relationship-uk-eu-mandates.

2. HM Government, Political Declaration setting out the framework for the future relationship between the European Union and the United Kingdomm, 19 October 2019, https://assets.publishing.service.gov.uk/government/uploads/system/uploads/attachment_data/file/840656/Political_Declaration_setting_out_the_framework_for_the_future_relationship_between_the_European_Union_and_the_United_Kingdom.pdf.

3. Institute for Government, "UK–EU future relationship".

4. EPP Group, "Extension of Brexit transition is the responsible thing to do", 30 March 2020, https://www.eppgroup.eu/newsroom/news/extension-of-brexit-transition-the-responsible-thing-to-do.

5. M. Settle, "UK Govt rejects Michael Russell's plea to extend Brexit transition period for maximum two years", *The Herald*, 20 April 2020, https://www.heraldscotland.com/news/18391128.uk-govt-rejects-michael-russells-plea-extend-brexit-transition-period-maximum-two-years/.

6. "IMF boss says UK should seek longer Brexit transition", Reuters, 16 April 2020, https://www.reuters.com/article/us-britain-eu-imf/imf-boss-says-uk-should-seek-longer-brexit-transition-idUSKCN21Y0LT.

7. "UK will refuse any EU offer to extend Brexit transition", *Financial Times*, https://www.ft.com/content/3c006614-767f-4447-8136-97987045517f.

8. Article 126, Withdrawal Agreement, https://ec.europa.eu/commission/sites/beta-political/files/draft_withdrawal_agreement_0.pdf.

9. European Union (Withdrawal Act) 2020, 15A: Prohibition on extending implementation period "A Minister of the Crown may not agree in the Joint Committee to an extension of the implementation period", http://www.legislation.gov.uk/ukpga/2020/1/part/4/crossheading/other-matters/enacted.

10. "Why the government will not ask for a Brexit extension", *The Economist*, 18 April 2020.

11. Press statement by Michel Barnier following the second round of future relationship negotiations with the United Kingdom, 24 April 2020, https://ec.europa.eu/commission/presscorner/detail/en/statement_20_739.

12. O. English, "Cruel Britannia: coronavirus lays waste to British exceptionalism", *Politico*, 5 May 2020, https://www.politico.eu/article/cruel-britannia-coronavirus-lays-waste-to-british-exceptionalism/.

13. "Failure of oil price war may cost Putin dear", *Financial Times*, https://www.ft.com/content/fb501e7e-8a19-11ea-9dcb-fe6871f4145a.

14. J. Barnes, M. Rosenberg & E. Wong, "As virus spreads, China and Russia see openings for disinformation", *New York Times*, 28 March 2020, https://www.nytimes.com/2020/03/28/us/politics/china-russia-coronavirus-disinformation.html.

15. J. Stiglitz, "Internationalizing the crisis", *Project Syndicate*, 6 April 2020, https://www.project-syndicate.org/commentary/covid19-impact-on-developing-emerging-economies-by-joseph-e-stiglitz-2020-04.

16. International Monetary Fund, "The IMF's response to Covid-19", https://www.imf.org/en/About/FAQ/imf-response-to-covid-19#Q5.

17. "A solution to the looming debt crisis in emerging markets", *Financial Times*, https://www.ft.com/content/b97eb604-4f6b-49bc-b350-3287bbde00c9.

18. Y. Huang, "US dependence on pharmaceutical products from China", blog post, Council on Foreign Relations, 14 August 2019, https://www.cfr.org/blog/us-dependence-pharmaceutical-products-china.

19. "Covid-19 exposes EU's reliance on drug imports", *Financial Times*, https://www.ft.com/content/c30eb13a-f49e-4d42-b2a8-1c6f70bb4d55.

20. See, for example, J. Stiglitz, *Globalization and Its Discontents Revisited: Anti-Globalization in the Age of Trump* (New York: Norton, 2020).

21. "France to bolster anti-takeover measures amid foreign investment boom", Reuters, 19 July 2018, https://www.reuters.com/article/us-france-investment/france-to-bolster-anti-takeover-measures-amid-foreign-investment-boom-idUSKBN1K922D.

22. "Vestager urges stakebuilding to block Chinese takeovers", *Financial Times*, https://www.ft.com/content/e14f24c7-e47a-4c22-8cf3-f629da62b0a7.

23. "UK partial rail nationalisation to battle coronavirus", Rail Freight.com, 23 March 2020, https://www.railfreight.com/policy/2020/03/23/uk-partial-rail-nationalisation-to-battle-coronavirus/?gdpr=accept.

24. "Beggar-Thy-Neighbour is an expression in economics describing a set of policies that seek to benefit one country at the direct expense of others. In particular, beggar-thy-neighbour policies typically pertain to an international trade policy of competitive devaluation and increased protective barriers instituted at the expense of trading partners", https://www.guggenheimpartners.com/perspectives/global-cio-outlook/the-return-of-beggar-thy-neighbor.

25. "What should Britain's role in the world be after Brexit?", *Huffington Post*, 7 July 2018, https://www.huffingtonpost.co.uk/entry/brexit-uk-position-in-world_uk_5b4dc19de4b0fd5c73bec6b7?5g.

26. R. Saunders, "The myth of Brexit as imperial nostalgia", *Prospect*, 7 January 2019, https://www.prospectmagazine.co.uk/world/the-myth-of-brexit-as-imperial-nostalgia.

27. P. Hammond, UK Contribution to the Asian Infrastructure Investment Bank Special Fund: Written statement – HCWS573, https://www.parliament.uk/business/publications/written-questions-answers-statements/written-statement/Commons/2018-03-21/HCWS573/.

28. C. Packard, "Trump and Johnson can quickly strike a trade deal – if they avoid the pitfalls", *Foreign Policy*, 11 March 2020, https://foreignpolicy.com/2020/03/11/trump-johnson-us-britain-trade-agreement-fta/.

29. "UK trade talks with US begin Tuesday", *Politico*, 5 March 2020, https://www.politico.eu/article/uk-trade-talks-with-us-begin-tuesday/.

30. "Britain says need for global 'lessons learned' inquiry into pandemic", *U.S. News*, 30 March 2020, https://www.usnews.com/news/world/articles/2020-03-30/britain-says-need-for-global-lessons-learned-inquiry-into-pandemic.

31. "EU-China – a strategic outlook", European Commission/High Representative of the Union for Foreign Affairs and Security Policy, Strasbourg, 12 March 2019, https://ec.europa.eu/commission/sites/beta-political/files/communication-eu-china-a-strategic-outlook.pdf.

32. "Europe has been 'naive' about China, says Josep Borrell", *Politico*, 5 March 2020, https://www.politico.eu/article/europe-has-been-naive-about-china-josep-borrell/.

33. "EU trade chief urges tougher defences against foreign takeovers", *Financial Times*, 16 April 2020, https://www.ft.com/content/bf83fa94-1bcf-4532-a75a-50f41351c0d4.

34. R. Niblett, "Avoiding a virus-induced cold war with China", Chatham House Expert Comment, 17 April 2020, https://www.chathamhouse.org/expert/comment/avoiding-virus-induced-cold-war-china.

35. For a critical view of British exceptionalism see, F. O'Toole, "Coronavirus has exposed the myth of British exceptionalism", *Irish Times*, 11 April 2020, https://www.irishtimes.com/news/world/fintan-o-toole-coronavirus-has-exposed-the-myth-of-british-exceptionalism-1.4227086.

36. Institute for Government, "UK–EU future relationship: defence and security co-operation", https://www.instituteforgovernment.org.uk/explainers/future-relationship-defence-security-cooperation.

37. Institute for Government, "Brexit deal: Political Declaration on future UK-EU relationship", https://www.instituteforgovernment.org.uk/explainers/brexit-deal-political-declaration.

38. R. Mason, "Five reasons the Tories won the election", *The Guardian*, 13 December 2019, https://www.theguardian.com/politics/2019/dec/13/five-reasons-the-tories-won-the-election.

39. "Cummings role under scrutiny over delay to UK suppression policy", *Financial Times*, https://www.ft.com/content/623a86ec-6c4c-11ea-9bca-bf503995cd6f.

40. "Keir Starmer elected Labour leader with 56% of vote on first round – as it happened", *The Guardian*, 4 April 2020, https://www.theguardian.com/politics/live/2020/apr/04/labour-leadership-election-winner-keir-starmer-long-bailey-nandy-and-jeremy-corbyns-successor-to-be-announced-at-1045am-live-news.

41. S. Rodgers, "Corbynsceptics sweep the board in Labour's ruling body by-elections", *LabourList*, 4 April 2020, https://labourlist.org/2020/04/corbynsceptics-sweep-the-board-in-labours-ruling-body-by-elections/.

42. BBC News, "Post-Brexit talks: we'll find out what's going on, TUC boss warns PM", 28 February 2020, https://www.bbc.com/news/uk-politics-51622348.

43. "'Confused, dangerous, flippant': rest of world pans PM's handling of coronavirus", *The Guardian*, 24 March 2020, https://www.theguardian.com/world/2020/mar/24/confused-dangerous-flippant-worlds-media-pans-pms-handling-of-coronavirus-boris-johnson?CMP=share_btn_link.

44. "A post-Brexit agreement for research and innovation – outcomes from a simulated negotiation process", Wellcome, 28 January 2020, https://wellcome.ac.uk/reports/post-brexit-agreement-research-and-innovation-outcomes-simulated-negotiation-process.

45. Revised Protocol on Ireland and Northern Ireland included in the Withdrawal Agreement, European Commission website, 17 October 2019, https://ec.europa.eu/commission/publications/revised-protocol-ireland-and-northern-ireland-included-withdrawal-agreement_en.

46. "Oven-ready or half-baked? Implementing the Northern Ireland Protocol", UK in a Changing Europe, 17 February 2020, https://ukandeu.ac.uk/oven-ready-or-half-baked-implementing-the-ireland-northern-ireland-protocol/.

47. "Brits increasingly don't care whether Northern Ireland remains in UK", YouGov, 22 April 2020, https://yougov.co.uk/topics/politics/articles-reports/2020/04/22/brits-increasingly-dont-care-whether-northern-irel.

48. White paper on the future of Europe: Five scenarios, European Commission website, https://ec.europa.eu/commission/future-europe/white-paper-future-europe/white-paper-future-europe-five-scenarios_en.

49. See, for example, "President Macron gives speech on new initiative for Europe", Elysee, 26 September 2017, https://www.elysee.fr/emmanuel-macron/2017/09/26/president-macron-gives-speech-on-new-initiative-for-europe.en.

50. "Macron pour une Europe forte, unie et souveraine", *Euronews*, 4 March 2019, https://www.youtube.com/watch?v=hMrOxWn9Cqw.

51. "Shaping the Conference on the Future of Europe", press release, 22 January 2020, https://ec.europa.eu/commission/presscorner/detail/en/ip_20_89.

52. "An uncertain future for Conference on Future of Europe", *The Parliament*, 23 March 2020, https://www.theparliamentmagazine.eu/articles/news/uncertain-future-conference-future-europe.

53. J. Monnet, *Mémoires* (Paris: Fayard, 1976).

54. "Coronavirus crisis lays bare the risks of financial leverage, again", *Financial Times*, https://www.ft.com/content/098dcd60-8880-11ea-a01c-a28a3e3fbd33.

55. "Merkel warns of Europe's collapse", *Spiegel International*, 13 May 2020, https://www.spiegel.de/international/germany/merkel-warns-of-europe-s-collapse-if-euro-fails-so-will-the-idea-of-european-union-a-694696.html.

56. "Bruno Le Maire: 'L'Union européenne est une protection, pas un problème'", *Liberation*, 3 May 2020, https://www.liberation.fr/planete/2020/05/03/bruno-le-maire-l-union-europeenne-est-une-protection-pas-un-probleme_1787208.

57. "Italy's Conte warns of EU collapse ahead of crucial financial talks", *Politico*, 9 April 2020, https://www.politico.eu/article/italys-conte-warns-of-eu-collapse-ahead-crucial-financial-talks-coronavirus/.

58. "EU project in danger if no solidarity on coronavirus crisis, says economy chief Gentiloni", *EuroNews*, 30 March 2020, https://www.euronews.com/2020/03/30/eu-project-in-danger-if-no-solidarity-on-coronavirus-crisis-says-economy-chief-gentiloni.

59. On this last point, see I. Krastev & S. Holmes, *The Light that Failed* (London: Penguin, 2019).

60. "La defiance s'installe dans opinion", *Le Monde*, 22 April, 2020, http://www.sciencespo. fr/cevipof/sites/sciencespo.fr.cevipof/files/MLMQ_20200422_page008.pdf.

61. "Coronavirus lockdown: 10 things that may never be the same again from travel to shops", *The Mirror*, 4 April 2020, https://www.mirror.co.uk/news/uk-news/coronavirus-lockdown-10-things-never-21812500.

62. On this latter point see E. Jones, "This is what European disintegration looks like", IISS, The Survival Editor's Blog, 28 April 2020, https://www.iiss.org/blogs/survival-blog/2020/04/europe-disintegration-covid-19.

63. "Die EU braucht eine neue Verfassung", *Zeit Online*, 28 June 2018, https://www.zeit.de/politik/2018-06/europaeische-integration-eu-verfassungaenderung-recht-asylpolitik.

64. See, for example, Jacques Delors' comments: "Pour Jacques Delors, l'Europe est 'au bord du gouffre'", *France Soir*, 18 August 2011, http://archive.francesoir.fr/actualite/politique/pour-jacques-delors-l-europe-est-au-bord-du-gouffre-128734.html.

65. European Commission, 2017, White Paper on the Future of Europe: Reflections and Scenarios for the EU-27 by 2025, Brussels, 1.3.2017, COM(2017) 2025 final.

66. Albena Azmanova, "The nascent paradigm shift in the EU", *Social Europe*, 28 April 2020, https://www.socialeurope.eu/the-nascent-paradigm-shift-in-the-eu.

67. A. Bradford, *The Brussels Effect: How the European Union Rules the World* (Oxford: Oxford University Press, 2020), x.

68. *Ibid.*

69. *Ibid.*, 1.

INDEX

Note: italic page numbers indicate figures; bold page numbers indicate tables; numbers in brackets preceded by *n* refer to notes.